MODERN
BALLROOM
DANCING

MODERN BALLROOM DANCING

Victor Silvester

Officer of the most excellent Order of the British Empire (OBE)

Winner of the World's Dancing Championship

President of the Imperial Society of Teachers of Dancing Incorporated

His world-famous Orchestra featured on television and radio,
and recorded exclusively for the Pye Record Company

STANLEY PAUL
LONDON

3 5 7 9 10 8 6 4 2

Copyright © Victor Silvester 1977, 1982, 1990, 1993

Victor Silvester has asserted his right under the Copyright, Designs
and Patents Act, 1988 to be identified as the author of this work

First published in the United Kingdom in 1977 by
Barrie & Jenkins Ltd
Reissued by Stanley Paul & Co Ltd 1982
Reprinted 1982, 1985, 1987
Revised edition 1990, reprinted 1990
Revised edition 1993

Stanley Paul & Co Ltd
Random House, 20 Vauxhall Bridge Road, London, SW1V 2SA

Random House Australia (Pty) Limited,
20 Alfred Street, Milsons Point, Sydney,
New South Wales 2061, Australia

Random House New Zealand Limited,
18 Poland Road, Glenfield,
Auckland 10, New Zealand

Random House South Africa (Pty) Limited
PO Box 337, Bergvlei, South Africa

Random House UK Limited Reg. No. 954009

A CIP catalogue record for this book
is available from the British Library

ISBN 0 09 178193 0

Typeset by Hope Services (Abingdon) Ltd.
Printed and bound in Portugal by
Printer Portuguesa

Contents

Acknowledgments

(TO FIRST EDITION)

The historical section in this book is a revised and
updated version of the opening chapters of *The Art
of the Ballroom*, now out of print, which I wrote
jointly with my friend the late Philip J. S.
Richardson, formerly editor of *The Dancing Times*.
I wish to express my thanks to Mary Griffith for
her invaluable editorial assistance in the revision
of both the historical and practical sections, and
my appreciation and gratitude to Norma Noble
for her great help in the revision of the Latin-
American section.

V. S.

Reviser's Note

The whole history of modern ballroom dancing follows the history of Victor Silvester very closely. He was in the forefront of dance and its music and played a major role in the development of social dancing. Right up to his death in 1978 he included all styles of dance in his work both as an author and with his world-famous orchestra.

The Victor Silvester Television Dancing Club ran for seventeen years and his Orchestra featured in more than 6500 broadcasts for BBC Radio. Some years ago his record sales were in excess of 75 million!

Together with Philip Richardson of *The Dancing Times*, Victor Silvester started the movement to standardize technique and form an official board which gave rise to the British Council and the International Council. This was indeed a chance meeting of two great men at the right time!

It gave me great pleasure to revise and update this book. It also gave me a great surprise for there was so little to be changed and what better testimony could there be to the thoroughness of the original work. But changes do take place all the time. The great impact of Disco dancing, with its solo style, is now complemented by the 'new' style of people dancing together. The latest craze is to dance in 'the old-fashioned way'! From my work with the International Council of Ballroom Dancing, I know of the influence of the Tango Argentine style and of the renewed interest in the Square Rumba for social dancing. Dancing is taking place in hotels and restaurants again and smaller floors have meant some alterations to dance performance which is reflected in this book.

The photographs, which are truly inspirational, were specially taken by Shaun Botterill of Allsport at the 1993 UK Open Championships. I think it is fair to say that the skill and artistry displayed on this and many other occasions has been built upon the foundations laid down by Victor Silvester. You can feel confident that study of this book will give you a fine start whether dancing for social enjoyment or planning more advanced competitive performance.

The wheel keeps turning. People have always danced and Victor Silvester has helped so many. I hope you enjoy his book.

BRYAN ALLEN
LEICESTER DANCE CENTRE, ENGLAND

Part I:
History

Kai Lillebo and Monica Rotvold of Norway are a talented couple who competed in the 1993
United Kingdom Amateur Modern Championship.

1

The Development of the Two Techniques

1 Old Time

The desire to dance is one of the primitive instincts of mankind. It has been said that 'dancing is older than anything except eating, drinking and love', and that 'rhythm is life' . . . and rhythm is the basis of dancing.

It is a fact that emotion stimulates the body into movement. Civilization and conditioning have taught people to suppress this natural response, but the primitive desire is there all the same. Prehistoric man expressed his emotions by movement in the days when speech had hardly been born. Primitive cave-drawings depict men dancing, and their dances are nearly always a kind of mime – an acting-out of their deepest thoughts and wishes.

As time went on language was developed and the immediate need for mime and gesture no longer existed. However, the expressive movements of early man continued, though they ceased to be spontaneous and became first formal and, finally, traditional. They were adapted as part of the customs of the tribe and, although often their origins were forgotten, they themselves lived on and became the foundation of folk dances.

The desire to move in response to emotion is a physiological fact which will survive, no matter how it may be suppressed, as long as people exist. The persistence of rhythm and its intimate association with sex and life itself is undeniable, and when rhythm and movement come together, dancing is born.

It was doubtless this desire for rhythmic movement combined with the communal instinct which is innate in almost every human being that enabled these crude folk dances to survive that dull period of history known as the Dark Ages. 'Throughout these earlier dark or middle ages,' writes Mr Perugini in his *Pageant of the Dance and Ballet*, 'dancing itself was always to be found in every country, in the form of traditional "folk" or national dances, indigenous to the soil: and moreover, dancing was a regular feature of most of the Church Festival days, especially in Italy, France and England. The dance may have languished during those dark or early middle ages, but it certainly did not die. What the dances of that lengthy period were – roughly from the dawn of the Christian Era to the fourteenth century – we do not know, or less surely at any rate than we do those of ancient Greece, simply from lack of those pictorial representations in which the Hellenic period of the dance was so rich. Indeed it is not really until the fifteenth century that we begin to find reliable records of the actual dances then in vogue, or any considerable testimony as to the popularity of dancing save in the form of ecclesiastical permission, or proscription.'

We gain our first authoritative knowledge of the earliest ballroom dances towards the end of the sixteenth century from a priest, one Jehan Tabourot, who, under the *nom de plume* 'Thoinot-Arbeau', published in 1588 his 'Orcheso-graphie'. Cyril Beaumont's excellent translation of this work into English should be known to every dancing teacher.

Arbeau himself lived at a time of transition when the rather solemn *basse danse* which had held sway for so long was gradually giving way to the livelier *branle*. It is interesting to note that each province had its own particular *branle* and that the Gavotte, which is described by Arbeau, was a branle of Provence danced originally by the inhabitants of Gap, and the Minuet a branle of Poitou. Amongst other dances described by Arbeau are the *pavane* and the *galliarde*. Shakespeare called this the cinq pace as it was made up of five steps.

Even in the days of which Arbeau writes a technique was slowly being formed by the dancing masters of the period, but it was not until the latter half of the seventeenth century, after Louis XIV had founded his 'Académie Royale de Musique et de Danse', that hard and fast rules for the execution of every dance were laid down by the members of the 'Académie' and the 'five positions' of the feet were formulated for the first time. These were the palmy days of the Minuet and the Gavotte. The Minuet, originally a peasant or folk dance of Poitou, was introduced into Paris in 1650 and later set to music by Lully and danced by the King in public. It may be said to have dominated the ballroom from that time until the close of the eighteenth century.

The ballets presented in the days of Louis XIV of France consisted of a series of 'entrées' such as the Minuet and other dances of the period. These dances were therefore spectacular as well as personal and, being spectacular, they had to be based on a technique which was to some extent artificial. The legs, for instance, had to be turned out, so as to provide a more graceful 'line', and many purely 'decorative' steps such as entrechats and cabrioles were executed.

The first definite cleavage between the ballet and the ballroom came when professional dancers appeared in the ballets and the ballets left the Court and went to the stage, but the influence of the ballet technique lingered for over two centuries and at the close of the Victorian era the dancing masters still based their tuition on the 'turned out' five positions of the stage.

2 Modern

When the ballet moved to the stage its technique became considerably enriched and though the *danse du salon* followed the instructions of the dancing masters, who also ruled the ballet, the coming of a new technique was already foreshadowed. It was, however, not until nearly two hundred and fifty years later that this new technique actually came into being.

We saw the first beginnings of modern dancing when, in 1812, the modern hold made its appearance in our ballrooms in the Waltz. We all know the storm of protest that this aroused at the time.

There has in the past been some difference of opinion as to the origin of the Waltz. The French trace it back to the Volta, a turning dance in triple time which came into Provence from Italy some time before Arbeau wrote his 'Orchesographie' in which it is fully described. The Volta is mentioned by Shakespeare and was a favourite dance of both Mary, Queen of Scots and Queen Elizabeth. Owing to the method in which the man swung his partner round in the *Saut Major*, the Volta, if we are to believe Arbeau, was a somewhat indelicate dance. It is more usual today to trace the origin of the Waltz to the Ländler of Southern Germany and it first came into notice about the year 1780.

Thomas Wilson, an English dancing master from the King's Theatre, in a book on Waltzing published in 1816 writes: 'Waltzing is a species of Dancing that owes its origin to the Germans, having been first introduced in Swabia, one of the nine circles of Germany; and from its introduction from thence into the neighbouring provinces, and afterwards, throughout the European Continent, its original manner of performance has been not only greatly improved, but such considerable additions upon its primitive principles have been made to it, so as to render it the most fashionable and agreeable species of Dancing.'

At the close of the eighteenth and in the early years of the nineteenth centuries, the Waltz, danced to tunes generally in three-eight time, was rather like a set dance. The couples stood in a circle around the room, partners held one another, generally by the hands only, and the dance consisted of several different figures. These are well shown in the plate which accompanies Wilson's book, and in an old print dated 1802 from a pamphlet entitled 'A Party of Pleasure to Paris' and also in a drawing by Thomas Rowlandson, published in 1806.

It was about 1812 that the Waltz with its modern hold took root in England, and it was about this time that Carl Maria von Weber, the composer of 'Der Freischütz' and 'Oberon', wrote his famous 'Invitation à la Valse', which, to quote Grove's Dictionary, 'marks the adoption of the Waltz form into the sphere of absolute music'.

The dance met with tremendous opposition. 'No event ever produced so great a sensation in English Society as the introduction of the German Waltz,' says a writer of the period. 'The Anti-Waltzing party took the alarm, cried it down, mothers forbade it, and every ballroom became a scene of feud and contention, sarcastic remarks flew about, and pasquinades were written to deter young ladies from such a recreation.' We are all familiar with Lord Byron's remarks about the dance, when, on entering a London ballroom, expecting to see a country dance, he (writing under the nom de plume Horace Hornem) discovered the partner of his joys and sorrows in the embrace of a 'huge hussar-looking gentleman, turning round and

round to a d—d see-saw, up and down sort of a tune like two cockchafers spitted upon the same bodkin'.

Other well-known people agreed with him. 'I am happy,' wrote Sir W. Elford to Miss Mitford in 1813, 'that you think with me about waltzing. Have you seen Sir H. Englefield's verses? They appear to me perfect as touching forcibly the proper points. They are supposed to be indignantly addressed to the man who is found waltzing with the poet's mistress:

What! The girl I adore by another embraced!
What! The balm of her breath shall another man taste?
What! Pressed in the dance by another man's knee!
What! Panting recline on another than me!
Sir, she is yours; you have pressed from the grape its fine blue,
From the rosebud you have shaken the tremulous dew;
What you've touched you may take, pretty waltzer – adieu!'

This state of things lasted but a brief while, and society surrendered to the new dance when the Emperor Alexander of Russia was seen waltzing round the room at Almack's, the highly exclusive assembly rooms.

The next advance towards what we call modern dancing was made in the 1840s when several new dances made their appearance in the ballroom. These included the Polka, Mazurka and the Schottische. At the same time there was a very strong tendency to drop all 'decorative' steps such as *entrechats* and *ronds de jambes* which found a place in the Quadrilles and other dances. Cellarius, a famous dancing master of the period, was one of the moving spirits in the reformation and some of his remarks in his book *Fashionable Dancing* (1848) are very interesting. He writes:

'The youthful dancers of the present day who are so often accused of walking, instead of dancing, are they so wrong in renouncing *entrechats*, *ronds de jambes* and other complicated steps in use in former days which had the serious inconvenience of recalling to one, most imperfectly and often most ridiculously, those which are exhibited every day on the boards of the theatre, with all the perfection of the art?'

At the close of the Victorian era ballroom dancing was inclined to stagnate, possibly owing to the absence of any new developments. The Two-Step was with us from New York but was still an academic *chassé à trois pas*: the Washington Post had had a season's fame and the Barn Dance a certain amount of popularity. It was not however until the present century was some years old that a new way of dancing to waltz music, known at the time as the Boston, and the coming of the Rag put fresh life into a stagnating art. These innovations appealed to the younger generation who had wearied of the eternal fast Waltz played by the many-hued Hungarian orchestras, and ballroom dancing took a fresh lease of life.

The younger generation, however, who danced at the clubs before the 1914 War, rebelled against the artificial technique of the old-time teachers with its five positions and 'pretty' movements. The coming of the First World War, when old institutions went by the board, encouraged this rebellion and there was introduced by the dancers themselves – not by the teachers, mark you – a free and easy go-as-you-please style based more or less on the natural movements used in walking. The coming of the Foxtrot in 1914 fanned this rebellion and killed the sway of the old-time technique.

For a time a state of chaos existed, but a few years after the Armistice the love of order which seems to be innate in the English asserted itself. A lead was given to dancers by a widely attended Informal Conference of Teachers called by *The Dancing Times* in 1920 at which some attempt was made to standardize the basic steps of the Foxtrot and One-Step. A new hierarchy of ballroom teachers arose. These particular teachers were the first dancers in the world to recognize the break with the old tradition and to evolve and codify a modern ballroom technique based on natural movement, with the feet in alignment.

They formed the first Committee of the 'Ballroom Branch' of the Imperial Society of Teachers of Dancing. The style which they codified and which has since been so highly developed is what we today call the 'English Style' and, with the possible exception of the United States of America, it has influenced modern ballroom dancing throughout the world.

2

How Dances Begin

In Chapter One we described the difference between old-time and modern dancing and how the later style evolved from the earlier. This chapter explains how our popular dances have reached the ballroom.

Ballroom dancing is not an activity which is cut off from the world, but a living thing influenced by events and sensitive to what is going on all around. A change of fashion, war, an upsurge of interest in a particular foreign country, pop music, increased opportunities for travel, social upheavals, the popularity of film or television music – all these have had repercussions on the dancing scene.

A dance, like any other living thing, must either develop or disappear; it cannot remain unchanged. The moment a popular dance becomes so standardized that it can develop no further its days are numbered. It will go on the shelf with the Minuet, the Gavotte, the Polka and other one-time favourites.

What then must be the characteristics of a new dance before it can hope to become the hit of the moment? The first is an easily recognizable and ear-catching rhythm which must be absolutely new to the ballroom, for a new dance is born of a new rhythm. We can trace no example of any rhythm ever returning to take on a second lease of life.

The old dances such as the Minuet, Gavotte and Polka, also the Waltz, Tango and Foxtrot, were all rhythms new to the ballroom when they were introduced. They were also all in a familiar time – 2/4, 3/4 or 4/4 – and one can discover no rhythm in an unusual time making any lasting appeal.

Another characteristic of a successful new dance is that it is a rhythm to which the steps of no existing dance can be satisfactorily fitted without some subtle change which alters the whole nature of the steps. For instance, there was difficulty in popularizing the Rumba until bands began to play it with the true feeling of Latin America and not as a dance very much like a Foxtrot.

And now consider the most important point of all: where does the rhythm come from which makes the new dance?

As far as it can be traced, in every case it comes from a folk dance.

Before the influence of North America had made itself felt Europe looked to the people of its own countries for these basic rhythms. Over the centuries every kind of rhythm was tried out, some being discarded, others going on to become popular dances.

The Minuet, most stately of all Court dances, originally came from the peasants of Poitou, the Gavotte from the people of Provence, both in France, the Waltz from the Ländler or folk songs of southern Germany and the Polka from Bohemia. When the possibilities of Europe had been exhausted the white population of North America turned to the rhythms at their own doors, and from the coloured people of the States came the Foxtrot – a rhythm which really had its origin in Africa.

Since then the dances of Latin America have gained tremendous popularity in the ballroom: the Tango from the gauchos of the Argentine, the Rumba, the Cha-Cha-Cha, the Samba. And now from its home in Spain has come the dazzling exhibition dance, the Paso Doble.

Strange as it may seem, the actual steps of a new dance are not particularly important. In the past, the steps associated with a new dance in the early days of its ballroom career rarely proved a permanent part of the dance. Quite often they were complicated and sometimes positively eccentric. Even when taken from the original folk dance they needed a good deal of adaptation to become acceptable in the smart ballrooms of their day.

The original steps of the Minuet, the Gavotte, the Waltz, the Polka, the Tango and the Foxtrot differed considerably from those used when the dances were at the height of their popularity. However, although the first steps are not of prime importance, of course they must be in keeping with the spirit of their times; no one would expect the mincing steps of the Minuet to last five minutes in the ballroom today.

As soon as a new dance appears its steps are tried by hundreds of dancers and teachers. In the light of their impressions modifications will probably be made: movements changed or omitted, or new ones included, much as it happened in the days of the Minuet.

The manner in which a new dance spreads socially is interesting; in its country of origin, from being a folk dance of the people, a simple, fascinating rhythm moves on to be taken up, in a modified form, by the sophisticated. In other countries the very opposite happens. The dance is picked up on its own ground by holidaymakers and travellers and taken back, to catch on in their home countries.

For the last four or five hundred years this has been the pattern of movement followed by all successful ballroom dances.

3

Just Before the 1914 War

1 The Waltz

Modern dancing was beginning to take definite shape in this era and much of its development depended on the conditions existing in London at that time.

Before 1914, at any rate in London, there was no equivalent of the modern dance hall. At a few English seaside resorts where many people took their holidays at that time, such as Blackpool, Douglas, Isle of Man, Morecambe, Great Yarmouth and Margate, large popular dance halls existed. In London, people who could only afford a little for their dancing were catered for by the old-time 'sequence' teacher who held dances in his own 'academy'. Possibly, once or twice a week, he organized an

'Assembly' in some Town Hall or similar place. At all these dances the 'sequence' and the 'set' dance flourished.*

The first modern 'Palais' to be opened was the Hammersmith** 'Palais de Danse' in 1919, soon to be followed by the 'Palais de Danse' at Birmingham under the same management. These Palais and the many others which sprang up differed from the old popular 'Assemblies' not only in their size and their equipment but also in their programme. The Palais provided an up-to-date programme with an up-to-date orchestra instead of the programme largely made up of sequence dances and played by a 'Quadrille Band' given at the old Assemblies.

Innumerable Subscription Dances, organized

---

* In a sequence dance the various movements have to be made in a set order. As a result the same step is being executed by all the couples in the room simultaneously. Sequence dances have generally been invented or arranged by teachers. Notable examples are the Veleta, the Military Two-Step and the Maxina. Before the First World War they were hardly ever on the programmes of the 'smart' dances but were confined to the 'Assemblies' organized by teachers. The last sequence dance to find any popularity in the smart ballrooms was the Barn Dance.

** Reviser's Note: Hammersmith Palais closed in 1987 and a new banqueting and conference suite is to be built on

the site. The last important dancing event to be held there was in November 1986 and I had the honour of being the Chairman of the Judges. The organizers, Philip and Pam Wylie, invited the Chairman of the British Council of Ballroom Dancing (who is also the President of the International Council of Ballroom Dancing) to address the large audience. Leonard Morgan detailed the history of the Palais from its days as a tram shed to that last, sad occasion. On a happier note, big bands such as Joe Loss, Rus Mitchell and Tony Evans have been engaged to play at the new Hammersmith Palais this season.

either in aid of charity or by some tennis, cricket or rowing club, were held in the ballrooms attached to the big hotels.

In addition there were numerous 'Dance Clubs'. These were not clubs in the usual acceptance of the term, as they owned no premises, but made use of some large ballroom. Each one was really a series of weekly – and sometimes bi-weekly – dances with a subscription covering the series. It was at these dances that one met the best dancers of the day and found well-known bands playing the most up-to-date music.

At the beginning of the twentieth century the Waltz was supreme. Since it was first introduced into London ballrooms it has passed through many changes, mostly of a fleeting nature such as in the late 1840s, when for a time the *valse à deux temps* was fashionable. Later on there were 'Hop Waltzes', 'Slow Waltzes' and even a strange melancholy affair known as the 'Kensington Crawl'. On the whole, however, the steps of the *valse à trois temps* as described by Carlo Blasis in 1830 more or less held good, with slight modifications.

By 1910 the Waltz was the unchallenged Queen of the Ballroom and in a programme of twenty-four dances eighteen might be Waltzes. The remaining numbers would be Two-Steps and Lancers, though at what may be called 'dancers' dances' the Lancers was never danced, and by 1911 the Two-Step had given way to the One-Step.

But if in 1910 Waltz music was supreme, the old-time Rotary Waltz was fighting for its life and a fierce battle was raging between the 'old-stagers' and the younger generation of those days as to how the music should be interpreted by the dancers.

It must be remembered that at this time it was only at the popular Assemblies and Academies that the Waltz was played slowly. Everywhere else, at the smart private dances, at the leading subscription dances, at the Hunt and Country Balls and at the dance clubs, the music was played at a considerable speed.

The ostensible quarrel between the two parties was a divergence of opinion as to whether one should do the old-time Rotary Waltz to this fast music or adopt the form of rectilinear Waltzing generally called the Boston.

But if that was the immediate cause of the dispute – a dispute in which the Press supported the old-timers and poked all the fun it could at the imagined eccentricities of the Boston – the real trouble lay deeper. It was, in fact, the beginning of the revolt by the younger generation of dancers against the rather stereotyped technique of the Victorian teacher with its 'turned-out' five positions and 'pretty' movements, which resulted shortly after the First World War in the foundation of modern technique based on natural movement.

Temporarily the Boston triumphed, and by 1912 at any of the Club dances in town we doubt if a Rotary Waltzer would have been seen – he only flourished at the private dance, the ordinary subscription dance, the Hunt and Country Ball and, of course, at the popular Assembly.

There may in the past have been many forms of Boston but the particular one in question was engendered by the fast music as it enabled the dancers to move at a more leisurely speed. It made its first appearance about 1902 at the 'K.D.S.' (Keen Dancer Society) dances. It differed greatly from the Waltz: in fact, except that both dances were done to music in triple time they had little in common.

In the Boston, partners held each other in the then American fashion hip to hip. The lady was on the man's right and both his feet were outside his partner. The rhythm or relative time duration in the Boston was not dactylic (long, short, short) as in the Waltz but all three steps were of equal time length and, moreover, occupied two bars of music. The six steps necessary for the full turn thus took four bars of music – twice the time required in the Rotary Waltz. The actual steps were taken as much on the flat of the foot as possible.

The basic movements of the Boston were

known as the Zigzag, the Turn (both Natural and Reverse) and the Crab, and there was something extraordinarily fascinating in doing them to a good swinging Waltz tune. As a well-known teacher of the day wrote at the time: 'It is to the melody one dances in the Boston, the steps and the movements are absolutely one with it, and that being so there is an independence of the exact attention to the beat required by the old Waltz. It is an impossibility to make beginners grasp this until they feel it for themselves. No amount of reading or writing on the subject will make the novice understand and it is this rhythm which is the great difficulty to the would-be pupil. The latest tendency has been to copy the Skating Waltz by using a great deal more swing during the turn, and in the reverse the actual Drop Three Skating Waltz is used.'

The Boston brought in its wake the usual number of variations such as the 'Double Boston', the 'Triple Boston' and the 'Royal Boston', of which only the first cut any ice at all.

The Boston died after a short but meteoric career some time in 1914. We are inclined to think that the crowded floors at the then smart places such as the Lotus, Ciro's, and the 400 where the Rag was the popular dance of the day did a great deal to kill it. It wanted too much space.

In the meantime the Tango – the pre-1914 Tango with its countless steps – had swept the country and a combination of the corté of this Tango with the Boston gave us the 'Tango Waltz' and the beginnings of the Hesitation. This was first tried in the Boston or 'hip to hip' position, but probably for the reason stated above a return was made to the classic Waltz hold. Writing about this dance in 1915, P. J. S. Richardson said: 'The Hesitation, I am told, is an American invention. Personally I do not think anyone has "invented" it in the strict sense of the word: it has been evolved out of the efforts of certain dancers to do Tango steps to Waltz time.'

2 The Tango

It is generally accepted that the Tango originated among the lower classes in the neighbourhood of Buenos Aires, particularly in the ill-famed 'Barrio de las Ranas', the most disreputable quarter of the city, when it was in the first instance known as *baile con corté* – the 'dance with a stop'. The girls wore very full skirts and the men the gaucho costume, with high top boots and spurs, and the attempt to dance in this cumbersome gear brought about several movements which afterwards became associated with the Tango.

The gallants of the town saw this dance and introduced it into their own favourite cafés, also of doubtful respectability, making two changes. To produce a more dreamy effect they substituted the *habanera* rhythm, and to show that their dance was no longer the common *baile con corté* they called it the Tango. For many years it was never danced by anybody in Buenos Aires who had his or her good name at heart.

It was probably towards the close of the nineteenth century that the Tango was first heard of in Europe, and after 1900 several sporadic attempts were made by amateurs from the Argentine to show it in Paris.

Among those who picked up the dance and were impressed with its immense possibilities was Monsieur Camille de Rhynal, who was afterwards to become well known as a dancer, a composer, a writer, and the organizer of countless dancing competitions.

It was in 1907 that he thought of the Tango he had seen in the Argentine, and proposed to Mr George Edwardes that an attempt should be made to introduce it on the London stage. Mr Edwardes at once sent for Miss Gabrielle Ray – then at the height of her fame as a musical comedy singer and dancer – and M. de Rhynal, with her assistance, gave the impresario an idea of the dance. Whilst all agreed that there were immense possibilities in it, it was at once realized that in its form at that moment it could not possibly be presented to a London audience.

M. de Rhynal in that same year found himself at the Imperial Country Club at Nice, and he gathered round him a few enthusiasts, including the Grand Duchess Anastasie of Russia. They set to work to experiment with the Tango, and very soon – shorn of its objectionable features – it became a dance possible for the ballroom. It even became possible for him to institute in that same year (1907) a Championship Contest.

The new dance soon found its way to Paris and for a time its headquarters were at a café then known as La Feria, afterwards Zelli's, which was in the rue Fontaine up at Montmartre. Such rapid strides did the Tango make in Paris that in 1909, when the paper *Excelsior* held a big dancing competition, the Tango was included, and this event was won by M. de Rhynal, who had Mado Minty for his partner.

The story is well known of the introduction of the Tango into England. A description of the dance was given in England in February 1911, but it was not until after the summer holidays of the following year that those who had seen it danced at Deauville, Dinard, and other casino towns, began to ask for it in London, and Tango Teas became the rage.

George Grossmith gave the first big fillip to the Tango in this country when he danced it with Phyllis Dare in 1912 at the Gaiety Theatre in 'The Sunshine Girl'. In a letter to P. J. S. Richardson he told how he first learned the dance, and threw an interesting light on the beginning of 'restaurant dancing'.

George Grossmith wrote: 'It was in the winter of 1911 when I had my first lesson in the Tango from Mme. Jean de Reszke at her house in Paris in the Rue de la Faisanderie. She was then an old lady, but danced like a girl of eighteen. It was she who actually started the dance craze in Society, and it became suddenly fashionable in Paris, and later in London, to have "Tango parties" in drawing-rooms with an Argentine boy playing the piano, in place of the usual "at homes".

'At this time also they began to introduce dancing couples into restaurants, and I think I was one of the first among the ordinary people watching to get up myself with a lady and dance on the floor between the tables. Other spectators followed suit. The restaurants welcomed this innovation (I was playing in Paris at the time), and began to clear a small space in the middle of the room. The Savoy was the first to do this in London.

'I may mention that I was the first to dance the Maxixe on the stage in London – with Kitty Mason at the Palace; the Cake-Walk with Florrie Ward in "The Toreador", and the Two-Step with Gertie Millar in "Our Miss Gibbs".'

The Tango of pre-1914 days was a very different affair from the Tango we know today. Not only was it danced to the *habanera* rhythm, but it was a dance of almost countless steps and figures. No two teachers taught exactly alike, and no serious attempt was ever made to standardize the dance. Sometimes the figures were called by their Spanish names, sometimes by their French, and this served to add to the confusion, a state of affairs that was not improved when one journalist announced that there could be found a new Tango step for each day of the year.

When Maurice and Florence Walton at Her Majesty's special request danced the Tango before Queen Mary at a ball given by the Grand Duke Michael at Ken Wood, Hampstead, in the summer of 1914, the actual figures which they made use of were El Paseo (the Slow Walk), La Marcha (the Quicker Walk), El Corte, Paseo con Golpe (the Walk with a Stamp), La Media Luna, Las Tijeras (the Scissors), La Rueda (the Wheel) and El Ocho (the Eight), and these represented the figures in general use at that time.

During the early years of the present century the only dances to be found on 'smart' programmes apart from the Waltz were the Two-Step, the Lancers, occasionally the Barn Dance, and sometimes as a finale the Galop. The Galop and the Barn Dance were on their last legs and

the Lancers was beginning to lose favour at 'dancers' dances'; they were, however, found on the programmes of all Hunt and Country Balls and also at many Private Subscription Dances until 1914. The Polka and the Quadrille were still retained on the programme of the State Balls.

About 1910 the Two-Step gave way to the One-Step, which brought in its train the Judy Walk, Turkey Trot, and Bunny Hug, but with the coming of syncopation and that remarkable tune 'Alexander's Ragtime Band' this had in its turn by 1912 become the 'Rag' and one of the most popular dances on the programme, particularly at the smart dance clubs.

It is interesting to note that before the coming of the Rag London was influenced by Paris: from this time onwards until after the First World War, when London herself took the lead, our dancing was swayed by that of New York.

With the ebbing of the Tango craze in the early days of 1914 we had for a time the strenuous Maxixe, which readers of today must not confuse with the Maxina, a sequence dance.

The wane of the Tango and the Boston – the latter with its hip-to-hip hold requiring too much space for the Dance Club – and the predominance of the Rag, set the teaching profession vainly searching for a new dance, and abortive attempts were made to introduce such freak affairs as the Furlana (on a reputed recommendation from the Pope), the Lulu-Fado, the Roulli-Roulli, the Argentine Polka (the most likely of them all but still too difficult), and the Ta-tao, described at the time as 'mere Chinese bunkum'.

In the meantime, and just before the outbreak of the war, quite unheralded, the Foxtrot crept in from America.

Mark Plant and Melanie Scott of England generate Tango atmosphere, dramatic feeling and total commitment on this Elevated Leg-Line. Very different from the Tango of earlier days!

4

Jazz

If it is agreed that Man was originally a primitive savage, then there was a time, countless ages ago, when he had no music at all. Eventually, with the passing of innumerable years, came the first natural rhythms – stamping the feet, clapping the hands, and the beating of drums.

In the East and Europe, Man, as he progressed towards civilization, evolved more complicated music for its own sake, but in Africa the Negro developed something quite different. He wedded his music to his dancing and his dancing to his religion. The drum in Africa became more diverse in form and complex in structure than all the musical instruments of the Western world put together.

True Jazz is the product of these centuries of evolution in drum playing, brought to its highest form in the school of the African jungle under the critical and sensitive ears of the highly emotional Negro people.

The Negro peoples of Africa, especially of the West African forests, have a most highly complicated religion, involving the recognition of countless gods, spirits, taboos and festivals. At these gatherings, the medium the people employ to express their emotions is the dance. Every tribe and sub-tribe has its own set of dances, each with its own dance rhythms – one for every occasion. They change according to the season, yet each is absolutely unique. No two are identical, even in part, though some may take over four hours to perform in full.

For a period of about three hundred years Europeans were involved in the West African slave trade. With their aptitude for wholesale organization, they were responsible for transporting hundreds of thousands of Negroes across the Atlantic. Those who survived the indescribable conditions of the slave ships were sold to white masters in the New World. What is not always realized, however, is that those slave owners were not only Englishmen and Anglo-Americans, but Frenchmen, Spaniards and Portuguese. Thus the Negroes in the New World, during their bondage and since their emancipation, have come under the influence of four distinct European cultures. The diverse results of these contacts were brought to our notice through the medium of their dances.

The slaves landed in America, looked for, and found, the same kinds of woods and clays as they had used in Africa to make their cooking pots and their drums. They reproduced their old customs, religions and festivals as much as they were allowed to do so. In fact, they succeeded in creating a new Africa, but for one important exception: in the New World, Africans of all tribes were thrown together. Customs, festivals and dance rhythms that had previously been separated by hundreds, even thousands, of tribal barriers were mixed indiscriminately. Language communication broke down also, and European languages had to be used. And for the first time in history, Negro Jazz began to circulate everywhere.

The history of Jazz in America has followed a different course under the influence of the four main European colonizers. In Portuguese and Spanish dependencies much intermarriage took place, which brought a rapid adoption by the Negroes of the cultures of these peoples. They heard old Spanish hill songs, remnants of flamenco and age-old serenades, and reproduced the melodies, or parts of them, as well as they could with their own instruments. They experimented with the dances of old Spain, but could not resist the temptation of invigorating them, repeating them again and again, introducing more and more of that pulsating rhythm which permeated the whole being of the Negro people – the heritage of Africa's tribal traditions.

New dances were thus born, the now-forgotten Son, and the Rumba, combinations of the colour and temperament of Spain with the powerful movement and rhythm of African Jazz. In some, the Spanish element prevails, while others, like the real Rumba, remain pure West African dances in every way except the melody. The double hip movement of the Rumba, completed in two and a half beats, is a highly complicated basic dance rhythm transported unadulterated from a tribe of Southern Nigeria.

In the French West Indian dependencies vigorous dances also evolved. As in the colonies of old Spain and Portugal, the Negroes under French rule reproduced their African culture as well as they could. They learned the beautiful anthems sung in the churches and strove to imitate them in their forest villages on their own instruments and any others they could muster, including old pianos and army bugles. When these dances burst upon the world at the Colonial Exhibition in Paris in 1931, the Beguine was paramount amongst them.

The love of the Negro in North Africa for dancing and his keen musical sense made themselves apparent from the first. Long before the days of the earliest Ragtime, the Negroes of the Southern states were adapting cowboy songs, hymns, sea shanties and even light operas to their own inimitable method of interpretation. The stirring pulse of the rhythmical drumming is so ingrained in the very soul of the African that it remains for him his universal means of expression.

Thus the white man became aware of that elemental thing called Jazz which the coloured man had to offer, and the Anglo-Saxons probably noticed it first because they lacked virile dances of their own such as other people possess traditionally.

From the time that the white man in North America became aware of Jazz music, the history of the dances that accompanied it became somewhat involved. The adoption of dances of diverse origins and their conversion to syncopated rhythms by artists of stage and cabaret led to further complications; for example, tap dancing – derived from clog dancing – was brought from northern England, the Cake-Walk from South Africa, and even the One-Step and similar so-called dances were pressed into service.

These complications took place for a variety of reasons: first, no community has ever long existed without the emotional outlet of dancing, which the Anglo-Saxons of North America lacked at that time. Secondly, the Americans, being a young nation, were keen to adopt anything new. Thirdly, and most important of all, was the fact that although the white people learnt the rudiments of syncopation, and some Negro songs, they either did not take the trouble to learn their dances, or entirely failed to realize that there were already any in existence.

In fact the discovery of Jazz produced a proliferation of dances, followed and even initiated by distinctive music that can only be classed together under the heading of 'syncopated' rhythm as opposed to unsyncopated. The Two-Step, the Bunny Hug and similar primitive forms of Jazz were introduced into the ballrooms of England, dances that were accompanied by the Ragtime bands. These originated in America where, at the same time, Negro laments were christened the Blues.

These early syncopated dances gradually replaced older dances until the First World War brought public dancing in restaurants. This gave a great impetus to the development of Jazz, which became a craze. During the war, also, American artists were much to be seen in the English theatre, and through them some understanding of Jazz was brought to this country.

By the time the war was over, the origin and true nature of Jazz had become obscured, while in America the gulf between the dancing of the Negro and the white communities had been considerably widened, both on the stage and on the dance floor.

The white man had acquired nothing but the novelty of syncopation, whereas the Negro had advanced to a moderate complexity of dances and music which varied in the fundamentals of their rhythmic construction. The 'Strut', the 'Shuffle' and the 'Drag' of the Negro were really different, whereas the imitation dances of the white people were so only in their high-sounding names. The adoption of the Blues by both communities marked the first real break with the old tradition, and when the Charleston was forced upon an apparently unwilling world some years later, in 1925, a new vista opened up. Co-operation between the Negro and the white man began again, largely due to the influence of one man alone: Paul Whiteman.

Musicians other than Negroes had by this time learnt to play Jazz, and Paul Whiteman revolutionized this music by first orchestrating certain numbers. From that time until 1934 the Negro again took second place, though he provided all the novelty in dancing, for which he was not given the credit.

New dances with extravagant names were advertised, most of which died without so much as being noticed, leaving no trace. The only examples that survived or exerted any lasting influence on Jazz dancing as a whole are those which are Negroid in origin, like the Charleston, the Black Bottom, and the Rumba.

5
1914–1918

When the war broke out the Tango and the Boston, already on their last legs, were completely forgotten. The Waltz very nearly died too, but in its 'Hesitation' form was occasionally danced. The highly syncopated One-Step or Rag more than held its own, but it was the Foxtrot, which was heard of for the first time only about a month before the outbreak of war, that was the rage of the ballroom. The reason is easily understandable.

When war came the most popular form of relaxation for the men on leave, either from France or the training camps in England, was a dance. Many of these men were almost fresh from school and had had no dancing experience. Their older relatives, so as to be with them as much as possible, also took up dancing again.

These people had not time to learn the intricacies of the Waltz or the Tango, but the fascinating lilt of the Foxtrot tunes and the informal nature of the steps appealed to them so much that in a few months the Foxtrot swept all other dances except the Rag off the floor.

It was during the summer of 1914 that the Foxtrot made its first appearance in the States. It was the result of the Negro influence referred to in the previous chapter and was, as a dance, the direct offspring of the One-Step and the Rag, and the tendency then very much in fashion on the other side of the Atlantic to introduce 'canters' and 'trots'. Its immediate forerunners were the 'Horse Trot' and the 'Fish Walk' of the preceding year.

It has an eponymous hero in the person of one Harry Fox, who was among the first to introduce it to the vaudeville stage, but the suggestion that it was named after the gait or pace of the horse, known in the West as a 'Foxtrot', is a much more plausible one.

Its original rhythm, with its tied notes after the second beat, came from the Negroes, and it was danced by the coloured population of New York for some time before it took white America by storm.

For the first few months of its existence the Foxtrot was a real 'go-as-you-please' dance, with no definite routine of steps. Such steps as were used were taken on the ball of the foot with a springy action, and were either slow (two beats) or quick (one beat). One basic movement was: 'Walk four slow steps (2 bars), then take a run of seven quick steps, bringing the right foot to the back of the left on the eighth beat.'

It should be remembered that when the Foxtrot came in the popular dances in the States were the One-Step and the Hesitation Waltz, with the Maxixe third and the Tango just past the crest of its popularity. As there were no definite Foxtrot steps, a free call was made on these established dances to supply movements.

In fact, one prominent American teacher, in reply to a request for a definition of the basic steps, wrote at the time: 'There are but two things to remember; first a slow walk, two counts to a step; second a trot or run, one count to each step. Any teacher teaching you more steps than this is drawing upon his inventive mind and mixing you a dose to take, consisting of Tango, Maxixe, Castle Walk and One-Step.'

In the early stages of its existence in England the stage gave the Foxtrot a big fillip and by the beginning of 1915 it was being played fairly regularly at the majority of dance places. As early as May that year the very first 'Foxtrot Ball and Competition' was announced.

The dance slowly lost its very 'fluid' condition and became slightly more stabilized. The slow walk and quicker 'trot' remained; a Butterfly figure became popular and the Twinkle made its appearance. Some curious figures had a vogue for a time, and much use was made of the Chassé, both for progression and for turning. The speed was about 32 bars per minute.

Towards the end of 1916 the dance had been in existence for two years, and after dancers had gone through a whole range of hops, kicks and capers, they showed a slight tendency to be bored and they let off steam by exaggerating many of the steps. This was counteracted by the arrival of a very smooth tune called 'Underneath the Stars', which became the rage.

To distinguish the smooth Foxtrot, which could be danced to this, *The Dancing Times* invented the name 'Saunter'. This form of the dance became quite popular in many quarters, and did a lot to eliminate freak steps and lay the foundation of that smooth-flowing Foxtrot for which English dancers were afterwards to become famous.

The year 1917 and the first half of the following year were almost a blank as regards ballroom dancing, and it is only towards what proved to be the final months of the war when such of our ballrooms as were open were crowded with American soldiers that the Foxtrot began a fresh phase of its existence.

Towards the end of 1917 'Jazz Music' was first heard, then described as the 'delirium tremens of syncopation . . . an attempt to reproduce the marvellous syncopation of the African jungle'.

In this country for quite a long time the term Jazz was thought to be the name of a new dance or a new routine of steps. Bands which in place of the 'strings' of pre-war days featured banjos, saxophones, and trap drummers became known as Jazz Bands, and the general public, who forgot that the old Quadrille Band played music other than Quadrilles, ran away with the idea that these orchestras 'jazzed' every tune.

Towards September 1918 'dips' and twinkles began to go out of fashion, and the Foxtrot showed a strong tendency to develop into a really smooth dance.

With the coming of Jazz music also arrived a new step which was destined to exercise an enormous influence on the Foxtrot: it was originally known as the Jazz Roll, and it was, undoubtedly, the forerunner of the Three-Step.

The basis of this movement, which, at that time, was introduced as frequently into the Rag as into the Foxtrot, was a series of three steps occupying four counts of the music. These steps could be taken both forwards and backwards, and also, when forwards, with a slight crossing of the feet, thus producing in a modified form the 'Dutch Roll' of skaters.

6

1918 to the First 'Worlds'

1 The Waltz

During the war the Waltz nearly died. After the war came a new generation of dancers who knew nothing of it. Waltzes were seldom played and the one Waltz tune that did make a real hit in Armistice days, 'Missouri', had a distinct Mazurka rhythm.

The German and Hungarian Orchestras who had set the fashion of speed vanished during the war. New bands arose who seemed to take their cue for the Waltz from the slow tempo that still survived at the popular Assemblies. A Rotary Waltz with a Hesitation movement was danced: there was a considerable amount of reversing, but the complete Natural Turn was generally conspicuous by its absence.

The reason for this was somewhat curious: everybody in those days Foxtrotted but in those early days of the Foxtrot, though the open or Foxtrot turn was used by all in the Natural direction, on the Reverse the Waltz turn was used by the majority. The result was that all those who had never been taught the Waltz could do the Reverse Turn but were not able to dance the Natural.

On the few occasions when Waltzes were played many dancers used Foxtrot steps, a complete Natural Turn was seldom performed, and the spirit of the Waltz was in grave danger of being lost. This was revived by the Informal Conference called by *The Dancing Times* in 1921, which defined the basis of the modern Waltz as 'step – step – feet together', and especially by the great Waltz Competition organized in the winter of that year by the *Daily Sketch*, but even in that the Waltzing reached only a very low standard and it is doubtful if the winners did one complete Natural Turn.

Apart from the absence of the Natural Turn the Waltz of those days was in many respects similar to that of today except that one crossed in the first part of the Reverse Turn and used a Heel Pivot in the last part. The first three steps of the Natural Turn were used, but this was followed by a Backward Change. The Change steps were taken with the feet passing on the third, and a number of Hesitation movements found favour. This was the Waltz which my partner and I used in the first competitions which we won.

The feeling that something was lacking in this dance spread abroad, but my partner and I were the first among the post-war English dancers to master the full Natural Turn and introduce it into the Waltz at the first World Championships ever held in London, which we were very proud to win.

That was in December 1922, and on that day the modern Waltz – as it is danced by so many professional couples today – was born.

2 The Foxtrot

In 1920 the speed of the Foxtrot was inclined to quicken, and tempi varied from 34 to 42 bars a minute. The Run – one short step on the ball of the foot to each count – about this time practically disappeared, and there came a 'cross behind' step introduced into the Chassé which held sway in some form or other for some time – in fact, until the introduction of the Feather. For the turns the Waltz step was used a lot, especially for the Reverse Turn.

This year, 1920, was an important one in the history of the Foxtrot, as it witnessed the first *Dancing Times* Informal Conference. This was attended by nearly three hundred teachers, and was made memorable by the attack made upon Maurice, who, with Leonora Hughes, had given a demonstration.

On the Continent there had been a determined attack by the Church and Press against the indelicacies of modern dancing and there was a certain amount of justification for the uproar. The Informal Conference was called to prevent such a state of affairs occurring in this country.

The teachers agreed:

To do their very best to stamp out freak steps in the ballroom, particularly dips and steps in which the feet are raised off the ground, and also side steps and pauses which impede the progress of those who may be following.

The 'side step' reference was to a modified form of the 'shimmy' then coming into vogue, and it was hoped that in future this would be taken at an angle of forty-five degrees instead of at right-angles to the line of dance. A sub-committee was appointed to consider the basic steps of each of the popular dances of the day. This committee submitted its report to a second Informal Conference, at which it was announced that the basic steps of the Foxtrot were three in number: the Foxtrot Walk (one step to two beats), the Chassé and the Three-Step.

In this year, 1920, an Open Foxtrot Competition was held. The judges awarded the very handsome prize to a then entirely unknown couple – Miss Josephine Bradley and Mr G. K. Anderson. Their steps were very simple: just a Walk, the Three-Step, a Cross Behind, and a side-step done at an angle of forty-five degrees with a slow drag of the foot not unlike the Change of Direction step.

This couple followed up their success by winning the first 'Ivory Cross All England Competition'.

So successful was this particular competition that the 'Ivory Cross' launched another one on similar lines, for which heats were held in London and several important provincial centres. The 'Grand Finals' were ultimately held on 9 December 1921.

The result of these three competitions at once made the hitherto unknown Miss Josephine Bradley an acknowledged authority on the dance, and since that day she has always held her position as a brilliant dancer and one of the leading protagonists of modern ballroom technique.

We are now approaching the era of the first big 'national' competition – that organized by the *Daily Sketch* – and the days when the modern technique began to take a definite shape.

During 1921 there was a further Informal Conference, when nearly three hundred teachers were present, and though a good deal was said about the threatened 'shimmy' step, actual decisions were left to a small committee with instructions to report in the autumn. As a result of her recent brilliant competition successes, Miss Josephine Bradley was for the first time in considerable demand as a demonstrator, particularly for the Foxtrot as then danced.

Professional dancers from Japan, Kozo and Masako Kodama, show expert balance, control and foot usage as they move between steps 3 and 4 of the Feather Step in the Foxtrot.

In October this Committee issued a report which stated:

They recommend that the basic steps of the Foxtrot be as arranged a year ago, namely, the Foxtrot Walk, the Chassé and the Three-Step, with the addition of the 'Cross Behind step', which has been seen in all recent competitions, and also of 'toddle' movements (to be done with a soft knee), and of the so-called 'shimmy' step, which takes the form of a forward and backward Chassé when the partners are partly facing the line of dance. No shoulder movement to accompany this step.

In 1922, partly as a result of the big *Daily Sketch* competition, the Foxtrot became a little 'over-standardized'. The only departure from the routine of the previous year was the gradual dropping of the Cross Behind step and the occasional introduction of the 'rhythmic walk' – sometimes called the 'camel' or 'collegiate walk' – which was then having a certain vogue in the States. This was due to the fact that a few bands, notably the American bands in the West End of London, were already beginning to play at a faster speed than the then orthodox 48 bars a minute, and the coming of the Quickstep was foreshadowed.

The Foxtrot of 1922–3, as described at the time, consisted of the Passing Three-Step, the Open Turn in both directions, and the Backward Wave. The Change of Direction step might have been added.

The beautiful, slow, smooth Foxtrot was now reaching the zenith of its career. It had ruled the ballroom since the early days of the First World War, but from this time onward it had to battle for its position with the Blues on the one hand and the dance that was to be called the Quickstep on the other. The Blues, like the Tango, had periodic 'revivals', but it never made any serious headway because its slow tempo required a balance and accuracy of footwork which the ordinary dancer does not possess.

In March 1922 there was held the first major competition in this country to determine the best 'all-rounder' dances in three dances. These were, on this occasion, the Waltz, Foxtrot and One-Step.

Later that year a World Championship was held in this country for the first time, organized by M. Camille de Rhynal, who had held similar events for several years in France.

The Championship dances were the Waltz, Foxtrot, One-Step and Tango. Couples danced two, sometimes three, at a time. There were three categories: Amateur, Professional and Mixed, and the winners in each category, together with the seconds and thirds, danced in the grand finals for the World Championship.

3 The Tango

The story of the Tango after the First War, at any rate in England, was rather an anti-climax. There was no recurrence of the great uproar which had greeted the dance in 1913 when crowded 'Tango Teas' were held in every hotel and special 'Tango Matinées' in half a dozen theatres. A dozen or so Tango 'teams' had disappeared, to give way to an occasional demonstration by a teacher. The Tango had ceased to be spectacular.

Actually, when war descended upon Europe, every ballroom dance, with the exception of the Foxtrot which was then at the beginning of its meteoric rise to fame, was blotted out. The Waltz was seen occasionally, but the Tango seemed to have gone for ever. However, the eclipse proved temporary; a year or two after the Armistice, when restrictions on dancing were at last removed in Paris, English dancers were surprised to hear that the Tango was once again the most popular dance there.

It was a chastened version, however. As was written at the time: 'There has been a marked alteration in the character of the music; the beat is more even and more subdued than before. There is more variety in the accompaniment to the air, and the general effect is one of great smoothness . . . This evolution in the music is paralleled by, probably occasioned by, an analogous change in the style of the dance. The exotic original of the gaucho estancias and Boca cafes has been remoulded more in accordance with the standards of the less ingenuous civilizations of Europe.'

By degrees the modern Tango drifted across the Channel from Paris to London, and a feature was made of it by many teachers and at a few of the dance places. At any rate, sufficient interest was taken in the dance – by the profession at least – for *The Dancing Times*, which had been a staunch supporter of it ever since 1912, to organize in May 1922 the first of its very successful 'Tango Balls'. It was attended by nearly three hundred teachers and others who came from all parts of the country. The chief attraction at this ball was the demonstration of the Tango by Marjorie Moss and Georges Fontana, and the competition which they judged.

In the course of the demonstration five figures were used. The following is a rough description of them written at the time: 1. The Simple Walk, performed with a peculiar drag of the sole of the foot; 2. The Argentine Walk – right, left, right to the side, close left to right; 3. The Promenade (very little 'opening out') – left to the side, right over left, left to the side, close right; 4. The Demi-Vuelta – best described as a half a Waltz Reverse Turn, ending with the left foot crossed in front of the right; 5. The

Lace Step – a walking step in various directions.

The next event in the story of the Tango in England was the appearance in London of Carlos Cruz, who was one of the foremost exponents of the dance in Paris; he exercised a good deal of influence on the Tango in this country.

In October 1922 over three hundred teachers attended the Informal Conference called by *The Dancing Times* to discuss the Tango. The main speakers were M. Camille de Rhynal, who explained the musical differences between the pre- and post-war Tango; M. Pierre, who showed certain steps; M. Carlos Cruz and Mr Georges Fontana, who both gave demonstrations of the sequence of steps generally in use at that time in Paris.

The result of this Conference was far-reaching. It was agreed that care should be taken to use only the modern tunes, and that the best tempo was about 30 bars per minute. It was pointed out that the feet must be kept straight and not turned out. (This statement would be astonishing today, but in 1922 modern ballroom technique had not been codified.)

It was also decreed that all the figures, with the exception of the Promenade, should be completed in an exact number of bars; the Promenade was different because it occupied a bar and a half.

From this moment, the Tango may be said to have been stabilized in this country.

7

The Coming of Technique

We have now reached a critical period in the history of modern ballroom dancing and before developments in the Waltz are considered and the division of the Foxtrot into Foxtrot and Quickstep, it will be as well to say a few words about an event which has had as great an influence on ballroom dancing as did the founding of the Académie Royale by Louis XIV of France on the ballet: this was the formation of the Ballroom Branch of the Imperial Society of Teachers of Dancing in 1924.

The 'Imperial' had been in existence for a number of years and in a loose kind of way had catered for all styles of dancing. In 1924, however, it was decided to remodel the Society and make each branch representative of the particular style of dancing to which it was dedicated.

The immediate reason for forming a special Ballroom Branch, however, was the news that P. J. S. Richardson, with several of the leading London ballroom teachers, none of whom was a member of the 'Imperial', contemplated forming a new Society of Teachers of Ballroom Dancing. He was interviewed by the Secretary of the 'Imperial' and gave an undertaking that if the 'Imperial' would take the matter out of his hands there would be no need for a new Society.

The result was that Miss Josephine Bradley, Miss Eve Tynegate-Smith, Miss Muriel Simmons, Mrs Lisle Humphreys and I were at once approached and became the first Committee of the Ballroom Branch of the Imperial Society and by the end of the year the Society's official publication *The Dance Journal* contained the syllabus of the examination which the candidates for admission to the new branch would have to pass.

This required:

1. A rudimentary knowledge of music as required for modern ballroom dancing.

2. Carriage of the arms, head and body.

3. A knowledge of the basic steps of the Foxtrot, Waltz, One-Step and Tango. Candidates were allowed to bring their own partners to assist them to demonstrate their ability to perform the dances in good style.

The same issue of *The Dance Journal* contained a detailed description of the steps required.

For a number of years, in fact from the time of the coming of the Boston and the Rag, it was obvious to everybody that ballroom dancing was passing through an immense change, but the five teachers who formed the first Ballroom Committee of the 'Imperial' were the first people in the world to analyse that change and discover exactly what it was. They pointed out that the old ballet technique had been passed by and that the modern technique was based entirely upon natural movement. As a result of their efforts and their own experience they were able to codify that technique and to set out the laws which governed such subtleties as body sway, contrary body movement, and rise and fall. It was not the work of a week, nor of a year. With the help of others who have joined their Committee the work has been constantly going on until today the technique of ballroom dancing is as precise as that of the ballet.

It is undoubtedly owing to the work of these teachers that the 'English Style' has made such great headway and is so much in demand all over the world today.

English Style is Perfected

The dancing of the leading professionals in the 'Worlds' towards the close of 1922 went a long way towards establishing the modern Waltz more or less as we know it today. It was then a very simple dance – just the Natural and Reverse Turns and the Forward and Backward Changes. It was not until two years later that Hesitation steps again made their appearance and Maxwell Stewart introduced the Double Reverse Spin.

About this time, very largely to help those inexpert dancers who could not make a complete turn, the diagonal Waltz, in which only three-quarters of a turn was necessary, came into being, and the Forward Change which previously had been three passing steps was altered to 'step, side, close'. A few years later, particularly in the diagonal Waltz, the crossing of the feet in the third step of the Reverse Turn went out of fashion and they were placed side by side.

In the meantime those same World Championships of 1922 saw the end of the Cross Behind step in the Foxtrot, and the substitution of the Feather.

The following year, 1923, was an eventful one in the ballroom. Paul Whiteman and his band were heard for the first time in this country; there was a considerable demand for Blues and fast Foxtrot and the cleavage between the slow and fast Foxtrot became more apparent.

Towards the end of the year Miss Bradley, writing in *The Dancing Times*, after commenting upon the total elimination of the Chassé and naming the principal Foxtrot steps then in use, said: 'Some American bands play very fast time indeed in the Foxtrot – over 50 bars a minute. To this fast music it is better to discard the passing Three-Step and to use the rhythmic walk, i.e., steps rather shorter than usual and with a slight rise on the ball of the foot at each step. The effect must be smooth, however, not jerky.'

The following year this tendency became even more pronounced and at a Dancers' Circle Dinner it was agreed by the profession that the fast Foxtrot should be known as the quick Foxtrot. This new dance practically displaced the One-Step, which had been carrying on a precarious existence for some time. The One-Step was still included as one of the four standard dances at the second and third World Championships held in London in 1924 and 1925, but after that it dropped out of the competitions in this country and at the 1925 World Championships a special competition in the quick Foxtrot was held.

Nineteen twenty-five witnessed the first of the big competitions organized by the *Star* newspaper which were held for the next seven years. Whilst they lasted they were recognized as the event of the ballroom year and the equivalent of a British Championship. They played an important part in the development of the English Style, as the very best movements that came into fashion during the year were crystallized in the dancing at these finals.

In 1925 there was a further revival of interest in the Tango and a big competition with a motor-car as first prize was featured at the Empress Rooms in the autumn.

It was this same year that saw the beginning of the Charleston craze. The Midnight Follies had introduced the rhythm, but it was at a special Tea Dance at the Carnival Club in Dean Street that Annette Mills and Bobbie Sielle, fresh from a trip through the States, introduced the teachers to its ballroom possibilities, and from then onwards for nearly two seasons the Charleston carried all before it. C. B. Cochran organized the enormous 'Charleston Ball' at the Royal Albert Hall and it became necessary to popularize a slogan 'P.C.Q.' (Please Charleston Quietly) as so many folk received physical injuries. There were all sorts of Charleston, including the 'Flat Charleston'. After people had temporarily tired of the new dance it became absorbed in the Quickstep and so gradually drifted away.

Writing about the Quick-time Foxtrot and Charleston – as the Quickstep was first called – Frank Ford said:

'It was obvious, however, that this dance [the Charleston] could not hope to survive in its original form: it was too crude, too wild to be a continued success so the process of taming was inevitable ... One could see it was difficult to progress in this dance; couples danced in a restricted area and held up other couples. We now had two new dances, the Quick-time Foxtrot and the Charleston, and somebody had an idea. At the 1927 Star Championships a new dance was introduced: on the programmes it was christened Q.T.F.T. and C. which meant Quick-time Foxtrot and Charleston. The ideal construction would therefore seem to be lots of Q.T.F.T. with splashes of Charleston here and there to liven it up. In the Star of 1927 and 1928 (when the same title for the dance was used) the leading professional couples evolved a rather smooth rhythmical dance, the wild Charleston having almost disappeared, a subtle knee action applying the rhythm.'

Mr Ford, it should be mentioned, won the Q.T.F.T. and C. in 1927 – in fact he won the Star Championship that year. He did not compete the following year, but in 1929 when the dance was for the first time in the Star Championships known as the Quickstep, he was again successful. On both occasions he was dancing with Molly Spain.

It was in the summer of 1927 that Miss Bradley, lecturing at one of the Imperial Society's Technical Schools, said:

'In addition to the lilting Quickstep of last year, with its open chassés and rhythmic movement produced by the flexing and straightening of the knees, the Quickstep is now also done smoothly. In the smooth Quickstep the feet in the chassé turns are closed and rise and fall is obtained from the ball of the foot instead of the flexing and straightening of the knee. A good deal more ground is covered with this type of Quickstep and, being in some respects reminiscent of the slow Foxtrot, it produces a pleasant contrast to the Charleston.'

In 1927, when the Charleston craze was over and the Charleston was becoming linked up with the Quickstep, we had that strange dance the Black Bottom which, although never a success in the ballroom, has exercised a considerable influence on other dances.

It was in 1927 in an effort to preserve the Foxtrot that the 'Ancient Order of Foxtrotters' was founded by Michael Stokes with the help of The Dancing Times. This 'Order' demanded that bands should play Foxtrots at the then recognized speed, namely 48 bars per minute.

The same year witnessed an attempt to launch a complicated number, the Heebie Jeebies, and a considerable upsurge of interest in the Blues. A routine for this dance, known as the 'Yale Blues', had a really remarkable success all over the country.

Nineteen twenty-eight was a year of freak dances, none of which made any serious headway, and many new variations of purely transient interest were introduced into both the Foxtrot and the Quickstep. The Dancing Times in conjunction with the Imperial Society organized a British Professional Championship. This was won by that sterling dancer Maxwell Stewart dancing with Pat Sykes. In the hope of interesting the West End public the preliminary heats were held at hotels instead of in the more popular Palais. This turned out to be a mistake and the competition proved a heavy loss. In the same year and also in the following one Santos Casani, on behalf of the Columbia Gramophone Company, organized an important Amateur Championship which took place at the Royal Albert Hall in London.

8

The 1930s to the Present Day

The more recent period of the history of ballroom dancing started with the Waltz, Foxtrot, Quickstep and Tango generally recognized as the four standard dances, although the name 'Quickstep' for the fast Foxtrot was not universally accepted.

It was a time of controversy: on what may be described as the 'social' side it saw the division of the dancing world into two factions – the casual, social occasion dancers, and the 'competition' or Palais-style dancers who frequented the larger dance halls.

During these years, the late 1920s and the 1930s, came the systemization of competition dancing under the Official Board and the National Society of Amateur Dancers and, in 1929, the important Informal Conferences called by The Dancing Times which resulted in the formation of the Official Board of Ballroom Dancing. This organization is now known as The British Council of Ballroom Dancing.

Many of the bands were then playing a Foxtrot – especially in the smart hotels – at a speed midway between the Quickstep and the true Foxtrot, which was becoming slower and slower each season. Many abortive attempts were made by the profession to establish the 'midway' tempo and in 1930 a routine of steps known as 'Midway Rhythm' was officially proposed, but the public did not take it up.

In Britain the dancing in the hotels and restaurants, and the 'competition' style in favour with good dancers in the spacious dance halls, tended to drift farther and farther apart. The 'Social' style became known as 'Crush' dancing because of crowded ballrooms and restricted space, and later acquired the name still in use, of 'Rhythm' dancing. With the closure of all the large public ballrooms the competition style of dancing is now seen at special promotions only. The space needed by the leading exponents is not normally available at public dances and therefore the dancing is more of the social style. Pop music featured from the mid 1960s and produced the Disco style of dancing whilst the commercial promotion of dancing produced very small floors and greater space for eating and drinking. There is evidence of a much greater interest in social dancing at tea dances and it would appear that the dinner dance scene has remained almost unchanged. The smaller floors present little problem for the

In the Shadow Position in the Latin dances, the man is slightly behind the lady. This is an advanced development in many figures – particularly the Samba – note how the couple are still very much 'together'.

dancers although the social style has become more compact. Perhaps history is starting to repeat itself and we may see, as reported by George Grossmith in his letter to P. J. S. Richardson in 1912 and recounted on page 19, people who go out to eat and drink starting to get up and dance between the tables!

The 1930s also brought a series of Party or 'Romping' dances, starting in 1937 when the musical *Me and My Girl* with Lupino Lane featured the Lambeth Walk. Certainly 'You'll find them all Doing the Lambeth Walk' was true, for with its easy-to-remember tune and cheeky novelty it caught the mood of the moment.

It was followed by other 'fun' dances on the less serious side, involving more or less prescribed actions rather than progress round the dance floor: the Chestnut Tree came at this time, also Boomps-a-Daisy and the immortal Knees Up, Mother Brown, still to be seen and heard at the less sober end of the evening at innumerable parties and in countless pubs.

On the Latin-American side, that delightfully light-hearted dance, the Samba, arrived in Europe from South America in the late 1930s, but only caught on generally in this country after the Second War. Its popularity was helped by some immensely attractive music and its lively rhythm. For any dance to find favour with the general public it must have a distinctive and easily definable rhythm. It is on this account that such dances as the Beguine, the Mambo and the Bossa Nova have not been generally accepted although their music has been, and still is, exceedingly popular all over the world.

Swing music, Jitterbug and Boogie-Woogie were names which had already arrived in Britain from America before the war, but the new, exciting style of dancing really came over with the American and Canadian Servicemen from 1940 onwards. But Jitterbugging, with its wild, uncontrolled movements and compulsive Boogie-Woogie music, soon had a bad name: it was thought to be too abandoned and dangerous for public dancing, and most ballrooms

banned it altogether. However, the professional dancing world, seeing that it could not be kept down, set about taming it and making it an acceptable ballroom dance with properly worked out, teachable figures. In this modified form, to its exciting music and under its new name, Jive, it flourished, eventually becoming a standard dance in the Latin-American group.

However, the general dancing public was looking around for something new, and within a few years it had arrived: Bill Haley and his Comets playing 'Rock Around the Clock'. Audiences went wild. Wherever the powerful beat of Rock music was heard youngsters leapt to their feet and danced – not only on dancefloors but in cinema aisles and everywhere else where the music was played. Although Rock 'n' Roll is related to Jive and danced to the same rhythm, the style is simpler and can be less energetic. The era of Pop music really began with Rock 'n' Roll and the early Rock groups which were featured in films and on records at this time.

In the early 1950s there were many big ballroom championships and competitions throughout the country. The British Championship at Blackpool, which was started early in the 1930s, is still going as strongly as ever today. The *Star* Championships, which had been held since the late 1920s, were terminated, sadly, at the beginning of the 1950s. In 1953 came the International Championships held every year at the Albert Hall in London and promoted by Elsa Wells, an event which is as successful as ever today although they are now organized jointly by Elsa Wells and Bobby Short. Bobby Short is the Chairman of *Dance News*, a weekly dance paper which celebrated its golden jubilee in 1988. All profits from these championships go to charity and, over the past thirty and more years, many thousands of pounds have been raised.

Old-time and sequence dances, which continue to be tremendously popular, particularly in the North of England, are rarely featured in smart ballrooms, or dance halls which cater for modern dancing. Old-time dancing is more or less exclusively British. It is on occasions featured to a limited extent in Australia and New Zealand, but it is never seen or heard of on the Continent or in the USA, or anywhere else for that matter. Where it is popular its wide appeal stems from the fact that every couple dances the same steps at the same time, usually to sixteen-bar sequences. In consequence of this it does not demand such a high standard as is required for the best dancers in the modern style who have to improvise and think for themselves.

There was change in the air once more as the new decade opened and when Chubby Checker's 'Let's Twist Again' arrived in 1961 the dance world seized upon it. Condemned as improper and worse, like the Charleston thirty-five years earlier, it went from strength to strength. Easy to learn, fun to dance with its distinctive beat, young and old Twisted the night away. The Twist brought with it a new idea: the dancers did not have to have partners, girls did not have to wait to be asked to dance; everyone could join in. At first there were definite, easily recognizable figures, but as the dance took root innumerable variations developed until everyone's style was personal and unique. The influence of the Twist spread: dresses were made with little pleats at the hem which flicked as the wearer Twisted; fashion

models posed in the Twist stance; there were complaints of aching muscles and painful backs; but its popularity was supreme.

In 1962, following the excitement of the Twist, another and totally different dance was steadily making headway: the Cha-Cha-Cha. It is derived from the Mambo, which has too difficult a rhythm for the general dancing public. The Cha-Cha-Cha, with its sophisticated, easily counted beat and distinctive, easily recognizable rhythm, arrived from the USA and soon was heard everywhere. It is an adaptable dance which can be a flamboyant competition number, as effective in showing off the man as the girl, or equally it can be tremendously subtle and sexy on a tiny night-club floor.

Finally there is the form of dancing which is now internationally popular, to the exclusion of almost everything else amongst the young people – Beat or Disco dancing. A derivative of the irresistible rhythm of the Twist, danced individually and apart, style and movement are entirely what the dancer makes them. It does not progress and there are no set steps; almost all the expression is in the movement of body and arms.

Disco dancing is the other end of the line from the formal dance patterns of the past with their standardized figures: the ultimate free-for-all of the twentieth century.

Part II:
Practice

This position is 'The Spanish Drag' in the Tango, showing the development of the 'Big Top Line' or wide look between the man and his partner, though body contact is still well maintained.

41

9

On Dancing

Ballroom dancing is one of the most popular leisure time activities in the world. It has universal appeal, for dancing is both tremendously enjoyable and a great social asset.

In the average ballroom the words 'modern ballroom dancing' all too often mean a shuffle round the floor. Most couples, if they could see themselves, would be so surprised that they would quickly set about improving their standard of dancing.

However little you may know about dancing technique, you will certainly be able to pick out of a crowd those who are really enjoying not only the music and excitement and each other's company, but the dancing itself. These are the people who move easily and in rhythm with the music. They may dance only a few different steps, but these will be basic figures which do not change from one year to the next, and they will be danced neatly and simply.

Few people are 'natural' dancers, but with a little instruction everyone can dance well enough to be a social asset in any ballroom and to get pleasure out of every moment.

Few ballrooms today are large and the aim of good dancers should be to make the best use of what space is available rather than to get round the floor quickly. This means that the 'Rhythm' style should be used for every type of Foxtrot, at whatever speed it is played – slow, medium or quick. Only if there is plenty of room may the orthodox Foxtrot be danced.

Most people enjoy a Waltz, whether modern slow-tempo or Viennese-style. In their advanced form all these need space, but their more simple figures are quite suitable for any size of dance-floor.

The Tango tends to put the beginner into a panic, yet its strongly marked beat is a help, and it is not too difficult to dance. It is well worth learning some of the easy figures so that you can dance to the exciting music of the Tango.

These are the standardized dances in the English style, and then of course there are the Latin-American dances which have caught on all over the world.

Sequence and old-time dances have a good following in many places in Britain. They are easier to learn than the modern dances because they are often made up of set figures repeated to eight, sixteen or thirty-two bars of music, whereas in modern dances it is left to the individual dancers to improvise and amalgamate the figures.

The English style of ballroom dancing has been copied by practically every good teacher throughout the world simply because it is acknowledged to be the best. This book will set you on the road to acquiring it yourself.

In the following pages I have chosen dances from the modern group which are suitable for beginners, bearing in mind that the 'social' dancer does not need to learn detailed technique. I have included some hints which have proved useful in teaching beginners. For each dance there is a simple syllabus of figures; from experience I know these to be perfectly adequate for the average dancer who just wants his dancing to be correct, enjoyable and suitable for any size of ballroom. These figures form a sound foundation for the ambitious beginner who can move on to more advanced figures and dances. Teachers of beginners in private lessons and classes will also find them useful.

Of Basic Importance

The Hold
The correct hold for each dance is described at the beginning of the chapter on each dance's figures.

Balance
Important rules to remember are: when you are moving forward, keep your feet in a straight line; do not try to avoid your partner's feet by walking outside them. When moving backwards, keep the feet in line in the same way – imagine you are 'walking the dotted line'.

Good balance is really a matter of practice in correct walking. When you are walking along the street, you do not push your feet out in front and allow your body to follow. So, in dancing, carry your weight forward with the moving foot. When moving backwards, step back on to the toes, bringing the weight gradually back with the forward foot before taking the next step. Good balance comes with control of movement, and this will improve as your dancing progresses. A more detailed description of walking steps is given for each dance.

The Head
Many dancers do not realize the great importance of head position for both partners. A tendency to look down, besides spoiling the appearance of the couple, throws out true balance because the head is heavy compared with the other parts of the body. Keep the head up, the chin held naturally in; it is a good idea to keep the eyes at their usual level. The man's head should be held so that he looks straight over his partner's right shoulder. The lady should look over the man's right shoulder.

The Body
Many dancers look either stiff or uncontrolled. Those who look stiff are keeping their muscles taut instead of holding the body in a natural, erect position, without raising the shoulders or pushing out the chest. On the other hand, sagging shoulders, floppy arms and slack stomach muscles give an uncontrolled appearance. The arms and elbows should be held up without raising the shoulders. The lady must not hang on her partner, either weighing him down with heavy arms or holding him tightly. Her left hand should rest lightly on his right upper arm, fingers neatly closed together. It is a good idea to think of the diaphragm muscles as the centre point of control of the whole body.

The Legs
Faults that apply to the body apply also to the legs; that is to say, over-stiffness or lack of control. Movement of the legs should be free and from the hips, not the knees. A natural bracing and relaxing movement should be used in each step. In all English-style dances – where there is room to move – the knees, generally speaking, are at their straightest – but not stiff – at the full extent of a stride, and relax slightly as the weight is taken on the foot.

The Feet
As described under 'Balance', the feet should be kept straight. Out-turned toes are a common fault amongst beginners: to correct a tendency

to this, practise walking properly along the street. If you can do this you will dance infinitely better. Try to feel your feet brushing past each other as you dance both forward and backward steps.

Proper use of the ankles is important too. When you have reached the full extent of a stride forward, the ankle of your back foot should be stretched with only the toes touching the floor, not the ball of the foot, before you move the front foot into its next position.

Leading

Quite a number of men who learn to dance the figures reasonably well still find that their partners complain: 'He does not lead me.' The man cannot concentrate on leading until he has mastered the figures and their amalgamation, but he should then learn to lead so that his partner can follow with confidence, and not have to guess what is coming next. On the other hand, he must never allow himself to be led into a figure by his partner anticipating his next move and pulling him into it.

The man must take his steps with decision. Even if they are incorrect, it is better to move firmly than to dither. The lady is more likely to follow and you will not fall over each other. In fact, if you lead well, she may not even realize that anything is wrong.

Apart from indicating by the movement of body and legs the direction of the next step, the man should use his right hand to help to lead the lady – except in Latin-American dances, where often both hands are used to lead. If he wants his partner to stay in the basic dancing position, almost square in front of him, the man should keep his right hand curved naturally on her back with even pressure along the hand; if the lady is to step outside her partner, he should press slightly with the fingers of his right hand; to turn the lady into Promenade Position (that is, where the couple open out fan-wise to form a 'V' and the man's right side only is in contact with, or close to, the lady's left side), he should apply slight pressure with

the base of the hand. To turn her to face front once more, the man presses slightly with his fingers again. All of this will of course be done almost unconsciously after some practice.

The Music

Time, tempo and rhythm are dealt with separately for each dance described in this book. However, here is some advice for beginners who find it difficult to hear the beat of the music. Listen as you wait to move off with your partner; count at least one bar of music, or more than one, to yourself. There is no need to hurry. Make sure your weight is off the foot you intend to move first. There is no rule about whether you should step off with your left foot or your right. As long as the man makes his intention clear by taking his weight on to the non-moving foot in a momentary pause before he moves off, which foot he steps on first is immaterial.

To help you to hear the beat, get someone to count the beats for you to the music; then practise counting them aloud yourself until the rhythm becomes fixed in your mind and you can keep time without thinking about it. It is quite common to see couples dancing out of time with the music, and not even noticing it. Train your ears, and after some practice you will find that keeping time has become quite automatic.

Ballroom Etiquette

It is the man's privilege to ask a lady to dance with him. He should ask politely, using some such expression as 'Would you like to dance?' or simply, 'Shall we dance?' The lady should always accept willingly, unless there is a very good reason for not doing so. She may have seen that he has bad manners on the dance-floor, or that he has had too much to drink. In this case she may say 'No, thank you.' Normally, however, she will accept, and if she later finds that her partner is not a very good dancer, she must put up with it cheerfully and do her best to follow him.

If a lady refuses a dance because she wants to rest for a few minutes, she must not change her mind and accept another partner until that particular dance is over.

Once on the floor, consideration must be given to the other dancers. Avoid collisions wherever possible. If there is a collision, apologize even if it was not your fault. At the end of the dance, everyone should applaud in appreciation of their partner and to encourage the band. The man should then thank his partner and escort her to her seat.

Men look their best on the dance-floor neatly dressed, in a suit or tidy casual clothes, or a dinner jacket. Tails are worn only on very formal occasions and, of course, as a kind of uniform for all major competitions and championships.

As he moves on to the dance-floor, a man should always, automatically, button his jacket.

A dress is more comfortable for the ladies to dance in than separates, which tend to come apart in the middle. A long dress may be worn at almost any time these days, and a simply cut one looks most attractive. You will have no difficulty in dancing in a long dress, but if the skirt is a little narrow for the longer steps, it can be slit to the knee at the side seams. Never try to dance clutching your handbag behind your partner's back, or swinging it from your right hand.

How to Read the Diagrams

In the diagrams the right foot is illustrated thus –

and the left foot –

The dotted outline of the foot is the position of that foot after you have turned on it.

The above denotes a turn on the ball of the right foot as it occurs in the diagrams given with each dance.

The above denotes a turn on the heel of the left foot.

In nearly all the figures each foot is moved alternately, just as when you walk; that is, you take a step with the left foot and then a step with the right foot (or vice versa). In following the diagrams, it will help the reader if he or she remembers this point, or it will be noticed that if the numbering 1, 3, 5, 7 is, say, the left foot, then 2, 4, 6, 8 will be the right foot (or vice versa).

You will find the diagrams easier to follow if you always face the direction in which the toes are pointing. As you turn, turn the diagram as well.

Let your feet follow along the lines in which the arrows are pointing.

The diagrams are not intended to be mathematically exact, but merely to show the pattern made in the different figures. The left side of the page on which each diagram is drawn represents the middle of the ballroom, whilst the right side of the page represents the outside – the wall. The top of the page is equivalent to the line of dance. From this the reader will be able to understand which way he or she should be facing on each step.

Explanations of Abbreviations used in Diagrams and Descriptions of Figures

S – A slow step

Q – A quick step

R – Right

L – Left

RF – Right foot

LF – Left foot

RS – Right shoulder

LS – Left shoulder

Diag. – Diagonally

LOD – The line of dance. (This means the direction that one takes when dancing round a ballroom anti-clockwise.)

CBM – Contrary body movement

CBMP – Contrary body movement position

PP – Promenade position. A position in which the partners open out fanwise to form a 'V' shape, the lady's left side remaining in contact with, or close to, the man's right side.

CPP – Counter promenade position. A position opposite to that of promenade position. The man's left side and the lady's right side are in contact with or close to, each other, and the opposite sides of the bodies turned out to form a 'V' shape.

FAP – Fall away position. This is the promenade position in which the couple travel backwards.

Fig. – Figure

Natural Turn – Right-handed turn

Reverse Turn – Left-handed turn

OP – Outside partner

PO – Partner outside

H – Heel

T – Toe

B – Ball of foot

The Positions of the Feet in Relation to the Ballroom

(Remember that you dance anti-clockwise round the ballroom)

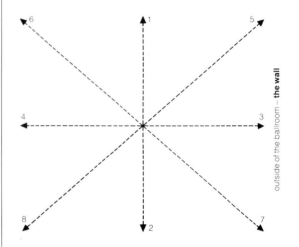

POSITIONS OF THE FEET *(Indicated by arrows)*

	counterpart	
1. Facing LOD		Backing LOD
2. Backing LOD	”	Facing LOD
3. Facing wall	”	Backing wall
4. Facing centre	”	Backing centre
5. Facing diag. to wall	”	Backing diag. to wall
6. Facing diag. to centre	”	Backing diag. to centre
7. Facing diag. to wall against LOD	”	Backing diag. to wall against LOD
8. Facing diag. to centre against LOD	”	Backing diag. to centre against LOD

Terms used in Describing the Direction of Steps

(Remember that you dance anti-clockwise round the ballroom)

DIRECTIONS OF STEPS *(Indicated by arrows)*

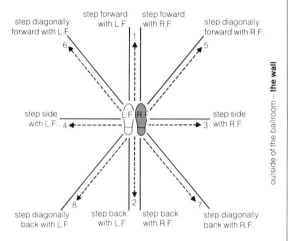

step diagonally forward with L.F.

step forward with L.F.

step foward with R.F.

step diagonally forward with R.F.

step side with L.F.

step side with R.F.

step diagonally back with L.F.

step back with L.F.

step back with R.F.

step diagonally back with R.F.

outside of the ballroom – **the wall**

1. Along LOD
2. Against LOD
3. To wall
4. To centre
5. Diag. to wall
6. Diag. to centre
7. Diag. to wall against LOD
8. Diag. to centre against LOD

Table Giving Times, Tempi and Rhythms

NOTE: As many dance bands play at varying tempi, I am giving in this table the ideal tempo for each dance as laid down by the International Council of Ballroom Dancing, and in parentheses the range of tempi to which it is possible to dance in comfort.

Dance	Time	Tempo	No. of Basic Rhythms Used
Waltz	¾	30 bars per min. (29 to 34)	One A step to each beat except when hesitation steps are introduced
Foxtrot	⁴⁄₄	30 bars per min. (28 to 36)	Two 1. Slow 2. Quick, quick, slow (Chassé) (Slows take 2 beats of the music. Quicks take 1 beat.)
Quickstep	⁴⁄₄	50/52 bars per min. (38 to 54)	Two 1. Slow 2. Quick, quick, slow (Chassé) (Slows take 2 beats of the music. Quicks take 1 beat.)
Tango	²⁄₄ (sometimes ⁴⁄₈)	33 bars per min. (28 to 34)	Two 1. Slow (walk) 2. Quick, quick, slow (Slows take 1 beat. Quicks take ½ beat.)
Viennese Waltz	¾	60 bars per min. (44 to 64)	One A step to each beat of the music
Rumba	⁴⁄₄ (sometimes ²⁄₄)	27 bars per min. (24 to 44)	One Quick, quick, slow (Slows take 2 beats, quicks take 1 beat in ⁴⁄₄ time. This is halved in ²⁄₄ time: slows 1 beat, quicks ½ beat.)
Samba	²⁄₄ (sometimes ⁴⁄₄)	50 bars per min. (45 to 65)	Four 1. Slow, slow 2. Slow, quick, quick 3. Slow 'and' slow. (The value of the first slow is ¾ beat, the 'and' ¼ beat, the final slow 1 beat in ²⁄₄ time. This is doubled in ⁴⁄₄ time: 1 ½, ½ and 2 beats.) 4. Quick, quick, quick, quick (Slows take 1 beat, quicks ½ beat in ²⁄₄ time. Slows take 2 beats, quicks 1 beat in ⁴⁄₄ time)
Cha-cha-cha	⁴⁄₄ (sometimes ²⁄₄)	32 bars per min. (30 to 40)	One Slow, slow, quick, quick, slow. (Slows take 1 beat, quicks ½ beat in ⁴⁄₄ time. This is halved in ²⁄₄ time: slows ½ beat, quicks ¼ beat.)
Paso Doble	²⁄₄ (sometimes ¾ or ⁶⁄₈)	62 bars per min. in ²⁄₄ time (58–66)	One A step to each beat of the music in ²⁄₄ or ¾ time. One step for each three beats of music in ⁶⁄₈ time.
Rock 'n' Roll	⁴⁄₄	40 bars per min. (30 to 50)	One Slow, slow, quick, quick (Slows take 2 beats, quicks take 1 beat.)
Jive	⁴⁄₄	44 bars per min. (30 to 50)	Two 1. Quick, quick, quick and quick 2. Quick, quick, quick and quick, quick and quick (Quicks take 1 beat, the 'and' takes ¼ the value of the preceding quick.)

10

Social Dancing: Slow and Quick Rhythm

These two dances are the 'rhythm' or crowded ballroom form of Foxtrot and Quickstep. 'Rhythm' dancing can be danced to any tempo 4/4 music (four beats in a bar). The standardized Foxtrot and Quickstep require a more strict tempo.

Quick Rhythm would be danced to any tempo faster than about forty bars per minute, Slow Rhythm to any tempo slower than forty bars per minute. The accented beats in 4/4 music are the first and third, and with a little practice the beginner will soon learn to pick out the beats.

To make the figures easier to learn, teachers substitute the use of 'slows' and 'quicks' in place of musical beats, and the pupil has only to remember that 'slow' = two beats and 'quick' = one beat. One 'slow' = two 'quicks', and vice versa. I have found with some pupils that even if they say 'slow' they are still inclined to take the step at the speed of a 'quick'; it is a good idea for a beginner who has this fault to say 'slowly' instead of just 'slow'; it takes him longer to say, and will thus slow him down a little.

The hold is the same for Quick and Slow Rhythm. The man places his right hand just under the lady's left shoulder-blade (a little farther round her back, if it is very crowded in the ballroom), with the fingers close together and the hand curved naturally onto her back. The left arm is raised so that his hand is a little above his shoulder level, with the forearm curved at the elbow, so as to appear natural and comfortable. He holds the lady's right hand in his left hand, palm to palm, thumbs crossed. Both elbows should be raised slightly, but without raising the shoulders. His partner should be held as squarely in front of him as possible, though if the room is very crowded and he holds his right hand a little farther round the lady she will tend to be a little more towards his right side. The lady raises her right arm to the level of her partner's left arm and places her right hand in his left, as described above. She places her left hand lightly on the man's right upper arm without spreading the fingers, and keeps her elbows up a little so as not to hang, or weigh down his arm.

All 'slow' steps forward and backward are danced like walking steps, and it is an excellent exercise for a beginner to practise correct walking steps before learning the figures, which will also improve balance. It is advisable to practise 'walks' even after the figures have been mastered.

The walk forward is based on a natural walking movement – the only difference being that the feet skim lightly along the floor instead of being lifted for each step. The moving foot is pushed forward first with the ball of the foot skimming the floor, going on to the heel as it passes the toes of the other foot; at this point the back heel begins to leave the floor. Continue to the extent of the stride on the heel of the moving foot, gradually releasing the back foot to the ball and then to the toes. At the end of the stride, lower the front toes to the floor, drawing the back foot up from the toes to the ball of the foot, ready for the next walk. Remember to keep the feet in a straight line, turned neither in nor out. For Slow Rhythm, the length of stride can be taken as in a natural walk; but if the room is very crowded, it should be shorter. For Quick Rhythm, the stride should be short – very short when the music is rather quicker than a normal tempo.

The walk backward is also based on the natural movement. The moving foot goes back onto the ball of the foot and then onto the toes, going gradually to the ball again as the front foot is brought back with pressure on the heel, with the toes slightly raised from the floor, until it reaches the back foot, when the toes are lowered, so that the foot is then flat. At this point, and not before, the heel of the back foot reaches the floor. The length of stride should be adapted as for the forward walk.

Each walking step is counted 'slow' and takes up two beats of music, so that two walks would take up one bar of music, that is, 'slow', 'slow' = 1,2, 3,4 (one bar).

Note: All steps taken in a sideways direction are taken onto the ball of the foot, and then the heel is lowered, as the whole weight is taken onto the foot.

Differences Between Slow and Quick Rhythm Dancing

Most of the figures described for Slow Rhythm may be danced in Quick Rhythm except the Side Step. The Slow Rhythm Side Step is counted as six 'quicks' and is therefore not so well suited to Quick Rhythm, as it is rather a rush to get it in at the faster speed. The only other figure which differs is the Twinkle. The timing is changed for Quick Rhythm, all 'slow' timing being much more attractive if applied to the quicker music.

On closing steps in Slow Rhythm, the feet are brought close together. In Quick Rhythm, on the closing steps which occur on a 'quick' count, the feet are not brought close together but are only nearly closed; but when a close occurs on a 'slow' count in Quick Rhythm, the feet are closed right together.

The steps are usually taken slightly longer for Slow Rhythm than Quick Rhythm.

Body Sway in Rhythm Dancing. This should not be attempted by beginners until they have achieved a reasonable standard of execution of the figures, but body sway will give style and softness to the various movements if applied thus: when a step is taken with the right foot, sway slightly from the hips towards the right; when a step is taken with the left foot, sway slightly from the hips towards the left. Briefly, sway slightly towards the stepping foot.

Quarter Turns

MAN

Begin facing diag. to wall.

1. Forward RF	S
2. Side LF ⎫	Q
3. Close RF to LF ⎬ Make ¼ turn to R	Q
4. Side LF (slightly back)	S
5. Back RF	S
6. Side LF ⎫	Q
7. Close RF to LF ⎬ Make ¼ turn to L	Q
8. Forward LF	S

Finish facing diag. to wall.

LADY

Begin backing diag. to wall.

1. Back LF	s
2. Side RF $\Big\}$ Make ¼ turn to R	Q
3. Close LF to RF	Q
4. Diag. forward RF	s
5. Forward LF	s
6. Side RF $\Big\}$ Make ¼ turn to L	Q
7. Close LF to RF	Q
8. Back RF	s

Finish backing diag. to wall.

This fig. may be preceded by:

(1) The Quarter Turns.
(2) The Natural Pivot Turn.
(3) A walk on the LF.

This fig. may be followed by:

(1) The Quarter Turns.
(2) The Natural Pivot Turn.
(3) The Reverse Pivot Turn, making the last step of the Quarter Turns the first step of the Reverse Pivot Turn.
(4) The Reverse Pivot and Rotary Chassé.

Natural Pivot Turn

MAN

Begin facing diag. to wall.

1. Forward RF	s
2. Side LF $\Big\}$ Make ¼ turn to R	Q
3. Close RF to LF	Q
4. Back LF	s

Repeat these four steps three times so as to make a complete turn to R and finish facing diag. to wall. If used at a corner repeat the four steps twice, making ¾ turn to R.

LADY

Begin backing diag. to wall.

1. Back LF	s
2. Side RF $\Big\}$ Make ¼ turn to R	Q
3. Close LF to RF	Q
4. Forward RF	s

Repeat these four steps three times so as to make a complete turn to R and finish backing diag. to wall. If used at a corner repeat the four steps twice, making ¾ turn to R.

This fig. may be preceded by:

(1) The Quarter Turns.
(2) A walk on the LF.

This fig. may be followed by:

(1) The Quarter Turns.

Reverse Pivot Turn

MAN

Begin facing diag. to wall.

1. Forward LF	s
2. Back on to RF $\Big\}$ Make ¼ turn to L	s
3. Side LF	Q
4. Close RF to LF	Q

Repeat these four steps three times so as to make a complete turn to L and finish facing diag. to wall.

LADY

Begin backing diag. to wall.

1. Back RF	s
2. Forward on to LF $\Big\}$ Make ¼ turn to L	s
3. Side RF	Q
4. Close LF to RF	Q

Repeat these four steps three times so as to make a complete turn to L and finish backing diag. to wall.

This fig. may be preceded by:

(1) Seven steps of the Quarter Turns.
(2) A Rotary Chassé.

This fig. may be followed by:

(1) A walk on the LF.
(2) A Rotary Chassé after the first two steps of the Reverse Pivot Turn when it has been danced in full once.

Rotary Chassé from Reverse Pivot Turn

MAN

Begin facing diag. to wall.

1.		s
2.	Dance the Reverse Pivot Turn,	s
3.	making ¼ turn to L	Q
4.		Q
5. Forward LF		s
6. Back on to RF		s
7. Side LF		Q
8. Close RF to LF	Make ¾ turn to L to	Q
9. Side LF	complete the whole turn	Q
10. Close RF to LF		Q
11. Side LF		Q
12. Close RF to LF		Q

Finish facing diag. to wall.

LADY

Begin backing diag. to wall.

1.		s
2.	Dance the Reverse Pivot Turn,	s
3.	making ¼ turn to L	Q
4.		Q
5. Back RF		s
6. Forward on to LF		s
7. Side RF		Q
8. Close LF to RF	Make ¾ turn to L to	Q
9. Side RF	complete the whole turn	Q
10. Close LF to RF		Q
11. Side RF		Q
12. Close LF to RF		Q

Finish backing diag. to wall.

This fig. may be preceded by:

(1) Seven steps of the Quarter Turns.
(2) The Reverse Pivot Turn.

This fig. may be followed by:

(1) A walk on the LF.
(2) The Reverse Pivot Turn.

Back Corté

MAN

Begin facing LOD.

1. Back RF	s
2. Side LF	Q
3. Close RF to LF	Q
4. Back LF	s

Finish backing LOD.

LADY

Begin facing LOD.

1. Forward LF	s
2. Side RF	Q
3. Close LF to RF	Q
4. Forward RF	s

Finish facing LOD.

This fig. may be preceded by:

(1) The first four steps of the Quarter Turns overturned so as to back LOD.
(2) The Double Chassé Back Corté.
(3) The first four steps of the Natural Pivot Turn.
(4) The Twinkle, making the last step of the Twinkle the first step of the Back Corté.
(5) The Back Corté.

This fig. may be followed by:

(1) The Back Corté (repeated).
(2) The Twinkle.
(3) The last four steps of the Quarter Turns.
(4) The Double Chassé Back Corté.

Double Chassé Back Corté

MAN

Begin backing LOD.

1. Back RF	s
2. Side LF	Q
3. Close RF to LF	Q
4. Side LF	Q
5. Close RF to LF	Q
6. Back LF	s

Finish backing LOD.

LADY

Begin facing LOD.

1. Forward LF	S
2. Side RF	Q
3. Close LF to RF	Q
4. Side RF	Q
5. Close LF to RF	Q
6. Forward RF	S

Finish facing LOD.

This fig. may be preceded by:

(1) The first four steps of the Quarter Turns over-turned so as to back LOD.
(2) The Back Corté.
(3) The first four steps of the Natural Pivot Turn.
(4) The Double Chassé Back Corté.
(5) The Twinkle, making the last step of the Twinkle the first step of the Double Chassé Back Corté.

This fig. may be followed by:

(1) The Back Corté.
(2) The Twinkle.
(3) The last four steps of the Quarter Turns.
(4) The Double Chassé Back Corté.

Chassé Reverse Turn

MAN

Begin facing LOD.

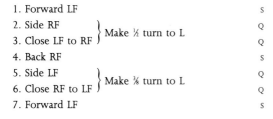

1. Forward LF	S
2. Side RF ⎫ Make ½ turn to L	Q
3. Close LF to RF ⎭	Q
4. Back RF	S
5. Side LF ⎫ Make ⅜ turn to L	Q
6. Close RF to LF ⎭	Q
7. Forward LF	S

Finish facing diag. to wall.

LADY

Begin backing LOD.

1. Back RF	S
2. Side LF ⎫ Make ½ turn to L	Q
3. Close RF to LF ⎭	Q
4. Forward LF	S
5. Side RF ⎫ Make ⅜ turn to L	Q
6. Close LF to RF ⎭	Q
7. Back RF	S

Finish backing diag. to wall.

This fig. may be preceded by:

(1) The Quarter Turns, making the last step the first step of the Chassé Reverse Turn, but having turned on steps 6 and 7 of the Quarter Turns to face LOD (⅜ turn instead of ¼).

This fig. may be followed by:

(1) The Quarter Turns.
(2) The Natural Pivot Turn.
(3) Five steps of the Quarter Turns into side step.
(4) Four steps of the Quarter Turns into the Back Corté, Back Corté and Twinkle, or Double Chassé Back Corté.

Six Quick Side Step (Slow Rhythm only)

MAN

Begin sideways on to LOD, toes pointing diag. to wall (PP).

1. Side LF	Q
2. Close RF to LF	Q
3. Side LF	Q
4. Close RF to LF without transferring weight on to it	Q
5. Side RF	Q
6. Close LF to RF without transferring weight on to it	Q

Finish facing in commencing position.

LADY

Begin sideways on to LOD, toes pointing diag. to centre (PP).

1. Side RF	Q
2. Close LF to RF	Q
3. Side RF	Q
4. Close LF to RF without transferring weight on to it	Q
5. Side LF	Q
6. Close RF to LF without transferring weight on to it	Q

Finish facing in commencing position.

This fig. may be preceded by:

(1) The first five steps of the Quarter Turns.
(2) The Six Quick Side Step.

This fig. may be followed by:

(1) The last three steps of the Quarter Turns.
(2) The Six Quick Side Step repeated once or twice.

Note: When the man dances the Quarter Turns into the Side Step (from the fifth step of the Quarter Turns) he must open his partner to PP. When following the Side Step with 6, 7, 8 of the Quarter Turns he must turn her square to him again. (See notes on Leading, page 44.)

The Twinkle (Slow Rhythm)

MAN

Begin backing LOD, having danced the Back Corté.

1. Forward on to RF	Q
2. Close LF to RF	Q
3. Back RF	S

Finish backing LOD.

LADY

Begin facing LOD, having danced the Back Corté.

1. Back on to LF	Q
2. Close RF to LF	Q
3. Forward LF	S

Finish facing LOD.

This fig. may be preceded by:

(1) The Back Corté.
(2) The Double Chassé Back Corté.

This fig. may be followed by:

(1) The Back Corté, making the last step of the Twinkle the first step of the Back Corté.
(2) The last three steps of the Quarter Turns.
(3) The Double Chassé Back Corté, making the last step of the Twinkle the first step of the Double Chassé Back Corté.

The Twinkle (Quick Rhythm)

MAN

Begin backing LOD, having danced the Back Corté.

1. Forward on to RF	S
2. Close LF to RF	S
3. Back RF	S

Finish backing LOD.

Note alteration of timing from Slow Rhythm.

LADY

Begin facing LOD, having danced the Back Corté.

1. Back on to LF	S
2. Close RF to LF	S
3. Forward LF	S

Finish facing LOD.

Note alteration of timing from Slow Rhythm.

This fig. may be preceded by:

(1) The Back Corté.
(2) The Double Chassé Back Corté.

This fig. may be followed by:

(1) The Back Corté.
(2) The last three steps of the Quarter Turns.
(3) The Double Chassé Back Corté.

Note 1 and 3. The last step of the Twinkle will be the first step of the following fig.

Side Step (Quick Rhythm)

MAN

Begin sideways on to LOD, toes pointing diag. to wall (PP).

1. Side LF	Q
2. Half close RF to LF	Q
3. Side LF	S
4. Close RF to LF	S

Finish facing in commencing position.

LADY

Begin sideways on to LOD, toes pointing diag. to centre (PP).

1. Side RF	Q
2. Half close LF to RF	Q
3. Side RF	S

4. Close LF to RF   S

Finish facing in commencing position.

This fig. may be preceded by:

(1) The first five steps of the Quarter Turns.
(2) The Side Step.

This fig. may be followed by:

(1) The last three steps of the Quarter Turns.
(2) The Side Step (repeated once or twice).

Note: When the man dances the Quarter Turns into the Side Step from the fifth step, he must open his partner to PP. When the man follows the Side Step with 6, 7 and 8 of the Quarter Turns he must turn his partner square again. (See notes on Leading, page 44.)

This Side Step may also be danced to Slow Rhythm, but the Six Quick Side Step is to be preferred.

The hold for Waltz, Foxtrot, Quickstep, and Viennese waltz

This photograph illustrates the correct way to hold your partner and the position of the man and lady in relation to each other. Advanced dancers and competition couples hold their arms higher than social dancers for greater impact. On crowded dance-floors the arms would be held nearer to the sides.

11

Easy Waltz

The modern Waltz can be danced in any ballroom and the figures described can be adapted for a crowded ballroom or a spacious one. If a ballroom is small or crowded, all the steps are taken very short and without any rise to the toes. If the ballroom is large and not crowded, all the steps should be long, and a gradual rise to the toes should be started at the end of the first beat and carried out to the end of the third beat of each bar of music, except where otherwise mentioned in the descriptions of the figures. At the end of the third beat, lower to the normal position by lowering the heel of the foot which is carrying the weight. The hold is the same as that described for Slow and Quick Rhythm.

Each step in the figures takes one beat of the music. The time of Waltz music is 3/4 (three beats to the bar). The speed of the Modern Waltz is thirty bars per minute and the accent is on the first beat. There will be no 'slows' and 'quicks' for beginners to worry about; they need only count in threes, but the count must be even, otherwise the steps will be hurried and the correct timing lost.

It is advisable for a beginner to pay special attention to counting the Waltz beats carefully before commencing the dance figures.

It will be seen from the description of the Natural Turn, Right Closed Change, Reverse Turn, and Left Closed Change that the steps in the turns have been numbered 1, 2, 3, 4, 5, 6; and the Changes 7, 8, 9. I have always found it easier if beginners count the numbers of the steps to themselves 1, 2, 3, 4, 5, 6, 7, 8, 9 for the Turns and the Changes rather than the musical timing, 1, 2, 3 1, 2, 3 1, 2, 3. They seem to get muddled with the pattern if they keep repeating the count 1, 2, 3, but by counting from 1 to 9 they remember when to turn and when to remain facing the same way. In the other figures, also, beginners will find this method helps them to know where a figure begins and ends.

When the figures have been mastered and there is plenty of room to 'step out' in the Waltz, a slight sway should be introduced not only to soften the look of the figures but also to assist the turns. The sway is unlike that used in Slow and Quick Rhythm in that it is retained to right or left for two beats of music in most figures. The general rule is: if you step with the right foot forward or backward on 1, you sway towards the right for 2 and 3; if you step with

Swinging into the Waltz, this professional couple hold their arms high with perfect poise in anticipation of the dance to come.

the left foot forward or backward on 1, you sway towards the left for 2 and 3. There is one exception in the figures described – there is no sway on 4, 5, 6 in the Natural Spin Turn.

Other figures and the standard variations will be found in Chapter 13 of this book.

Natural Turn (Right Turn) followed by Right Closed Change

MAN

Begin facing diag. to wall.   Music timing

1. Forward RF	Turning to R to back LOD	1
2. Side LF		2 } 1 bar
3. Close RF to LF		3
4. Back LF	Turning to R	1
5. Side RF		2 } 1 bar
6. Close LF to RF		3

Finish facing diag. to centre.

This fig. may be preceded by:

(1) The Left Closed Change.
(2) The Reverse Corté.

This fig. may be followed by:

(1) The Right Closed Change.

ADVANCED TECHNIQUE OF THE ABOVE FIGURE

(Not required by the beginner)

Amount of turn: Make ¼ turn to R between 1 and 2; make ⅛ turn to R between 2 and 3; make ⅜ turn to R between 4 and 5.
Footwork: 1.HT 2.T 3.TH 4.TH 5.T 6.TH.
Contrary body movement: Used on 1 and 4.
Body sway: Sway to R on 2 and 3; sway to L on 5 and 6.

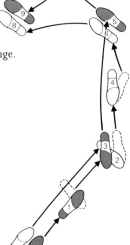

begin here

Right Closed Change

MAN

Begin facing diag. to centre.   Music timing

7. Forward RF	No turn	1
8. Side LF slightly forward		2 } 1 bar
9. Close RF to LF		3

Finish facing diag. to centre.

This fig. may be preceded by:

(1) The Natural Turn.

This fig. may be followed by:

(1) The Reverse Turn.
(2) 1, 2 and 3 of the Reverse Turn into the Reverse Corté.

ADVANCED TECHNIQUE OF THE ABOVE FIGURE

(Not required by the beginner)

Amount of turn: Nil.
Footwork: 1.HT 2.T 3.TH.
Contrary body movement: Used on 1 (slightly).
Body sway: Sway to R on 2 and 3.

Natural Turn (Right Turn) followed by Right Closed Change

LADY

Begin backing diag. to wall.   Music timing

1. Back LF	Turning to R to face LOD	1
2. Side RF		2 } 1 bar
3. Close LF to RF		3
4. Forward RF	Turning to R	1
5. Side LF		2 } 1 bar
6. Close RF to LF		3

Finish backing diag. to centre.

ADVANCED TECHNIQUE OF THE ABOVE FIGURE

(Not required by the beginner)

Amount of turn: Make ⅜ turn to R between 1 and 2; make ¼ turn to R between 4 and 5; make ⅛ turn to R between 5 and 6.

Footwork: 1.TH 2.T 3.TH 4.HT 5.T 6.TH.

Contrary body movement: Used on 1 and 4.

Body sway: Sway to L on 2 and 3; sway to R on 5 and 6.

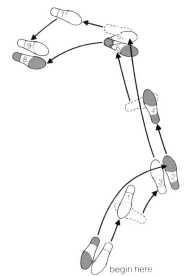

Right Closed Change

LADY

Begin backing diag. to centre.		Music timing	
7. Back LF		1	
8. Side RF slightly back	No turn	2	1 bar
9. Close LF to RF		3	

Finish backing diag. to centre.

ADVANCED TECHNIQUE OF THE ABOVE FIGURE

(Not required by the beginner)

Amount of turn: Nil.

Footwork: 1.TH 2.T 3.TH.

Contrary body movement: Used on 1 (slightly).

Body sway: Sway to L on 2 and 3.

Reverse Turn (Left Turn) followed by Left Closed Change

MAN

Begin facing diag. to centre.		Music timing	
1. Forward LF		1	
2. Side RF	Turning to L to back LOD	2	1 bar
3. Close LF to RF		3	
4. Back RF		1	
5. Side LF		2	1 bar
6. Close RF to LF		3	

Finish facing diag. to wall.

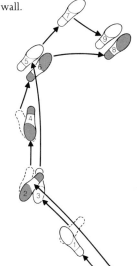

This fig. may be preceded by:

(1) The Right Closed Change.

(2) The Natural Spin Turn and 4, 5, 6 of the Reverse Turn danced on the side of the ballroom.

This fig. may be followed by:

(1) The Left Closed Change.

(2) 1, 2 and 3 of the Reverse Turn may be followed by the Reverse Corté.

ADVANCED TECHNIQUE OF THE ABOVE FIGURE

(Not required by the beginner)

Amount of turn: Make ¼ turn to L between 1 and 2; make ⅛ turn to L between 2 and 3; make ⅜ turn to L between 4 and 5.

Footwork: 1.HT 2.T 3.TH 4.TH 5.T 6.TH.

Contrary body movement: Used on 1 and 4.

Body sway: Sway to L on 2 and 3; sway to R on 5 and 6.

Left Closed Change

MAN

Begin facing diag. to wall.　　　　Music timing

7. Forward LF		1
8. Side RF slightly forward	No turn	2 } 1 bar
9. Close LF to RF		3

Finish facing diag. to wall.

ADVANCED TECHNIQUE OF THE ABOVE FIGURE

(Not required by the beginner)

Amount of turn: Nil.
Footwork: 1.HT 2.T 3.TH.
Contrary body movement: Used on 1 (slightly).
Body sway: Sway to L on 2 and 3.

This fig. may be preceded by:

(1) The Reverse Turn.
(2) The Natural Spin Turn and 4, 5 and 6 of the Reverse Turn (after the Spin).

This fig. may be followed by:

(1) The Natural Turn.
(2) The Natural Spin Turn.

Reverse Turn (Left Turn) followed by Left Closed Change

LADY

Begin backing diag. to centre.　　　Music timing

1. Back RF		1
2. Side LF	Turning to L to face LOD	2 } 1 bar
3. Close RF to LF		3
4. Forward LF		1
5. Side RF	Turning to L	2 } 1 bar
6. Close LF to RF		3

Finish backing diag. to wall.

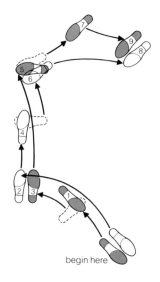

begin here

ADVANCED TECHNIQUE OF THE ABOVE FIGURE

(Not required by the beginner)

Amount of turn: Make ⅜ turn to L between 1 and 2; make ¼ turn to L between 4 and 5; make ⅛ turn to L between 5 and 6.
Footwork: 1.TH 2.T 3.TH 4.HT 5.T 6.TH.
Contrary body movement: Used on 1 and 4.
Body sway: Sway to R on 2 and 3; sway to L on 5 and 6.

Left Closed Change

LADY

Begin backing diag. to wall.　　　Music timing

7. Back RF		1
8. Side RF slightly back	No turn	2 } 1 bar
9. Close RF to LF		3

Finish backing diag. to wall.

ADVANCED TECHNIQUE OF THE ABOVE FIGURE

(Not required by the beginner)

Amount of turn: Nil.
Footwork: 1.TH 2.T 3.TH.
Contrary body movement: Used on 1 (slightly).
Body sway: Sway to R on 2 and 3.

12

More Advanced Technique

Chapters 9–11 of this book were addressed primarily to beginners in ballroom dancing. The basic technique and the figures described are all that are necessary for the beginner to learn to dance with confidence and enjoyment after only a little practice. But as his experience of the ballroom grows, the novice will naturally want to broaden his horizon. In the Waltz, for instance, he will see other dancers performing figures which are new to him, and the individual attractions of the Foxtrot, Quickstep, Viennese Waltz and the Latin-American dances will quickly make their appeal.

It is at this stage of the less experienced dancer's progress that the following section of this book becomes important. It deals with each of the dances in turn and introduces new aspects of technique – such as footwork, body sway and contrary body movement – with which the beginner has so far not had to concern himself. You will, I am sure, enjoy a feeling of accomplishment if you practise what is set out in the following pages.

How to Construct the Dances

When you have mastered a few figures of a dance it is time to think about the best way of amalgamating them – that is, joining them together so that you progress round the floor with one step following naturally upon another. The movement should flow, with no breaks to spoil the continuity.

The correct combinations or sequences are mostly a matter of experience and practice; but at first the man should learn which steps it is possible to link together. This will depend on which direction he is facing at the end of each figure, where his partner is in relation to him, and which foot his weight is on.

In this book each figure described for the man is followed by a note of the figures which will follow on most naturally. Other amalgamations may be tried later, but at the beginning it is best to keep to the usual, well-tried ones.

Footwork

Footwork refers to the rise and fall in the feet, indicating which part of the foot is in contact with the floor on each step or part step.

H–Heel (Note: This term, when used on its own, means 'Heel on to flat foot' as in a forward walk.)
T–Toe.
B–Ball of foot.
Inside edge of foot.
Inside edge of T (toe).

Inside edge of B (ball).
Whole foot.

Example:
The Quarter Turns

Footwork	Meaning of footwork
1. HT	Heel rising to toe.
2. T	Toe.
3. T	Toe.
4. TH	Toe lowering to heel.
5. TH	Toe lowering to heel.
6. H	Heel (then flat).
7. H (RF) pressure on T of LF	Heel of right foot with pressure on toe of left foot.
8. H	Heel (then flat).

Contrary Body Movement

Any dancer aiming at a high standard must understand the theory and practice of the use of Contrary Body Movement. It cannot be taught to beginners – good balance and movement must have been acquired first.

In ballroom dancing Contrary Body Movement is brought about by turning the body slightly, from the hips upwards, so that the opposite hip and shoulder are turned towards the moving leg; e.g., if the step is being taken forward on the right foot, the left shoulder and hip will be turned slightly forwards.

The four ways that Contrary Body Movement can be used are as follows:

Step forward with the RF, turning the L hip and shoulder forward.
Step forward with the LF, turning the R hip and shoulder forward.
Step back with the RF, turning the L hip and shoulder backward.
Step back with the LF, turning the R hip and shoulder backward.

Contrary Body Movement must not be used indiscriminately; it is something which should only be used in a natural, effortless manner. In the descriptions of the figures for each dance the proper use of Contrary Body Movement is shown where appropriate. It is, however, used on most turning figures in the 'moving' dances.

Remember that the opposite hip and shoulder should turn as the step is taken, not afterwards, and, once again, remember that the whole body from the hips upwards must be turned very slightly. It is a common fault to break at the waist, turning the shoulders only.

You can help the Contrary Body Movement by allowing the back foot to turn inwards very slightly. Actually it will only be pointing the way you are facing, but if you think of it as being turned inwards it will help to produce the Contrary Body Movement. There is a natural tendency to turn the back foot outwards; this must be corrected because it will prevent the hips turning together with the shoulders.

There is another form of Contrary Body Movement, called Contrary Body Movement Position. When you step across your body you will be in Contrary Body Movement Position. If you step forward with your right foot across your left, keeping your body facing the front, you will see that the effect is the same as if you had stepped straight forward with your right foot, at the same time turning your left hip and shoulder forward.

This form of contrary movement – Contrary Body Movement Position – is used on all 'outside' steps, i.e., whenever you step outside your partner or your partner steps outside you. It is often used in the Tango, especially in Promenade figures, and on occasions in other ballroom dances.

The borderline between Contrary Body Movement and Contrary Body Movement Position is so narrow that it is sometimes difficult to differentiate between them.

Body Sway

A slight sway of the body is introduced into the majority of turning figures in ballroom dancing to help to retain good balance. The inclination of the body should always be towards the centre of the turn that is being made. It also occurs in figures other than turns.

In a ballroom you always dance anti-clockwise and there are only two basic ways that you can turn – natural (right-handed) or reverse (left-handed). You will appreciate, therefore, that in a Natural Turn you always sway slightly towards the middle of the ballroom, and in a Reverse Turn you always sway slightly towards the outside of the ballroom – the wall. Another and perhaps easier way of thinking of this is as follows:

For the Quickstep and Foxtrot
If you have taken a 'slow' step forward or backward with your right foot, then you sway to the right on the two 'quick' steps following.
If you have taken a 'slow' step forward or backward with your left foot, then you sway to the left on the two 'quick' steps following.

For the Waltz
If you have taken the 1 forward or backward with your right foot, then you sway to the right for the 2 and 3.
If you have taken the 1 forward or backward with your left foot, then you sway to the left for the 2 and 3.

There are exceptions, but as a general rule the above applies. The sway when introduced in these dances should be carried from the feet upwards, so that the whole of your body – legs, hips, shoulders and head – is inclined towards the centre of the turn that you are making. If a straight line were drawn through your body as this slight sway was introduced, it should divide you equally in two parts.

Do not forget that the sway must be very slight. Should you have any doubt as to which way you should incline, leave it out altogether until you can get a professional to explain it to you. With experience you will find it comes naturally.

In the Tango, in basic figures, there is no body sway at all.

13

The Waltz

The fundamentals of the Waltz were described in Chapter 11 of this book. The pages which follow give details of a number of additional Waltz figures and the standard variations.

Natural Spin Turn

MAN

At a corner or along the line of dance.

Begin facing diag. to wall.

		Music timing
1. Forward RF	⎫ Turning to R to	1 ⎫
2. Side LF	⎬ back LOD	2 ⎬ 1 bar
3. Close RF to LF	⎭	3 ⎭
4. Back LF	⎫ Turning to R	1 ⎫
5. Forward RF in CBMP	⎬ to face original	2 ⎬ 1 bar
6. Side LF slightly back	⎭ facing position	3 ⎭

Finish in position, having made one complete turn to R.

ADVANCED TECHNIQUE OF THE ABOVE FIGURE

(Not required by the beginner)

Amount of turn: Make ⅜ turn to R between 1 and 3; make ⅜ turn to R on 4; make ¼ turn to R between 5 and 6.

Footwork: 1.HT 2.T 3.TH 4.THT 5.HT 6.TH.

Contrary body movement: Used on 1, 4 and 5.

Body sway: Sway to R on 2 and 3.

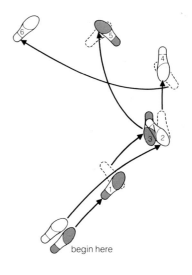

begin here

The Contra Check, performed here by Mark Lucas and Delia Grossley of England, is a figure often used by experts to follow figures such as the Double Reverse Spin.

Natural Spin Turn

LADY

At a corner or along the line of dance.

Begin backing diag. to wall. *Music timing*

1. Back LF	} Turning to R to face	1	}
2. Side RF	LOD	2	1 bar
3. Close LF to RF		3	}
4. Forward RF	Turning to	1	}
5. Back LF	R to back	2	1 bar
6. Brush RF towards LF	original		
and place it diag. forward.	position	3	}

Finish in position, having made one complete turn to R.

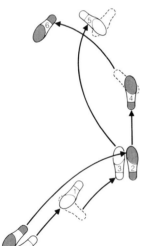

begin here

ADVANCED TECHNIQUE OF THE ABOVE FIGURE

(*Not required by the beginner*).

Make ⅜ turn to R between 1 and 2; make ⅜ turn to R on 4; make ¼ turn to R between 5 and 6.

Footwork: 1.TH 2.T 3.TH 4.HT 5.T 6.TH

Contrary body movement: Used on 1 and 4.

Body sway: Sway to L on 2 and 3.

(1) The Left Closed Change.
(2) The Reverse Corté.

This fig. may be followed by:

(1) 4, 5 and 6 of the Reverse turn:

(a) when the Spin is danced at a corner, dance 4, 5 and 6 of the Reverse

Turn with ¼ turn to L, ending diag. to *new wall*;

(b) when Spin is danced on the sides of the ballroom, dance 4, 5 and 6 of the Reverse Turn with ¼ turn to L to end diag. to centre.

(2) The Reverse Corté, making ¼ turn to L, on 1, 2 and 3 of the Reverse Corté.

Reverse Corté

MAN

Begin backing LOD, having danced 1, 2 and 3 of the Reverse Turn. *Music timing*

1. Back RF		1	}
2. Close LF to RF	Turning to	2	}
3. Hesitate, holding	L to face		1 bar
position with weight	diag. to wall	3	}
on RF			
4. Back LF in CBMP, PO		1	}
5. Side RF (in front of	No turn		1 bar
partner)		2	}
6. Close LF to RF		3	}

Finish facing diag. to wall.

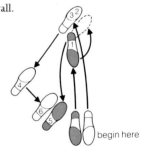

begin here

ADVANCED TECHNIQUE OF THE ABOVE FIGURE

(*Not required by the beginner*)

Amount of turn: Make ⅜ turn to L between 1 and 2.

Footwork: 1.TH 2.H of LF, then T of both F 3.TH of RF 4.TH 5.T 6.TH.

Contrary body movement: Used on 1 and 4 (slightly).

Body sway: Sway to R on 2 and 3; sway to L on 5 and 6.

This fig. may be preceded by:

(1) 1, 2 and 3 of the Reverse Turn.
(2) The Natural Spin Turn at a corner.
(3) The Natural Spin Turn on the sides of the ballroom, when the Corté will end facing diag. to centre.

This fig. may be followed by:

(1) The Natural Turn.
(2) The Natural Spin Turn.
(3) The Right Closed Change when the Corté has been danced following the Natural Spin Turn danced on the side of the ballroom.

LADY

Begin facing LOD, having danced 1, 2, 3 of the Reverse Turn.

		Music timing	
1. Forward LF	Turning to	1	
2. Side RF	L to back	2	1 bar
3. Close LF to RF	diag. to wall	3	
4. Forward RF in CBMP, OP		1	
5. Side LF (partner in front)	No turn	2	1 bar
6. Close RF to LF		3	

Finish backing diag. to wall.

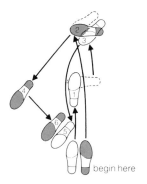

begin here

ADVANCED TECHNIQUE OF THE ABOVE FIGURE

(*Not required by the beginner*)

Amount of turn: Make ¼ turn to L between 1 and 2; make ⅛ turn to L between 2 and 3.

Footwork: 1.HT 2.T 3.TH 4.HT 5.T 6.TH.

Contrary body movement: Used on 1 and 4 (slightly).

Body sway: Sway to L on 2 and 3; sway to R on 5 and 6.

Hesitation Change

This figure is very useful in small or rather crowded ballrooms; it will change you quickly from the Natural into the Reverse Turn, but it needs very careful leading and so is not suitable for beginners.

MAN

Begin facing diag. to wall and finish facing diag. to centre.

1, 2, 3, 4. Dance 1, 2, 3, 4 of the Natural Turn, then:

Heel Pull
{
5. Pull RF back to side of LF, turning from L heel on to RF (feet slightly apart)
6. Hesitate, brushing LF to RF (weight on RF)
}

Amount of turn: Make ⅜ turn to R between 1 and 3; make ⅛ turn to R between 4 and 5.

Footwork: 1.HT 2.T 3.TH 4.TH 5.H, inside edge of foot, whole foot 6.Inside edge of T (LF).

Contrary body movement: Used on 1 and 4.

Body sway: 1, 2, 3, as in the Natural Turn. Sway to L on 5 and 6.

LADY

Begin backing diag. to wall and finish backing diag. to centre.

1, 2, 3, 4. Dance 1, 2, 3, 4 of the Natural Turn, then:

5. Side LF
6. Hesitate, brushing RF to LF (weight on LF)

Amount of turn: Make ⅜ turn to R between 1 and 2; make ⅛ turn to R between 4 and 5.

Footwork: 1.TH 2.T 3.TH 4.HT 5.TH 6.Inside edge of T (RF).

Contrary body movement: Used on 1 and 4.

Body sway: 1, 2, 3, as in the Natural Turn. Sway to R on 5 and 6.

This fig. may be preceded by:

(1) The Left Closed Change.
(2) The Reverse Corté.
(3) The Telemark.
(4) The Outside Spin.
(5) The Open Telemark.

This fig. may be followed by:

(1) The Reverse Turn.
(2) The Double Reverse Spin.
(3) The Telemark.
(4) The Open Telemark.
(5) The Drag Hesitation.

The Whisk

MAN

Begin and finish facing diag. to wall.

1. Forward LF
2. Side RF, slightly forward
3. Cross LF behind RF in PP

Amount of turn: Nil.
Footwork: 1.HT 2.T 3.TH.
Contrary body movement: Used on 1 (slightly).
Body sway: Sway to L on 2 and 3.

LADY

Begin backing diag. to wall and finish facing diag. to centre.

1. Back RF
2. Diag. back LF
3. Cross RF behind LF in PP

Amount of turn: Make ¼ turn to R between 1 and 2.
Footwork: 1.TH 2.T 3.TH.
Contrary body movement: Nil.
Body sway: Sway to R on 2 and 3.

This fig. may be preceded by:

(1) The Reverse Left Turn.
(2) The Double Reverse Spin (ended facing diag. to wall).

This fig. may be followed by:

(1) The Chassé from PP.
(2) The Wing.

Chassé from PP

This figure is preceded by the Whisk.

MAN

Begin and finish facing diag. to wall.

1. Step through with RF in PP and CBMP
2. Side LF slightly forward
&. Close RF to LF, turning partner to face you
3. Side LF, preparing to step outside partner

This figure is followed by a step forward RF outside partner into any Natural figure.

Amount of turn: Nil.
Footwork: 1.HT 2.T & T 3.TH.
Contrary body movement: Used on 1.
Body sway. Nil.

LADY

Begin facing diag. to centre and finish backing diag. to wall.

1. Step through with LF in PP and CBMP
2. Side RF slightly back
&. Close LF to RF, turning to face partner
3. Side RF

This figure is followed by a step back LF, partner outside, into a Natural figure.

Amount of turn: Make ¼ turn to L between 2 and 3.
Footwork: 1.HT 2.T & T 3.TH.
Contrary body movement: Used on 1.
Body sway: Nil.

Note: Both the man and lady dance four steps to three beats. The second beat is the split beat (not the third). It helps to count SQQS for this figure instead of 1, 2 &, 3.

Closed Telemark

The pattern is the same as that used in the Foxtrot but counted 1, 2, 3.

The Closed Telemark is usually preceded by the Wing, or the Double Reverse Spin.

It is followed by any Natural figure.

Impetus Turn

The pattern is the same as that used in the Foxtrot but counted 1, 2, 3.

The Impetus Turn is usually preceded by 1, 2, 3 of the Natural Turn, the Drag Hesitation or the Backward Lock.

It is followed by 4, 5, 6 of the Reverse Turn, or the Reverse Corté.

Open Telemark

MAN

Begin facing diag. to centre and finish diag. to wall in PP.

1. Forward LF
2. Side RF   } turning to L to back diag. to wall
3. Side LF, slightly forward, in PP

Amount of turn: Make ¼ turn to L between 1 and 2; make ½ turn to L between 2 and 3.
Footwork: 1.HT 2.T 3.TH.
Contrary body movement: Used on 1.
Body sway: Sway to L on 2.

LADY

Begin backing diag. to centre and finish in PP with feet pointing to LOD.

1. Back RF, turning to L
2. Close LF to RF (heel turn to face LOD)
3. Diag. forward RF, in PP, RS leading

Amount of turn: Make ⅜ turn to L between 1 and 2.
Footwork: 1.TH 2.HT 3.TH.
Contrary body movement: Used on 1.
Body sway: Sway to R on 2.

This fig. may be preceded by:

(1) The Right Closed Change.
(2) The Double Reverse Spin.
(3) The Natural Spin Turn, 4, 5 and 6 of the Reverse Left Turn (ended diag. to centre).
(4) The Wing.

This fig. may be followed by:

(1) The Wing.
(2) The Cross Hesitation.

Cross Hesitation

MAN

Begin and finish according to preceding and following figs.

1. Forward RF, in PP and CBMP
2. Close LF to RF (weight on RF)
3. Hesitate with weight on RF

Amount of turn: Nil or ¼ turn to L may be made between 1 and 2.
Footwork: 1.HT 2.T (both feet) 3.TH (RF).
Contrary body movement: Nil.
Body sway: Nil.

LADY

Begin and finish according to preceding and following figs.

1. Forward LF, and across in PP and CBMP
2. Side RF
3. Close LF to RF

Amount of turn: Make ¼ turn to L between 1 and 2; make ⅛ turn to L between 2 and 3.
Footwork: 1.HT 2.T 3.TH.
Contrary body movement: Used on 1.
Body sway: Sway to L on 2 and 3.

This fig. may be preceded by:

(1) The Open Telemark.
(2) The Whisk.
(3) The Open Impetus Turn.

This fig. may be followed by:

(1) LF back (lady RF forward) into 4, 5 and 6 of Reverse Corté.
(2) The Outside Spin.
(3) LF forward (lady RF back) into the Left Closed Change or the Whisk.

Notes: (1) No turn on the Cross Hesitation (for man) when used after the Open Telemark or the Whisk.
(2) ¼ turn to L may be made after the Open Impetus Turn has been danced into the Cross Hesitation, when the Cross Hesitation may be followed by the Backward Lock Step.

The Wing

This figure is usually preceded by the Open Telemark, taking the third step slightly farther back than normally.

MAN

Begin in PP after the Open Telemark and finish along LOD or diag. to centre.
1. Forward RF, and across in PP and CBMP (pointing to LOD)
2, 3. Keeping weight on RF, close LF to RF

Amount of turn: Make ⅛ turn to L between 3 of the Open Telemark and 1 of the Wing; make ⅛ turn to L between 2 and 3.
Footwork: 1.H 2, 3. Pressure on T of RF with F flat, and pressure on inside edge of T of LF.
Contrary body movement: Nil.
Body sway: Nil.

LADY

Begin in PP after the Open Telemark and finish facing against LOD or backing diag. to centre.

1. Forward LF, in PP and CBMP
2. Forward RF, preparing to step OP on his L side
3. Forward LF, in CBMP, OP on his L side

Amount of turn: Make ⅛ turn to L between 3 of the Open Telemark and 1 of the Wing; make ⅜ turn to L between 1 and 3 of the Wing.

Footwork: 1.HT 2.T 3.TH.
Contrary body movement: Used on 1.
Body sway: Sway to L on 2 and 3.

This fig. may be preceded by:

(1) The Open Telemark.
(2) The Whisk.

This fig. may be followed by:

(1) The Reverse Turn, taking first step OP (man).
(2) The Double Reverse Spin, taking first step OP.
(3) The Telemark, taking first step OP.
(4) The Drag Hesitation, taking first step OP.

Open Impetus Turn

This figure is preceded by 1, 2 and 3 of the Natural Turn.

MAN

Begin backing LOD and finish diag. to centre in PP.

1. Back LF, turning to R
2. Close RF to LF, turning from L heel on to RF (heel turn) to face diag. to centre
3. Diag. forward LF in PP, LS leading

Amount of turn: Make ⅜ turn to R between 1 and 2.
Footwork: 1.TH 2.HT 3.TH.
Contrary body movement: Used on 1.
Body sway: Sway to L on 2.

LADY

Begin facing LOD and finish diag. to centre in PP.

1. Forward RF }
2. Side LF } Turning to R to back diag. to centre
3. Brush RF to LF and step to side with RF in PP

Amount of turn: Make ⅜ turn to R between 1 and 2; make ⅜ turn to R between 2 and 3.
Footwork: 1.HT 2.T 3.TH.
Contrary body movement: Used on 1.
Body sway: Sway to R on 2.

Advanced dancers incorporate many Promenade Position figures in their choreography. This photograph shows the shape and position of step 3 of the Open Impetus Turn (above) or the Open Telemark (page 69).

This fig. may be preceded by:

(1) 1, 2 and 3 of the Natural Turn.
(2) The Drag Hesitation.
(3) The Backward Lock.

This fig. may be followed by:

(1) The Cross Hesitation.
(2) The Wing.
(3) The Right Closed Change, commenced in PP.

Drag Hesitation

MAN

Begin facing LOD, or diag. to centre, and finish backing diag. to wall.

1. Forward LF
2. Side RF
3. Close LF to RF, keeping weight on RF, preparing to lead PO on R side

Amount of turn: Make ⅜ or ¼ turn to L between 1 and 3.
Footwork: 1.HT 2.T 3.T (of both feet), then TH (RF).
Contrary body movement: Used on 1.
Body sway: Nil.

LADY

Begin backing LOD, or back diag. to centre, and finish facing diag. to wall.

1. Back RF
2. Side LF
3. Close RF to LF, keeping weight on LF, preparing to step OP on R side

Amount of turn: Make ⅜ or ¼ turn to L between 1 and 3.
Footwork: 1.TH 2.T 3.T (of both feet), then TH (LF).
Contrary body movement: Used on 1.
Body sway: Nil.

This fig. may be preceded by:

(1) The Hesitation Change.
(2) The Right Closed Change.
(3) The Double Reverse Spin.
(4) The Wing.
(5) 4, 5 and 6 of the Reverse Turn after the Natural Spin Turn.

This fig. may be followed by:

(1) 4, 5 and 6 of the Natural Turn.
(2) The Backward Lock.
(3) The Impetus Turn or the Open Impetus Turn.
(4) 4, 5 and 6 of the Hesitation Change.

Backward Lock

MAN

Begin and finish backing diag. to wall.

1. Back LF, in CBMP, PO
2. Back RF
&. Cross LF in front of RF
3. Diag. back RF, preparing to lead PO on R side.

Amount of turn: Nil.
Footwork: 1.TH 2.T, & T 3.TH.
Contrary body movement: Used on 1 (slightly).
Body sway: Nil.

LADY

Begin and finish facing diag. to wall.

1. Forward RF, OP, in CBMP
2. Forward LF
&. Cross RF behind LF
3. Diag. forward LF, preparing to step OP on R side

Amount of turn: Nil.
Footwork: 1.HT 2.T & T 3.TH.
Contrary body movement: Used on 1 (slightly).
Body sway: Nil.

Notes: (1) Both the man and lady dance four steps to three beats. The second beat is the split beat (not the third). It helps to count SQQS for this figure instead of 1, 2 & 3.

(2) While the man dances the Backward Lock backwards, the lady dances her steps forwards.

This fig. may be preceded by:

(1) The Drag Hesitation.

This fig. may be followed by:

(1) 4, 5 and 6 of the Natural Turn.

(2) The Impetus Turn or the Open Impetus Turn.

Double Reverse Spin

Although called the *Double* Reverse Spin, this does not signify that it must be used twice. More often than not, it is only used once at a time.

Whilst the man does three steps to three beats, the lady does four steps to three beats, that is why it is counted 1, 2 & 3.

MAN

Begin and finish according to preceding and following figs.

1. Forward LF } Turning to L to back diag.
2. Side RF } to wall

Toe { &. Close LF towards RF, turning on RF
Pivot { 3. Complete turn RF (retaining weight on RF)

Amount of turn: Make complete turn or ¾ turn to L, according to the preceding and following figs.

Notes: (1) When a complete turn is made: make ⅜ turn to L between 1 and 2, and make ⅝ turn to L between 2 and 3.

(2) When ¾ turn is to be made: make ⅜ turn to L between 1 and 2, and make ⅜ turn to L between 2 and 3.

Footwork: 1.HT 2.T, & 3.T of LF, then TH of RF.

Contrary body movement: Used on 1.

Body sway: Nil.

LADY

Begin and finish according to preceding and following figs.

1. RF back } Turning to L to
2. Close LF to RF (heel turn) } face LOD

&. Side RF slightly back

3. Cross LF in front of RF

Amount of turn: Make complete turn to L or ¾ turn, according to the preceding and following figs.

Notes: (1) When a complete turn is made: make ½ turn to L between 1 and 2; make ⅜ turn between 2 and &; and make ⅛ turn between & and 3.

(2) When ¾ turn is made: make ⅜ turn to L between 1 and 2; make ¼ turn between 2 and &; and make ⅛ turn between & and 3.

Footwork: 1.HT 2.T & T 3.TH.

Contrary body movement: Used on 1.

Body sway: Nil.

This fig. may be preceded by:

(1) The Right Closed Change.

(2) The Hesitation Change.

(3) The Natural Spin Turn and 4, 5 and 6 of the Reverse Turn.

(4) The Reverse Turn.

(5) The Double Reverse Spin.

(6) The Wing.

This fig. may be followed by:

(1) The Left Closed Change.

(2) The Double Reverse Spin.

(3) The Telemark.

(4) The Open Telemark.

(5) The Drag Hesitation.

(6) The Whisk.

Outside Spin

MAN

Begin and finish facing diag. to wall.

1. Very short step back LF, pivoting on it to R, PO, in CBMP
2. Forward RF, OP, in CBMP
3. Side LF, still turning, to end with LF back

Amount of turn: Make ⅜ turn to R on 1; make ⅜ turn to R between 2 and 3; make ¼ turn to R on 3.

Footwork: 1.THT 2.HT 3.TH.

Contrary body movement: Used on 1 and 2.

Body sway: Nil.

Outside Spin

LADY

Begin and finish backing diag. to wall.

1. Forward RF, OP, in CBMP
2. Close LF to RF, turning to face wall
3. Forward RF in front of partner, ending in CBMP

Amount of turn: Make ⅜ turn to R between 1 and 2; make ¼ turn to R between 2 and 3; make ⅛ turn to R on 3.

Footwork: 1.HT 2.T 3.TH.

Contrary body movement: Used on 1.

Body sway: Nil.

This fig. may be preceded by:

(1) 1, 2 and 3 of the Reverse Corté.
(2) The Open Telemark and the Cross Hesitation.
(3) The Open Impetus Turn and the Cross Hesitation.

This fig. may be followed by:

(1) Any Natural fig.

The Outside Change

This figure is usually preceded by 1, 2 and 3 of the Natural Turn.

MAN

Begin backing diag. to centre, and finish facing diag. to wall.

1. Back LF
2. Back RF
3. LF to side, slightly forward

} Turning to the L to almost face diag. to centre

Amount of turn: Make almost a ¼ turn to L between 2 and 3.

Footwork: 1.TH 2.T 3.TH.

Contrary body movement: Used on 2 (slightly).

Body sway: Nil.

LADY

1. Forward RF
2. Forward LF
3. RF to side, slightly back

} Turning to the L to almost back diag. to wall

Amount of turn: Make almost a ¼ turn to L between 2 and 3.

Footwork: 1.HT 2.T 3.TH.

Contrary body movement: Used on 2 (slightly).

Body sway: Nil.

This fig. may be preceded by:

(1) 1, 2 and 3 of the Natural Turn.
(2) The Reverse Corté, taking the first step with lady outside.
(3) 1, 2 and 3 of the Weave.
(4) The Cross Hesitation.
(5) The Progressive Chassé to R.

This fig. may be followed by:

(1) The Natural Turn.
(2) The Natural Spin Turn.
(3) May be ended in PP and then followed by the Weave from PP, the Wing, the Chassé from PP or the Cross Hesitation.

Note: This figure resembles the last 3 steps of a Weave in Waltz time, except that the first step is taken with the lady in line.

The Back Whisk

MAN

Begin backing diag. to centre against the LOD and finish facing diag. to wall.

1. Back LF in CBMP
2. Diag. back RF
3. LF crosses behind RF in PP

Amount of turn: Nil

Footwork: 1.TH 2.T 3.TH.

Contrary body movement: Used on 1 (slightly).

Body sway: Sway to L on 2 and 3.

LADY

Begin facing diag. to centre against the LOD and finish facing diag. to centre.

1. Forward RF in CBMP, OP
2. Side LF
3. Cross RF behind LF in PP

Amount of turn: ⅛ to R between 1 and 2, ⅛ to R between 2 and 3.
Footwork: 1.HT 2.T 3.TH.
Contrary body movement: Used on 1.
Body sway: Sway to R on 2 and 3.

This fig. may be preceded by:

(1) The Reverse Corté.
(2) 1, 2 and 3 of the Natural Turn.

This fig. may be followed by:

(1) The Chassé from PP.
(2) The Wing.
(3) The Cross Hesitation.
(4) The Weave from PP.

Progressive Chassé to the Right

MAN

Begin facing diag. to centre and finish backing diag. to wall.

1. Forward LF
2. Side RF
3. Close LF to RF
4. Side and slightly back RF

Amount of turn: Almost ¼ turn to L.
Footwork: 1.HT 2.T 3.T 4.TH.
Contrary body movement: Used on 1.
Body sway: Nil.
Rhythm: 1 2(½) & (½) 3.

LADY

Begin backing diag. to centre and end facing diag. to wall.

1. Back RF
2. Side LF
3. Close RF to LF
4. Side and slightly forward LF

Amount of turn: Almost ¼ turn to L.
Footwork: 1.TH 2.T 3.T 4.TH.
Contrary body movement: Used on 1.
Body sway: Nil.
Rhythm: 1 2(½) & (½) 3.

This fig. may be preceded by:

(1) The Hesitation Change.
(2) The Wing (the Progressive Chassé to R would then be taken OP on her L side).
(3) 4, 5 and 6 of the Reverse Turn taken after an underturned Natural Spin Turn.

This fig. may be followed by:

(1) The Backward Lock Step.
(2) The Back Whisk.
(3) The Underturned Outside Spin.
(4) The Open or Closed Impetus Turn.
(5) The Outside Change if the Progressive Chassé to R finishes backing diag. to centre.

The Weave from PP

MAN

1. Forward RF and across in PP and CBMP
2. Forward LF
3. RF to side and slightly back

Turning to the L to almost back LOD

4. Back LF in CBMP
5. Back RF
6. LF to side and slightly forward

Turning to the L to almost face diag. to wall

Amount of turn: Make ⅜ turn to L between 2 and 3. Make almost ⅜ turn to L between 4 and 6.
Footwork: 1.HT 2.T 3.TH 4.TH 5.T 6.TH.
Contrary body movement: On 2 and 5.
Body sway: Nil.

The Weave from PP

LADY

1. Step through with LF in PP and CBMP
2. Side RF slightly back
3. Side LF slightly forward
⎫ Turning to the L to almost face LOD

4. Forward RF in CBMP, OP
5. Forward LF
6. Side RF slightly back
⎫ Turning to the L to almost back diag. to wall

Amount of turn: Make almost ¾ turn to the L between 1 and 3. Make almost ¼ turn to L between 5 and 6.

Footwork: 1.HT 2.T 3.TH 4.HT 5.T 6.TH.

Contrary body movement: On 1 and 5.

Body sway: Nil.

This fig. may be preceded by:

The Weave from PP can be taken from any figure ended in PP, such as the Whisk, Open Impetus, Open Telemark etc.

This fig. may be followed by:

The Forward RF OP into any Natural figure, e.g. Natural Turn, Natural Spin Turn etc.

The Turning Lock

MAN

Taken after a Natural Spin Turn.
Begin backing diag. to centre and finish diag. to wall.

1. Back RF R shoulder leading
2. Cross LF in front of RF
3. Back RF moving it slightly to R
4. Side and slightly forward LF

Amount of turn: Make ¼ turn to L.

Footwork: 1.T 2.T 3.T 4.TH.

Body sway: Sway to L on 1 and 2.

Rhythm: 1 (½) & (½) 2 3.

Note: It is the first beat that is the split beat.

LADY

Begin facing diag. to centre and finish backing diag. to wall.

1. Forward LF L shoulder leading
2. Cross RF behind LF
3. Forward LF moving it slightly leftwards
4. Side and slightly back RF

Amount of turn: Make ¼ turn to L.

Footwork: 1.T 2.T 3.T 4.TH.

Body sway: Sway to R on 1 and 2.

Rhythm: 1 (½) & (½) 2 3.

Note: It is the first beat that is the split beat.

This fig. may be preceded by:

(1) The Natural Spin Turn.
(2) The Outside Spin at a corner.
(3) The Impetus Turn at a corner.

This fig. may be followed by:

(1) Any Natural fig.

Suggested amalgamations:

(1) Spin Turn: Turning Lock: Natural Turn.
(2) Spin Turn: Turning Lock ending in PP along LOD: Wing: Chassé to R.
(3) Overturn preceding Spin Turn by taking step 6 more across LOD. Take step 1 of Turning Lock back down LOD and turn to R on step 3 which will be a small step to side on RF to end with the body facing diag. to centre. The fourth step will be taken towards centre in PP by both man and lady. End by turning lady square for a Weave from PP.

The Weave

This figure is preceded by 1, 2 and 3 of a Reverse Turn, ended backing diag. to wall.

MAN

Begin backing diag. to wall and finish facing diag. to wall.

1. RF back
2. LF forward
3. RF to side
4. LF back in CBMP
5. RF back
6. LF to side and slightly forward

Amount of turn: Make ⅛ turn to L between 2 and 3; make ⅛ turn to L between 3 and 4 and ¼ turn to L between 5 and 6.

Footwork: 1.TH 2.HT 3.TH 4.TH 5.T 6.TH.

Contrary body movement: On 1, 2, 5.

Body sway: Nil.

LADY

Begin facing diag. to wall and finish backing diag. to wall.

1. LF forward.
2. RF back
3. LF to side
4. RF forward in CBMP, OP
5. LF forward
6. RF to side and slightly back

Amount of turn: Make ¼ turn to L between 2 and 3 and ¼ turn to L between 5 and 6.

Footwork: 1.H 2.T 3.TH 4.HT 5.T 6.TH.

Contrary body movement: On 1, 2, 5.

Body sway: Nil.

Notes: (1) It is better to commence facing LOD for the 3 steps of the Reverse Turn preceding this figure. A Double Reverse Spin ended facing the LOD is a good entry.

(2) If 1, 2, 3 of the Reverse Turn is ended backing the LOD (normal alignment) ⅛ turn will be made between steps 2 and 3 and no turn between 3 and 4.

This fig. may be preceded by:

(1) The Natural Spin Turn followed by 4, 5, 6 of the Reverse Turn ended facing the LOD.

(2) The Double Reverse Spin ended facing the LOD.

(3) The Hesitation Change at a corner and ended facing the new LOD followed by 1, 2, 3 of the Reverse Turn to back diag. to wall.

(4) The Reverse Pivot to face the LOD. Open Telemark and Wing to face LOD followed by 1, 2, 3 of the Reverse Turn to back diag. to wall.

This fig. may be followed by:

(1) Any Natural fig.

(2) May be ended in PP. Follow with Wing, etc.

14

The Foxtrot

The greater part of the technique of modern ballroom dancing has been formed out of this dance, and a thorough knowledge of it is essential to any serious dancer, or anyone who enters competitions or who intends to take up dancing professionally.

If you cannot give much time to this dance, I advise using the easier Slow Rhythm, the social dancer's Foxtrot.

The true Foxtrot is a dance for good dancers, and unfortunately it needs a great deal of space. It is popular in dance halls, which usually have large dance-floors, but it can rarely be used in restaurants and small nightclubs. Slow Rhythm is therefore more suitable for the beginner and for anywhere where there is not much space to move.

The Foxtrot is above all things a 'smooth' dance; the movement should be flowing, the weight of the body travelling continuously, the slows and quicks blending in an unbroken movement, the dancers completely relaxed and controlled. It is, as I have said, a dance for the experienced dancer who has acquired the ability to be both relaxed and perfectly controlled at the same time.

The fundamental movements of the Foxtrot are the Walk and the Three-Step; all the basic figures are built up from these two movements.

The Walk forward consists of long steps taken from the hips, the feet moving only just clear of the floor.

Begin with the feet together. Put the weight of the body on one foot, and with the other take a long smooth step forward, straight from the hip, with the ball of the foot skimming the floor, going on to the heel as it passes the toes of the stationary foot. The heel of the back foot should now be gradually released from the floor, the moving foot continuing forward on the heel to the full extent of the stride. The weight of the body is now central between the two feet – on the heel of the front foot and the ball of the back foot. The toes of the front foot are then immediately lowered on to the floor and the weight of the body is taken forward over the front foot. The back foot is then brought forward, moving from the toes on to the ball of the foot, until it reaches the front foot, from where the forward movement is repeated.

The walk backward. Swing the leg well back

Flowing movement in the Foxtrot is essential. The bodies should travel continuously together without apparent effort.

from the hip, going from the ball of the foot out on to the toes. The weight is on the front foot. Release the toes of the front foot (keeping the back heel up). The weight is now central between the two feet (on the heel of the front foot and the ball of the back foot). Pull the front foot back with light pressure on the heel, controlling the weight on the ball of the back foot so that the back heel does not lower until the front foot (which is now flat) passes underneath you. Repeat with alternate feet. Each walking step takes two beats of the music and is counted 'slow'.

Note: Walking steps are never used on their own, but all forward slow steps are based on the movement of the walk forward, and all slow steps backwards are based on the movement of the walk backward.

To develop good balance, movement and timing, practise walks forward and backward before attempting the figures.

Feather Step

MAN

Begin and finish either facing LOD, or diag. to wall, or diag. to centre.

1. Forward RF   S
2. Forward LF, preparing to step OP, LS leading   Q
3. Forward RF, OP, in CBMP   Q
4. Forward LF (in front of partner)   S

Amount of turn: This figure may curve very slightly to R.
Footwork: 1.HT 2.T 3.TH 4.H.
Contrary body movement: Used on 1 and 4.
Body sway: Sway to R on 2 and 3.

begin here

LADY

Begin and finish either backing LOD, or diag. to wall, or diag. to centre.

1. Back LF   S
2. Back RF, RS leading   Q
3. Back LF, in CBMP, PO   Q
4. Back RF (partner in front)   S

Amount of turn: The lady curves her steps slightly towards the wall.
Footwork: 1.TH 2.TH 3.TH 4.T.
Contrary body movement: Used on 1 and 4.
Body sway: Sway to L on 2 and 3.

This fig. may be preceded by:

(1) The Natural Turn.
(2) The Reverse Wave.
(3) The Change of Direction.
(4) The Telemark (first step OP).
(5) The Open Telemark (first step in PP)
(6) The Open Impetus (first step in PP).
(7) The Hover Telemark (first step OP).
(8) The Outside Swivel (first step in PP).

This fig. may be followed by:

(1) The Three-Step.
(2) The Reverse Wave (when Feather Step is danced diag. to wall or along LOD).
(3) The Change of Direction.
(4) The Reverse Turn (when Feather Step is danced diag. to centre).
(5) The Telemark (when Feather Step is danced diag. to centre).
(6) The Hover Telemark (when Feather Step is danced diag. to wall).
(7) The Open Telemark (when Feather Step is danced diag. to centre).

begin here

Three-Step

MAN

Begin and finish either facing LOD, or facing diag. to wall, or facing diag. to wall and curve to L to LOD.

1. Forward RF	Q
2. Forward LF	Q
3. Forward RF	S

Amount of turn: Nil; or if curved make about ⅛ turn to L between 1 and 3.

Footwork: 1.HT 2.TH 3.H (Note: When step 3 becomes first step of a Natural fig., footwork on 3 will be HT).

Contrary body movement: Used on 3.

Body sway: Sway to L on 1 and 2.

Note: When the Three-Step is joined to any Natural fig., the last step of the Three-Step becomes the first step of the Natural fig.

LADY

Begin and finish either backing LOD, or backing diag. to wall, or backing diag. to wall and curve to L to LOD.

1. Back LF	Q
2. Back RF	Q
3. Back LF	S

Amount of turn: Nil; or if curved make about ⅛ turn to L between 1 and 3.

Footwork: 1.TH 2.TH 3.T (Note: When step 3 becomes first step of a Natural fig., footwork on 3 will be TH).

Contrary body movement: Used on 3.

Body sway: Sway to R on 1 and 2.

Note: When the Three-Step is joined to any Natural fig., the last step of the Three-Step becomes the first of the Natural fig.

This fig. may be preceded by:

(1) The Feather Step.
(2) The Reverse Turn or any Feather Finish.
(3) The Hover Feather.
(4) The Natural Telemark.
(5) The Natural Twist Turn.
(6) The Weave.
(7) The Top Spin.

This fig. may be followed by:

(1) Any Natural Turn (i.e. the Natural Twist Turn, etc.).

Natural Turn

MAN

Begin facing either LOD, or diag. to wall, and finish facing diag. to centre.

Note: The third step of the Three-Step becomes the first of the Natural Turn.

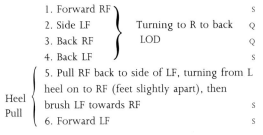

1. Forward RF		S
2. Side LF	Turning to R to back	Q
3. Back RF	LOD	Q
4. Back LF		S
Heel Pull { 5. Pull RF back to side of LF, turning from L heel on to RF (feet slightly apart), then brush LF towards RF		S
6. Forward LF		S

Amount of turn: Make ⅜ or ½ turn to R between 1 and 3; make ⅛ turn to R between 4 and 5.

Footwork: 1.HT 2.T 3.TH 4.TH 5.H, inside edge of foot, whole foot, then inside edge of LF 6.H.

Contrary body movement: Used on 1, 4 and 6.

Body sway: Sway to R on 2 and 3; sway to L on 5.

Note: The Natural Turn can be danced along the sides of the room, or round a corner, when less turn would be made.

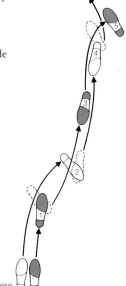

begin here

Natural Turn

LADY

Begin backing LOD, or backing diag. to wall, and finish backing diag. to centre.

Heel Turn	{ 1. Back LF 2. Close RF to LF, turning from L heel on to RH	Turning to R to face LOD	S Q
	3. Forward LF		Q
	4. Forward RF, turning to R		S
	5. Side LF, then brush RF to LF		S
	6. Back RF		S

Amount of turn: Make ½ turn to R between 1 and 2; make ⅜ turn to R between 4 and 5.

Footwork: 1.TH 2.HT 3.TH 4.HT 5.TH, then inside edge of T of RF 6.T.

Contrary body movement: Used on 1, 4 and 6.

Body sway: Sway to L on 2 and 3; sway to R on 5.

This fig. may be preceded by:

(1) The Three-Step, making last step the first of the Natural Turn.
(2) The Telemark, making last step the first of the Natural Turn, but outside partner.

This fig. may be followed by:

(1) The Feather Step.
(2) (In a small ballroom.) Making last step of the Natural Turn first step of any Reverse figure.
(3) The Hover Feather from fifth step.
(4) The Impetus Turn, the Open Impetus, or the Outside Swivel after third step.

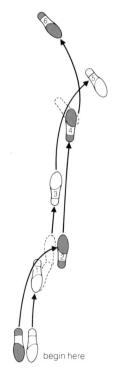

Reverse Turn

MAN

Begin facing diag. to centre and finish facing diag. to wall.

	1. Forward LF		S
	2. Side RF	Turning to L to back LOD	Q
	3. Back LF		Q
	4. Back RF		S
Feather Finish	{ 5. Side LF slightly forward		Q
	6. Forward RF, OP, in CBMP		Q
	7. Forward LF (in front of partner)		S

Amount of turn: Make ⅜ turn to L between 1 and 3; make ⅛ turn to L between 4 and 5.

Footwork: 1.HT 2.T 3.TH 4.THT 5.T 6.TH 7.H.

Contrary body movement: Used on 1, 4 and 7.

Body sway: Sway to L on 2 and 3; sway to R on 5 and 6.

Note: The Reverse Turn is danced along the sides of the room only and used round a corner.

Steps 5, 6 and 7 are similar to 2, 3 and 4 of the Feather Step and are therefore called a Feather Finish.

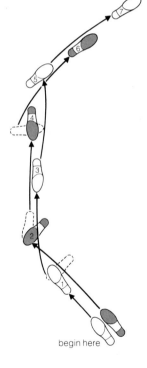

The Feather Step into the Three Step in a classic Slow Foxtrot as danced by Ian Hayes and Sasha McKee of England always looks easy but you must retain perpetual motion.

Reverse Turn

LADY

Begin backing diag. to centre and finish backing diag. to wall.

Heel Turn
{
1. Back RF — s
2. Close LF to RF, turning from R heel on to LF — Turning to L to face LOD
3. Forward RF — Q
}

4. Forward LF, turning to L — s

Feather Finish
{
5. Side RF — Q
6. Back LF, in CBMP, PO — Q
7. Back RF (partner in front) — s
}

Amount of turn: Make ⅜ turn to L between 1 and 2; make ⅜ turn to L between 4 and 6.

Footwork: 1.TH 2.HT 3.TH 4.HT 5.TH 6.TH 7.T.

Contrary body movement: Used on 1, 4 and 7.

Body sway: Sway to R on 2 and 3; sway to L on 5 and 6.

This fig. may be preceded by:

(1) The Feather Step, danced diag. to centre.
(2) Change of Direction (last step becoming first of Reverse Turn).
(3) The Hover Feather.
(4) The Natural Telemark.
(5) The Natural Twist Turn.
(6) The Top Spin.

This fig. may be followed by:

(1) The Three-Step.
(2) The Reverse Wave.
(3) The Change of Direction.
(4) The Hover Telemark.
(5) The Top Spin after sixth step.

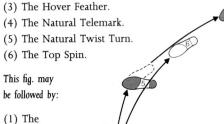
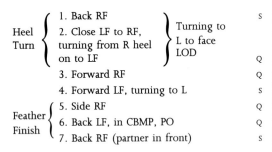
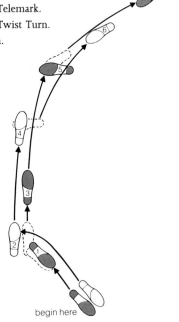

begin here

Reverse Wave

MAN

Begin facing LOD and finish facing diag. to centre.

1. Forward LF — s
2. Side RF — Turning to L to back diag. to wall — Q
3. Back LF — Q

4. Back RF — s
5. Back LF — Curving to L to back LOD — Q
6. Back RF — Q

Heel Pull
{
7. Back LF — s
8. Pull RF back to side of LF, turning from L heel on to RF (feet slightly apart), then brush LF towards RF — s
}

9. Forward LF — s

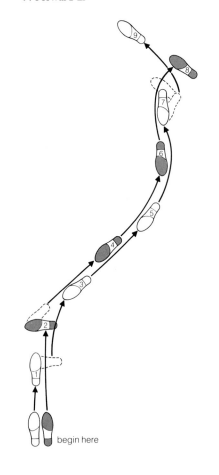

begin here

Amount of turn for sides of room (as above): Make ⅜ turn to L between 1 and 3; make ⅛ curve to L between 4 and 6; make ⅜ turn to R between 7 and 8.

Amount of turn round a corner (begin facing LOD): Make ⅜ turn to L between 1 and 3 to back diag. to wall; make ¼ turn to L between 4 and 6 to back diag. to wall of new LOD; make ¼ turn to R between 7 and 8 to finish facing diag. to centre of new LOD.

Footwork: 1.HT 2.T 3.TH 4.TH 5.T 6.TH 7.TH 8.H, inside edge of foot, whole foot, then inside edge of LF 9.H.

Contrary body movement: Used on 1, 4, 7 and 9.

Body sway: Sway to L on 2 and 3; sway to R on 5 and 6; sway to L on 8.

LADY

Begin backing LOD and finish backing diag. to centre.

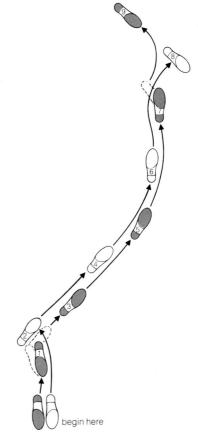

begin here

Heel Turn {
1. Back RF, turning to L
2. Close LF to RF, turning from R heel on to LH
} Turning to L to face diag. to wall   S

3. Forward RF   Q
4. Forward LF   Q
5. Forward RF } Curving to L to face LOD   S
6. Forward LF   Q
     Q
7. Forward RF   S
8. Side LF, then brush RF to LF   S
9. Back RF   S

Amount of turn for sides of room (as above): Make ⅜ turn to L between 1 and 2; make ⅛ curve to L between 4 and 5; make ⅜ turn to R between 7 and 8.

Amount of turn round a corner (begin backing LOD): Make ⅜ turn to L between 1 and 2 to face diag. to wall; make ¼ turn to L between 4 and 6 to face diag. to wall of new LOD; make ¼ turn to R between 7 and 8 to finish backing diag. to centre of new LOD.

Footwork: 1.TH 2.HT 3.TH 4.H 5.HT 6.TH 7.TH 8.TH, then inside edge of T of RF 9.T.

Contrary body movement: Used on 1, 4, 7 and 9.

Body sway: to R on 2 and 3; sway to L on 5 and 6; sway to R on 8.

This fig. may be preceded by:

(1) The Feather Step.

(2) The Reverse Turn (when more turn will be made between 1 and 3 of Reverse Wave).

(3) The Change of Direction, making last step first of Reverse Wave.

(4) The Hover Feather.

(5) The Natural Telemark.

(6) The Natural Twist Turn.

(7) The Weave.

(8) The Top Spin.

(9) Any Feather Finish.

This fig. may be followed by:

(1) The Feather Step.

(2) The Impetus Turn after sixth step of the Wave.

(3) The Hover Feather after eighth step of the Wave.

(4) The Weave after fourth step of the Wave.

(5) The Open Impetus after sixth step of the Wave.

Change of Direction

This figure is commenced on the last step of the Feather Step, or on the last step of the Reverse Turn, when at the end of the room, in a corner, or when you have not enough space to follow either of these figures with a Three-Step and Natural Turn.

MAN

Begin and finish according to the preceding and following figure.

1. Forward LF   s
2. Diagonally forward RF, RS leading   Q
3. Close LF to RF, slightly forward without weight (relaxing both knees)   Turning to L   or s
4. Forward LF, in CBMP   Q   s

Amount of turn: Make up to ½ turn (or less) to L.

Footwork: 1.H 2 and 3.Inside edge of T, H, then inside edge of T of LF 4.H.

Contrary body movement: Used on 1 and 4.

Body sway: Sway to L on 2 and 3.

Note: In standard technique, steps 2 and 3 are timed as one 'slow'.

LADY

Begin and finish according to the preceding and following figure.

1. Back RF   s
2. Diag. back LF, LS leading   Q
3. Close RF to LF, slightly back without weight (relaxing both knees)   Turning to L   or s
4. Back RF, in CBMP   Q   s

Amount of turn: Make up to ½ turn (or less) to L.

Footwork: 1.TH 2 and 3.T, inside edge of T, H, then inside edge of T of RF 4.T.

Contrary body movement: Used on 1 and 4.

Body sway: Sway to R on 2 and 3.

This fig may be preceded by:

(1) The Feather Step.
(2) The Reverse Turn.
(3) The Hover Feather.
(4) The Natural Twist Turn.
(5) The Natural Telemark.
(6) The Top Spin.
(7) The Weave.
(8) Any Feather Finish.

This fig. may be followed by:

(1) The Feather Step, or the last step of the Change of Direction may be used as first of a Reverse fig.

Note: After these figures have been mastered, you should have no difficulty in introducing more advanced figures such as the Telemarks and the Impetus Turns.

As far as possible try to use right-handed and left-handed turns alternately: this will make the dance much more effective.

Impetus Turn

MAN

Begin backing LOD and finish backing diag. to centre against LOD.

Heel Turn
1. Back LF   s
2. Close RF back to LF, turning from L heel on to RF   Turning to R to face diag. to centre   Q
3. Side LF slightly back   Q
4. Back RF   s

Amount of turn: Make ⅜ turn to R between 1 and 2; make ¼ turn to R between 2 and 3.

Footwork: 1.TH 2.HT 3.TH 4.T.

Contrary body movement: Used on 1 and 4.

Body sway: Sway to L on 2.

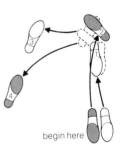
begin here

The Right Lunge can be performed in the Foxtrot, the Waltz or the Tango. In the Tango it often precedes The Drag (shown on page 40).

86

Impetus Turn

LADY

Begin facing LOD and finish facing diag. to centre against LOD.

1. Forward RF ⎫ Turning to R to   s
2. Side LF   ⎭ back diag. to centre   Q
3. Brush RF to LF and step diag. forward with it   Q
4. Forward LF   s

Amount of turn: Make ⅜ turn to R between 1 and 2; make ¼ turn to R between 2 and 3.

Footwork: 1.HT 2.T 3.TH 4.H.

Contrary body movement: Used on 1 and 4.

Body sway: Sway to R on 2.

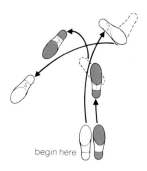

begin here

This fig. may be preceded by:

(1) Three steps of the Natural Turn.
(2) Six steps of the Reverse Wave.

This fig. may be followed by:

(1) A Feather Finish danced diag. to centre or diag. to wall if the Impetus Turn is danced at a corner.

(2) Two steps of a Feather Finish, check into a Top Spin.

Note: For a Feather Finish see 5, 6 and 7 of Reverse Turn (page 84).

The Telemark

MAN

Begin facing diag. to centre and finish facing diag. to wall.

1. Forward LF ⎫ Turning to L to almost   s
2. Side RF   ⎭ backing LOD   Q
3. Side LF, slightly forward   Q
4. Forward RF, OP, in CBMP   s

Amount of turn: Make almost ⅜ turn to L between 1 and 2; make just over ⅛ turn to L between 2 and 3.

Footwork: 1.HT 2.T 3.TH 4.H.

Contrary body movement: Used on 1 and 4.

Body sway: Sway to L on 2.

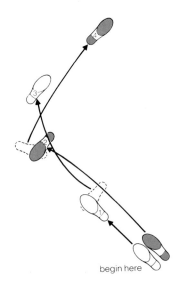

begin here

LADY

Begin backing diag. to centre and finish backing diag. to wall.

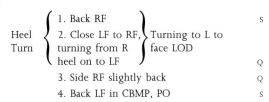

Heel Turn ⎧ 1. Back RF ⎫		s
⎨ 2. Close LF to RF, ⎬ Turning to L to		
turning from R ⎬ face LOD		
⎩ heel on to LF ⎭		Q
3. Side RF slightly back		Q
4. Back LF in CBMP, PO		s

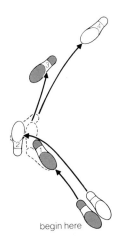

begin here

Amount of turn: Make ⅜ turn to L between 1 and 2; make ⅜ turn to L between 2 and 3.

Footwork: 1.TH 2.HT 3.TH 4.T.

Contrary body movement: Used on 1 and 4.

Body sway: Sway to R on 2.

This fig. may be preceded by:

(1) The Feather Step.
(2) The Change of Direction.
(3) The Reverse Wave.
(4) The Hover Feather.
(5) The Natural Telemark.
(6) The Natural Twist Turn.
(7) Any Feather Finish danced diag. to centre.

This fig. may be followed by:

(1) The Feather Step (last three steps).
(2) The Natural Turn (commenced on last step of the Telemark, outside partner).
(3) The Natural Telemark. As for Natural Turn (page 82).

Open Telemark (with a Feather Finish)

MAN

Begin facing diag. to centre and finish facing diag. to wall.

1. Forward LF ⎫ Turning to L to back		S
2. Side RF ⎭ diag. to wall		Q
3. Side LF slightly forward, in PP		Q
4. Forward RF in PP and CBMP		S
Feather ⎧ 5. Diag. forward LF, preparing to step OP in CBM		Q
Finish ⎨ 6. Forward RF, OP in CBMP		Q
⎩ 7. Forward LF		S

Amount of turn: Make ¼ turn to L between 1 and 2; make ½ turn to L between 2 and 3. (Turn partner square between 4 and 5.)

Footwork: 1.HT 2.T 3.TH 4.HT 5.T 6.TH 7.H.

Contrary body movement: Used on 1, 4 (slightly) and 7.

Body sway: Sway to L on 2; sway to R on 5 and 6.

LADY

Begin backing diag. to centre and finish backing diag. to wall.

Heel ⎧ 1. Back RF ⎫ Turning to L	S
Turn ⎨ 2. Close LF to RF, turning ⎬ to face LOD	
⎩ from R heel on to LF ⎭	Q
3. Diag. forward RF in PP, RS leading	Q
4. Forward LF and across in PP and CBMP	S
Feather ⎧ 5. Side RF, slightly back	Q
Finish ⎨ 6. Back LF in CBMP, PO	Q
⎩ 7. Back RF	S

Amount of turn: Make ⅜ turn to L between 1 and 2; make ¼ turn to L between 4 and 5; make ⅛ turn to L between 5 and 6.

Footwork: 1.TH 2.HT 3.TH 4.HT 5.TH 6.TH 7.T.

Contrary body movement: Used on 1, 4 and 7.

Body sway: Sway to R on 2; sway to L on 5 and 6.

This fig. may be preceded by:

(1) The Feather Step.
(2) The Hover Feather.
(3) The Natural Telemark.
(4) The Natural Twist Turn.

(5) The Top Spin ended diag. to centre.
(6) Any Feather Finish ended diag. to centre.

This fig. may be followed by:

(1) The Feather Finish as above (steps 5, 6 and 7).
(2) The Natural Turn from fourth step.
(3) The Natural Turn to the Outside Swivel (see Outside Swivel notes).
(4) The Natural Twist Turn from fourth step.
(5) The Natural Telemark from fourth step.

Natural Telemark

MAN

Begin facing diag. to wall and finish facing diag. to centre.

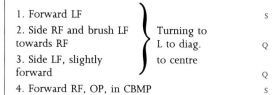

1. Forward RF — s
2. Side LF — Q
3. Side RF (small step) — Turning to R to face diag. to centre — Q
4. Diag. forward LF, preparing to step outside partner, LS leading — Q
5. Forward RF, OP, in CBMP — Q
6. Forward LF — s

Amount of turn: Make ¼ turn to R between 1 and 2; make ¼ turn to R between 2 and 3
Footwork: 1.HT 2.T 3.T 4.T 5.TH 6.H.
Contrary body movement: Used on 1 and 6.
Body sway: Sway to R on 2; sway to L on 4.
Note: At a corner ½ turn to R will be made between 1 and 3.

LADY

Begin backing diag. to wall and finish backing diag. to centre.

Heel Turn {
1. Back LF — s
2. Close RF to LF, turning from L heel on to RF — Turning to R to face LOD
3. Side LF, and RF brushes towards LF — Q
4. Diag. back RF, RS leading — Q
5. Back LF, in CBMP, PO — Q
6. Back RF — s
}

Amount of turn: Make ⅜ turn between 1 and 2; make ⅜ turn between 2 and 3.

Footwork: 1.TH 2.HT 3.T 4.TH 5.TH 6.T.
Contrary body movement: Used on 1 and 6.
Body sway: Sway to L on 2; sway to R on 4.

This fig. may be preceded by:

(1) The Three-Step.
(2) The Telemark, making last step the first of the Natural Telemark.
(3) The Open Telemark, making last step the first of the Natural Telemark.

This fig. may be followed by:

(1) Any Reverse fig. (e.g. the Reverse Turn, the Telemark, the Open Telemark).

Hover Telemark

MAN

Begin facing diag. to wall and finish facing diag. to centre.

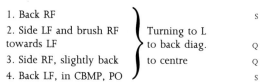

1. Forward LF — s
2. Side RF and brush LF towards RF — Turning to L to diag. to centre — Q
3. Side LF, slightly forward — Q
4. Forward RF, OP, in CBMP — s

Amount of turn: Make ¼ turn to L between 1 and 3.
Footwork: 1.HT 2.T of RF, then inside edge of T of LF 3.TH 4.H.
Contrary body movement: Used on 1 and 4.
Body sway: Sway to L on 2.

LADY

Begin backing diag. to wall and finish backing diag. to centre.

1. Back RF — s
2. Side LF and brush RF towards LF — Turning to L to back diag. to centre — Q
3. Side RF, slightly back — Q
4. Back LF, in CBMP, PO — s

Amount of turn: Make ¼ turn to L, between 1 and 3.
Footwork: 1.TH 2.T of LF, then inside edge of T of RF 3.TH 4.T.
Contrary body movement: Used on 1 and 4.
Body sway: Sway to R on 2.

This fig. may be preceded by:

(1) The Feather Step.
(2) The Reverse Turn or any Feather Finish ended diag. to wall.
(3) The Weave.
(4) The Top Spin.

This fig. may be followed by:

(1) The Feather Step (steps 2, 3 and 4).
(2) The Natural Turn.
(3) The Natural Telemark.

Hover Feather

The Hover Feather is introduced as an alternative ending to the Natural Turn, or the Reverse Wave; it is also used as an ending to the Natural Twist Turn.

(It is described after the fourth step of the Natural Turn.)

MAN

Begin backing to LOD, after 1, 2, 3 and 4 of the Natural Turn, and finish diag. to centre.

1. Dance a Heel Pull (turning to face diag. to centre)	Q	
2. Rising on RF to toes, brush LF slightly towards RF	Q	or s

Hover Feather	3. Diag. forward LF, preparing to step outside partner, LS leading	Q
	4. Forward RF, OP, in CBMP	Q
	5. Forward LF (in front of partner)	s

Amount of turn: Nil after the Heel Pull, which finishes diag. to centre.

Footwork on Hover Feather: 3.T 4.TH 5.H.

Contrary body movement: Used on 5.

Body sway: Sway to L on 1, 2 and 3.

Note: In standard technique, steps 1 and 2 are timed as one 'slow'.

LADY

Begin facing LOD, after 1, 2, 3 and 4 of the Natural Turn, and finish back diag. to centre.

1. Side LF	Q	
2. Rising on LF, brush RF towards LF	Q	or s

Hover Feather	3. Diag. back RF, RS leading	Q
	4. Back LF, in CBMP, PO	Q
	5. Back RF (partner in front)	s

Amount of turn: Nil, after the first step, which finishes backing diag. to centre.

Footwork: 1.TH 2.TH 3.T.

Contrary body movement: Used on 5.

Body sway: Sway to R on 1, 2 and 3.

This fig. may be preceded by:

(1) Any Heel Pull (e.g., five steps of the Natural Turn or eight steps of the Reverse Wave).
(2) The first four steps of the Natural Twist Turn.

This fig. may be followed by:

(1) The Reverse Turn.
(2) The Open Telemark.
(3) The Closed Telemark.
(4) The Change of Direction. (If the Hover Feather is danced near a corner it would end diag. to new wall.)
(5) The Three-Step (if the Hover Feather is danced near a corner).

Natural Twist Turn

MAN

Begin facing LOD and finish facing diag. to centre.

1. Forward RF } Turning to R to back		S
2. Side LF } diag. to centre		Q
3. Cross RF behind LF, slightly back		&
4. Twist to R on heel of LF and toe of RF (to face diag. to centre)		Q
5. Rise up on to toes, as in the Hover Feather		S
Hover Feather { 6. Diag. forward LF, preparing to step OP, LS leading		Q
7. Forward RF, OP, in CBMP		Q
8. Forward LF (in front of partner)		S

Amount of turn: Make ½ turn to R between 1 and 3; make ⅜ turn to R on the twist.

Footwork: 1.HT 2.TH 3.T 4. Twist on T of RF and H of LF with feet flat (end with weight on RF) 5.T of RF, with pressure on inside edge of T of LF 6.T 7.TH 8.H.

Contrary body movement: Used on 1 and 8.

Body sway: Sway to R on 2 and 3; sway to L on 5 and 6.

LADY

Begin backing LOD and finish backing diag. to centre.

Heel Turn { 1. Back LF } Turning to R to face LOD		S
2. Close RF to LF, turning from L heel on to RF		Q
3. Forward LF, preparing to step OP		&
4. Forward RF, OP, in CBMP		Q
5. Side LF, and brush RF towards LF		S
Hover Feather { 6. Diag. back RF, RS leading		Q
7. Back LF, in CBMP, PO		Q
8. Back RF (partner in front)		S

Amount of turn: Make ½ turn to R between 1 and 2; make ⅛ turn to R between 2 and 4; make ¼ turn to R between 4 and 5.

Footwork: 1.TH 2.HT 3.T 4.T 5.T, and inside edge of T of RF 6.TH 7.TH 8.T.

Contrary body movement: Used on 1, 4 and 8.

Body sway: Sway to L on 2 and 3; sway to R on 5 and 6.

This fig. may be preceded by:

(1) The Three-Step.

(2) The Telemark.

(3) The Open Telemark.

This fig. may be followed by:

(1) Any Reverse fig.

Top Spin

MAN

At a corner, begin facing diag. to wall and finish facing diag. to centre of new LOD.

	1. Back on to LF, in CBMP, PO	Q
	2. Back RF (partner in front)	Q
5, 6, 7 of the Reverse Turn {	3. Side LF, slightly forward	Q
	4. Forward RF, OP, in CBMP	Q
	5. Forward LF (in front of partner)	S

Amount of turn: Make ¼ turn to L between 1 and 2; make ¼ turn to L between 2 and 3.

Footwork: 1.T 2.T 3.T 4.TH 5.H.

Contrary body movement: Used on 2 and 5.

Body sway: Sway to R on 3 and 4.

LADY

At a corner begin backing diag. to wall and finish backing diag. to centre of new LOD.

	1. Forward RF, OP, in CBMP	Q
	2. Forward LF (partner in front)	Q
5, 6, 7 of the Reverse Turn {	3. Side RF	Q
	4. Back LF, in CBMP, PO	Q
	5. Back RF (partner in front)	S

Amount of turn: Make ¼ turn to L between 1 and 2; make ¼ turn to L between 2 and 4.

Footwork: 1.T 2.T 3.T 4.TH 5.H.

Contrary body movement: Used on 2 and 5.

Body sway: Sway to L on 3 and 4.

This fig. may be preceded by:

(1) Six steps of the Reverse Turn.
(2) Three steps of a Feather Step at a corner, danced diag. to wall.
(3) Six steps of the Weave.

This fig. may be followed by:

(1) Any Reverse fig. (e.g., the Reverse Turn, the Telemark, the Open Telemark).

Outside Swivel

MAN

Note: This figure is preceded by the Open Telemark making only half a turn to L on it, followed by 1, 2 and 3 of the Natural Turn commenced in PP.

Step 1	Forward and across RF in PP and CBMP	s
Step 2	Side LF	Q
Step 3	Back RF, RS leading	Q
	Making a quarter of a turn to R	

Begin backing diag. to wall and finish facing diag. to centre.

1. Back LF in CBMP, PO   Q
2. Cross RF loosely in front of LF, swivel-   } or s
ling partner into PP (without weight)   Q
3. Forward RF and across in PP and CBMP s
Follow with the Feather Finish taken

diag. to centre (turning partner square)   QQS

Amount of turn: Make ¼ turn to R by turning toe of LF inwards between 1 and 2.

Footwork: 1.TH 2.Pressure on T of RF 3.HT, Feather Finish, T, TH, H.

Contrary body movement: Used on 1 and 3.

Body sway: Nil.

Note: In standard technique steps 1 and 2 are timed as one 'slow'.

LADY

Note: This figure is preceded by the Open Telemark making only a quarter of a turn to L, followed by 1, 2 and 3 of the Natural Turn commenced in PP, the lady making no turn.

Step 1	Forward and across LF in PP and CBMP s	
Step 2	Forward RF	Q
Step 3	Forward LF preparing to step OP, LS leading	Q

Begin facing diag. to wall and finish backing diag. to centre.

1. Forward RF, OP, in CBMP   Q
2. Close LF to RF, slightly back,   } or s
without weight, opening to PP   Q
3. Forward LF and across in PP and CBMP   s
Follow with the Feather Finish diag. to centre
(turning square to partner)   QQS

Amount of turn: Make ½ turn to R between 1 and 2.

Footwork: 1.HTH 2.Pressure on inside edge of T of LF 3.HT, Feather Finish, TH, TH, T.

Contrary body movement: Used on 1 and 3.

Body sway: Nil.

Note: If the Outside Swivel is used at a corner the lady turns slightly less and the man makes no turn.

This fig. may be preceded by:

(1) 1, 2 and 3 of the Natural Turn after the under-turned Open Telemark (see note above).

This fig. may be followed by:

(1) The Feather Finish.

(2) The Outside Swivel, danced without any turn at a corner, and the following Feather Finish danced diag. to new centre.

(3) The Outside Swivel, danced without any turn, on the sides of the room, when it would be followed by a Feather Finish danced diag. to centre against LOD, into a Top Spin, making ½ turn to L to end diag. to wall.

(4) The Weave, when no turn is made on the Swivel.

The Weave

MAN

Begin facing diag. to centre, against LOD, and finish facing diag. to wall.

1. Forward on to LF	Turning to L	Q
2. Side RF	to back diag.	Q
3. Back LF, in CBMP, PO	to centre	Q
4. Back RF (partner in front)		Q
Feather Finish { 5. Side and slightly forward with LF		Q
6. Forward RF, OP, in CBMP		Q
7. Forward LF (in front of partner)		S

Amount of turn: Make ¼ turn to L between 1 and 3; make ¼ turn to L between 4 and 5.

Footwork: 1.HT 2.T 3.T 4.T 5.T 6.TH 7.H.

Contrary body movement: Used on 1, 4 and 7.

Body sway: Sway to L on 2 and 3; sway to R on 5 and 6.

This fig. may be preceded by:

(1) Four steps of the Reverse Wave.

(2) Four steps of the Reverse Turn, when the Weave will commence backing LOD, and less turn made on it between 1 and 3 unless danced at a corner.

(3) The Outside Swivel, danced without turning on swivel (lady will be turned square at end of 3 of the Outside Swivel into the Weave).

This fig. may be followed by:

(1) The Three-Step.

(2) The Change of Direction.

(3) The Wave (commenced diag. to wall, making ½ turn to L between 1 and 3 of Wave).

(4) The Hover Telemark.

LADY

Begin backing diag. to centre, against LOD, and finish backing diag. to wall.

1. Back on to RF	Turning to L	Q
2. Side LF	to face diag.	Q
3. Forward RF, OP, in CBMP	to centre	Q
4. Forward LF (in front of partner)		Q
Feather Finish { 5. Side RF, still turning		Q
6. Back LF, in CBMP, PO		Q
7. Back RF (partner in front)		S

Amount of turn: Make ¼ turn to L between 1 and 2; make ¼ turn to L between 4 and 6.

Footwork: 1.TH 2.T 3.T 4.T 5.TH 6.TH 7.T.

Contrary body movement: Used on 1, 4 and 7.

Body sway: Sway to R on 2 and 3; sway to L on 5 and 6.

For preceding and following figs. see beneath the description of man's steps.

Natural Weave

MAN

Begin and finish facing diag. to wall.

1, 2. Dance 1 and 2 of the Natural Turn (turning to back diag. to centre)	SQ
3. Back RF	Q
4. Back LF, in CBMP, PO	Q
5. Back RF, partner in front	Q
6, 7, 8. Dance 5, 6 and 7 of Reverse Turn (Feather Finish)	QQS

Amount of turn: Make ¼ turn to R between 1 and 2; make ¼ turn to L between 5 and 6.

Footwork: 1.HT 2.T 3.T 4.T 5.T 6.T 7.TH 8.H.

Contrary body movement: Used on 1, 5 and 8.

Body sway: Sway to R on 2 and 3; sway to R on 6 and 7.

LADY

Begin backing diag. to wall and finish backing diag. to wall.

1, 2. Dance 1 and 2 of the Natural Turn (turning to face diag. to centre)	SQ
3. Forward LF	Q
4. Forward RF, OP, in CBMP	Q
5. Forward LF (in front of partner)	Q
6, 7, 8. Dance 5, 6 and 7 of the Reverse Turn (Feather Finish)	QQS

Amount of turn: Make ¼ turn to R between 1 and 2; make ¼ turn to L between 5 and 7.

Footwork: 1.TH 2.HT 3.T 4.T 5.T 6.TH 7.TH 8.T.

Contrary body movement: Used on 1, 5 and 8.

Body sway: Sway to L on 2 and 3; sway to L on 6 and 7.

This fig. may be preceded by:

(1) The Three-Step.
(2) The Telemark, making last step of the Telemark first of the Natural Weave.

This fig. may be followed by:

(1) The Three-Step.
(2) The Reverse Wave.
(3) The Change of Direction.
(4) The Hover Telemark.
(5) The Top Spin after seventh step of the Natural Weave.

Open Impetus Turn

When used in the Foxtrot the Open Impetus Turn is counted sQQ. It is normally preceded by steps 1, 2 and 3 of the Natural Turn or steps 1 to 6 of the Reverse Wave. The normal endings are a Feather ending or the Weave from PP. The technique for the Open Impetus Turn is given in the Waltz section on page 70.

The Weave from PP

This figure follows an Open Impetus Turn.

MAN

Begin facing LOD and finish facing diag. to wall.

1. RF forward in PP and CBMP	S
2. LF forward	Q
3. RF to side and slightly back	Q
4. LF back in CBMP	Q
5. RF back	Q
6. LF to side and slightly forward	Q
7. RF forward in CBMP, OP	Q
8. LF forward	S

Amount of turn: Make ¼ turn to L between 2 and 3; make ⅛ turn to L between 3 and 4; make ⅜ turn to L between 5 and 6.

Footwork: 1.HT 2.T 3.T 4.T 5.T 6.T 7.TH 8.H.

Contrary body movement: Used on 2, 5 and 8.

Body sway: Sway to the L on 3 and 4; sway to the R on 6 and 7.

Note: On step 4 the footwork of TH may be used.

LADY

Begin facing diag. to centre and finish backing diag. to wall.

1. LF forward and across in PP and CBMP	S
2. RF to side and slightly back	Q
3. LF to side and slightly forward	Q
4. RF forward in CBMP, OP	Q
5. LF forward	Q
6. RF to side	Q
7. LF back in CBMP	Q
8. RF back	S

Footwork: 1.HT 2.T 3.T 4.T 5.T 6.TH 7.TH 8.T.

Contrary body movement: Used on 1, 5 and 8.

Body sway: Sway to the R on 3 and 4; sway to the L on 6 and 7.

Amount of turn: Make ⅜ turn to L between 1 and 2; make ⅜ turn between 2 and 3; make ¼ turn between 5 and 6; make ⅛ turn between 6 and 7.

This fig. may be preceded by:

(1) The Whisk.
(2) The Open Impetus Turn.
(3) The Open Telemark.
(4) The Outside Swivel.

This fig. may be followed by:

(1) The Three-Step.
(2) The Change of Direction.
(3) The Reverse Wave.
(4) The Hover Telemark.
(5) The Top Spin after sixth step.

Notes: (1) When the first and second steps of the Weave are taken in a direction to centre or diag. to centre against the LOD by the man the alignment of his third step will be backing LOD (lady's third step will be pointing diag. to centre). The fourth step will be taken diag. to centre.

(2) When taken after an Open Telemark, the man's first step (RF) will be pointing to LOD and he will make ⅛ turn between the preceding step and 1, ⅜ turn between 2 and 3 and ⅛ turn between 3 and 4. Foot positions as in the charts.

(3) Although the Weave normally commences with the LF the preceding step on RF is so important that it has been included in the charts.

15

The Quickstep

The Quickstep is undoubtedly the most popular dance today.

It is danced to the same music as Quick Rhythm, but played in stricter tempo at fifty to fifty-two bars per minute. If the band plays a very fast tempo, you will find it difficult to dance the Quickstep correctly, and in this event you will find it advisable to dance Quick Rhythm instead.

You can always mix Quickstep with Quick Rhythm, even when the band is playing a steady tempo. If when dancing the Quickstep you find yourself temporarily in a crowd, drop into Quick Rhythm and then go back to Quickstep when you find a clear space.

There are two fundamental movements in this dance, the walk and the Chassé, and all the basic figures are built up on these two movements.

The walk forward is the same as in the Slow Foxtrot, only danced more quickly.
The walk backward is also the same as in the Slow Foxtrot, only danced more quickly.
The Chassés may be danced in different ways, but they are always made up of three steps counted 'quick, quick, slow', and take four beats of the music. The feet are closed together on the second of the three steps. In the different figures where they are used, they are clearly described.

Quarter Turns

This is the most important figure in the Quickstep. It is called the Quarter Turns because usually a quarter turn to R is made on the first part, and a quarter turn to L on the last part.

MAN

Begin and finish facing diag. to wall.

Chassé	1. Forward RF	Turning to R	s
	2. Side LF	to back diag.	Q
	3. Close RF	to centre	
	to LF		Q
	4. Side LF, slightly back		s
	5. Back RF, turning to L		s
Heel	6. Close LF to RF, turning		
Pivot	7. to L on R heel		QQ
	8. Forward LF		s

Amount of turn: Make ¼ turn to R between 1 and 3; make ¼ turn to L between 5 and 7.

Today, many of the Chassé actions danced in the Quickstep are performed by experts in Promenade Position. They are sometimes called Scatter or Polka Chassés or simply slips, jumps and bounce actions.

If the Quarter Turns are preceded by a figure which ends facing LOD, make ⅜ turn to R, between 1 and 3; if to be followed by a reverse figure, make ⅜ turn to L between 5 and 7.

Footwork: 1.HT 2.T 3.T 4.TH 5.TH 6.H 7.H of RF, pressure on T of LF 8.H.

Contrary body movement:
Used on 1, 5 and 8.

Body sway: Sway to R on 2 and 3; sway to R on 6 and 7.

Note: On 6 and 7 the man is making one step, doing what is known as a Heel Pivot, while the lady is making two steps; that is why it is counted QQ.

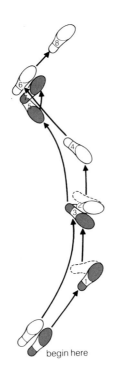

Quarter Turns

LADY

Begin and finish backing diag. to wall.

	1. Back LF	Turning to R to	S
	2. Side RF	face diag. to centre	Q
Chassé	3. Close LF to RF		Q
	4. Diag. forward RF		S
	5. Forward LF		S
	6. Side RF		Q
Chassé	7. Close LF to RF		Q
	8. Step back RF		S

Amount of turn: Make ¼ turn to R between 1 and 2; make ¼ turn to L between 5 and 7.

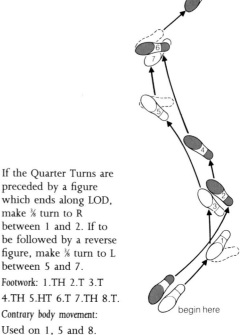

If the Quarter Turns are preceded by a figure which ends along LOD, make ⅜ turn to R between 1 and 2. If to be followed by a reverse figure, make ⅜ turn to L between 5 and 7.

Footwork: 1.TH 2.T 3.T 4.TH 5.HT 6.T 7.TH 8.T.

Contrary body movement:
Used on 1, 5 and 8.

Body sway: Sway to L on 2 and 3; sway to L on 6 and 7.

This fig. may be preceded by:

(1) The Chassé Reverse Turn.

(2) The Cross Chassé.

(3) The Progressive Chassé or any fig. ended diag. to wall leaving RF free (lady LF).

(4) The Zig-Zag or Running Zig-Zag when commenced along LOD.

(5) The Natural Turn.

(6) The Natural Pivot Turn.

(7) The Running Right Turn.

This fig. may be followed by:

(1) Any Natural fig. when ended diag. to wall.

(2) The Cross Chassé.

(3) The Change of Direction.

(4) The Cross Swivel.

(5) Any Reverse fig. when ended along LOD.

(6) The Progressive Chassé after the first four steps (very popular).

Progressive Chassé

This figure is really an ending to several others (see below, in column of preceding figs.).

MAN

Begin backing diag. to centre and finish facing diag. to wall.

Chassé
1. Back RF   Turning to L   S
2. Side LF   to face diag. to   Q
3. Close RF to   wall
LF   Q
4. Side LF, slightly forward   S
5. Forward RF, OP, in CBMP   S

Amount of turn: Make ¼ turn to L between 1 and 2.
Footwork: 1.TH 2.T 3.T 4.TH 5.H.
Contrary body movement: Used on 1 and 5.
Body sway: Nil.

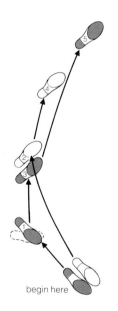

begin here

LADY

Begin facing diag. to centre and finish backing diag. to wall.

Chassé
1. Forward LF   Turning to L   S
2. Side RF   to back diag.   Q
3. Close LF to   to wall
RF   Q
4. Side RF, slightly back   S
5. Back LF, in CBMP, PO   S

Amount of turn: Make ¼ turn to L between 1 and 3.
Footwork: 1.HT 2.T 3.T 4.TH 5.T.
Contrary body movement: Used on 1 and 5.
Body sway: Nil.

This fig. may be preceded by:

(1) Four steps of the Quarter Turns.
(2) Three steps of the Quick Open Reverse Turn.
(3) Three steps of the Chassé Reverse Turn.
(4) The Natural Spin Turn.
(5) The Impetus Turn.
(6) The Quick Open Reverse Turn.

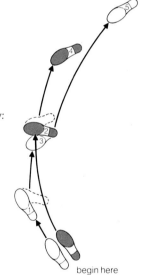

begin here

This fig. may be followed by:

(1) Any Natural fig.
(2) The Forward Lock Step.
(3) The Fish Tail.
(4) Any Reverse fig. if turned more to L.

Note: Most good dancers use this ending to certain figures in preference to using the Heel Pivot.

Lock Step Forward

This figure can be preceded by practically any figure which finishes forward with RF outside partner (lady–back, LF, partner outside). No. 1 described below is therefore the last step of the preceding figure.

MAN

Begin and finish diag. to wall.

1. Forward RF, OP, in CBMP	S
2. Diag. forward LF	Q
3. Cross RF behind LF	Q
4. Diag. forward LF	S
5. Forward RF, OP, in CBMP	S

Amount of turn: Nil.

Footwork: 1.HT 2.T 3.T 4.TH 5.H.

Contrary body movement: Used slightly on 1; used on 5.

Body sway: Nil.

Note: Although the feet are diag. to wall, the body faces a little more towards the wall throughout this fig.

LADY

Begin and finish backing diag. to wall.

1. Back LF, in CBMP, PO	S
2. Back RF	Q
3. Cross LF in front of RF	Q
4. Diag. back RF	S
5. Back LF, in CBMP, PO	S

Amount of turn: Nil.

Footwork: 1.TH 2.T 3.T 4.TH 5.T.

Contrary body movement: Used slightly on 1; used on 5.

Body sway: Nil.

Note: While man dances the Lock Step Forward, the lady dances the Lock Step Backward.

This fig. may be preceded by:

(1) The Progressive Chassé.
(2) The Cross Chassé.
(3) The Telemark.

This fig. may be followed by:

(1) The Quarter Turns.
(2) Any Natural Turn.

Natural Turn

This Natural figure is not as popular as the Natural Pivot or Spin Turn, but it is a good basic figure for the beginner because other figures have been built up from it.

MAN

Begin facing diag. to wall and finish facing diag. to wall of new LOD.

Chassé	1. Forward RF	Turning to R to	S
	2. Side LF	back LOD	Q
	3. Close RF to LF		Q
	4. Back LF		S
Heel Pull	5. Pull RF to side of LF, turning from L heel on to RF		S
	6. Forward LF		S

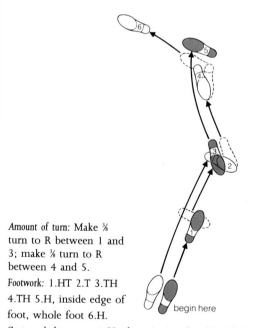

begin here

Amount of turn: Make ⅜ turn to R between 1 and 3; make ⅜ turn to R between 4 and 5.

Footwork: 1.HT 2.T 3.TH 4.TH 5.H, inside edge of foot, whole foot 6.H.

Contrary body movement: Used on 1, 4 and 6 (slightly).

Body sway: Sway slightly to R on 2 and 3.

Note: The Natural Turn, as described above, is for use at a corner. If commenced facing LOD, make ½ turn to R between 1 and 3.

LADY

Begin backing diag. to wall and finish backing diag. to wall of new LOD

Chassé {	1. Back LF	s
	2. Side RF } Turning to R to	Q
	3. Close LF to } face LOD	
	RF	Q
	4. Forward RF	s
	5. Side LF	s
	6. Back RF, brushing it past LF	s

Amount of turn: Make ⅜ turn to R between 1 and 2; make ⅜ turn to R between 4 and 6.

Footwork: 1.TH 2.T 3.TH 4.HT 5.TH 6.T.

Contrary body movement: Used on 1, 4 and 6 (slightly).

Body sway: Sway to L on 2 and 3.

This fig. may be preceded by:

(1) Any fig. ended diag. to wall, leaving RF free (lady LF) (e.g., the Quarter Turns, the Chassé Reverse Turn, the Cross Chassé, the Progressive Chassé etc.).

(2) The Zig-Zag or the Running Zig-Zag (when commenced along LOD).

(3) The Running Right Turn.

This fig. may be followed by:

(1) Any Natural fig. when ended diag. to wall.

(2) The Cross Chassé.

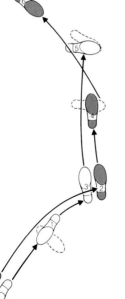

begin here

Chassé Reverse Turn

This is one of the popular left-handed turns used in the Quickstep.

MAN

Begin facing LOD, or diag. to centre, and finish facing diag. to wall.

Chassé {	1. Forward LF	s
	2. Side RF } Turning to L	Q
	3. Close LF to } to back LOD	
	RF	Q
	4. Back RF	s
Heel {	5. Close LF to RF, turning to	
Pivot {	6. L on R heel	QQ
	7. Forward LF	s

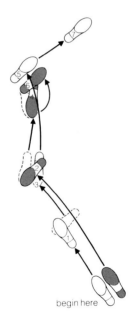

begin here

Amount of turn: Make ½ or ⅜ turn to L between 1 and 3; make ⅜ turn to L between 4 and 6.

Footwork: 1.HT 2.T 3.TH 4.TH 5.H 6.H of RF, pressure on T of LF 7.H.

Contrary body movement: Used on 1, 4 and 7.

Body sway: Sway to L on 2 and 3; sway to R on 5 and 6.

Note: On 5 and 6 the man is making one step, doing what is known as a Heel Pivot, while the lady is making two steps; that is why it is counted QQ.

Chassé Reverse Turn

LADY

Begin backing to LOD, or diag. to centre, and finish backing diag. to wall.

Chassé {	1. Back RF	Turning to L to face LOD	S
	2. Side LF		Q
	3. Close RF to LF		Q
	4. Forward LF		S
Chassé {	5. Side RF		Q
	6. Close LF to RF		Q
	7. Back RF		S

Amount of turn: Make ⅜ or ½ turn to L between 1 and 3; make ⅜ turn to L between 4 and 6.

Footwork: 1.TH 2.T 3.TH 4.HT 5.T 6.TH 7.T.

Contrary body movement: Used on 1, 4 and 7.

Body sway: Sway to R on 2 and 3; sway to L on 5 and 6.

This fig. may be preceded by:

(1) The Change of Direction.
(2) The Natural Turn ended on LOD.
(3) The Quarter Turns.
(4) The Progressive Chassé danced diag. to centre.

This fig. may be followed by:

(1) Any Natural fig.
(2) The Cross Chassé.
(3) The Change of Direction.
(4) The Cross Swivel.
(5) The Progressive Chassé after the first three steps. (Very popular.)

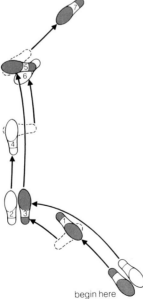

begin here

Cross Chassé

MAN

Begin and finish diag. to wall.

	1. Forward LF	S
Chassé {	2. Side RF (short step)	Q
	3. Close LF to RF	Q
	4. Forward RF, OP, in CBMP	S

Amount of turn: Nil.

Footwork: 1.HT 2.T 3.TH 4.H.

Contrary body movement: Used on 1 and 4.

Body sway: Sway to L on 2 and 3.

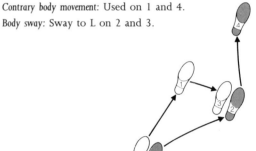

begin here

LADY

Begin and finish backing diag. to wall.

	1. Back RF	S
Chassé {	2. Side LF (short step)	Q
	3. Close RF to LF	Q
	4. Back LF, in CBMP, PO	S

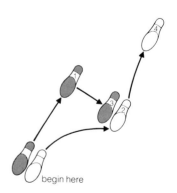

begin here

Amount of turn: Nil.

Footwork: 1.TH 2.T 3.TH 4.T.

Contrary body movement: Used on 1 and 4.

Body sway: Sway to R on 2 and 3.

This fig. may be preceded by:

(1) The Quarter Turns or any Heel Pivot.

(2) The Double Reverse Spin.

(3) The Reverse Pivot Turn.

(4) The Natural Turn.

This fig. may be followed by:

(1) Any Natural fig.

(2) The Quarter Turns.

(3) The Lock Step Forward.

(4) The Fish Tail.

The Zig-Zag

MAN

Begin and finish facing LOD.

1. Forward LF ⎫ Turning to L to back		S
2. Side RF ⎭ diag. to wall		S
3. Back LF, in CBMP, PO		S
Heel ⎰ 4. Pull RF to side of LF, turning from L		
Pull ⎱ heel on to RF		S
5. Forward LF		S

Amount of turn: Make ⅜ turn to L between 1 and 3; make ⅜ turn to R between 3 and 4.

Footwork: 1.HT 2.TH 3.TH 4.H, inside edge of foot, whole foot 5.H.

Contrary body movement: Used on 1, 3 and 5 (slightly).

Body sway: Nil.

Note: When used near a corner, make slightly less turn on 3 and 4 and finish facing diag. to wall of new LOD.

LADY

Begin and finish backing LOD.

1. Back RF ⎫ Turning to L		S
Heel ⎰ 2. Close LF to RF, turning ⎬ to face diag.		
Turn ⎱ from R heel on to LF ⎭ to wall		S
3. Forward RF, OP, in CBMP		S
4. Side LF		S
5. Back RF, brushing it past LF		S

Amount of turn: Make ⅜ turn to L between 1 and 2; make ⅜ turn to R between 3 and 5.

Footwork: 1.TH 2.H 3.HT 4.TH 5.T.

Contrary body movement: Used on 1, 3 and 5 (slightly).

Body sway: Nil.

Note: When used near a corner, make slightly less turn on 3, 4 and 5, and finish backing diag. to wall of new LOD.

This fig. may be preceded by:

(1) The Quarter Turns or any figure ending with a Heel Pivot.

(2) The Double Reverse Spin.

(3) The Reverse Pivot Turn.

This fig. may be followed by:

(1) Any Natural fig.

(2) The Quarter Turns.

(3) Most advanced dancers use the steps 1–4 of the Zig-Zag and follow with the Back Lock and Running Finish.

Natural Pivot Turn

This is a popular Natural Turn used in the Quickstep.

MAN

Begin facing diag. to wall and finish the pivot facing diag. to wall of new LOD.

Chassé	1. Forward RF		Turning to R to	S
	2. Side LF		Back LOD	Q
	3. Close RF to LF			Q
	4. Back LF, pivoting to R (keeping RF in front of you in CBMP)			S
	5. Forward on to RF			S

This figure is usually followed by the Quarter Turns, so 5 described above would be 1 of the Quarter Turns.

Amount of turn: Make ⅜ turn to R between 1 and 3; make ⅜ turn on 4.

Footwork: 1.HT 2.T 3.TH 4.THT 5.H.

Contrary body movement: Used on 1 and 4.

Body sway: Sway to R on 2 and 3.

LADY

Begin backing diag. to wall and finish backing diag. to wall of new LOD.

Chassé	1. Back LF		Turning to R to	S
	2. Side RF		face LOD	Q
	3. Close LF to RF			Q
	4. Forward RF, keeping LF behind you			S
	5. Back on to LF			S

This figure is usually followed by the Quarter Turns, so 5 described above would be 1 of the Quarter Turns.

Amount of turn: Make ⅜ turn to R between 1 and 2; make ⅜ turn to R on 4.

Footwork: 1.TH 2.T 3.TH 4.HTH.

Contrary body movement: Used on 1, 4 and 5.

Body sway: Sway to L on 2 and 3.

This fig. may be preceded by:

(1) Any fig. ended diag. to wall, leaving RF (lady LF) free.
(2) The Zig-Zag or the Running Zig-Zag when commenced along LOD.
(3) The Running Right Turn.

This fig. may be followed by:

(1) The Quarter Turns.
(2) The Natural Spin.

Note: The Natural Pivot Turn as described above is for use at a corner. If commenced backing LOD, make ½ turn to R between 1 and 3.

Natural Spin Turn

MAN

Begin backing diag. to wall and finish backing diag. to wall of new LOD (described for use at a corner).

1, 2, 3, 4. Dance 1, 2, 3 and 4 of the Natural Pivot Turn   SQQS

| Spin | 5. Forward on to RF in CBMP | S |
| | 6. Side LF, slightly back | S |

Amount of turn: 1, 2, 3 and 4 as for Natural Pivot Turn; make ¼ turn to R between 5 and 6.

Footwork: 1, 2, 3 and 4 as for the Natural Pivot Turn 5.HT 6.TH.

Contrary body movement: Used on 1, 4 and 5.

Body sway: 1, 2, 3 and 4 as in the Natural Pivot Turn; no sway on 5 and 6.

It's take-off time again in the Quickstep! Note the obvious spring in the dancers' legs and feet.

Natural Spin Turn

LADY

Begin backing diag. to wall and finish facing diag. to centre of new LOD (described for use at a corner).

1, 2, 3, 4. Dance 1, 2, 3 and 4 of the Natural Pivot
Turn   SQQS

Spin { 5. Back LF, slightly to L   S
6. Brush RF to LF and step diag. forward with it   S

Amount of turn: 1, 2, 3 and 4 as for the Natural Pivot Turn; make ¼ turn to R between 5 and 6.

Footwork: 1, 2 and 3 as for the Natural Pivot Turn 4.HT 5.T 6.TH.

Contrary body movement: Used on 1 and 4. (The lady loses CBM on 5.)

Body sway: 1, 2 and 3 as in the Natural Pivot Turn; no sway on 4, 5 and 6.

This fig. may be preceded by:

(1) Any fig. ended diag. to wall, leaving RF (lady LF) free.
(2) The Zig-Zag or the Running Zig-Zag, when the Natural Spin Turn will commence along LOD and more turn will be made on 1, 2 and 3.
(3) The Running Right Turn.

This fig. may be followed by:

(1) The last four steps of the Quarter Turns.
(2) A Reverse Pivot (like fourth step of the Reverse Pivot Turn).
(3) The Progressive Chassé.

Running Zig-Zag

MAN

Begin and finish facing LOD.

1. Forward LF   S
2. Side RF, slightly back } Turning to L to back wall   S

Running Finish { 3. Back LF, in CBMP, PO   Q
4. Side RF, slightly forward   S
5. Forward LF, preparing to step OP, LS leading   S
6. Forward RF, OP, in CBMP   S

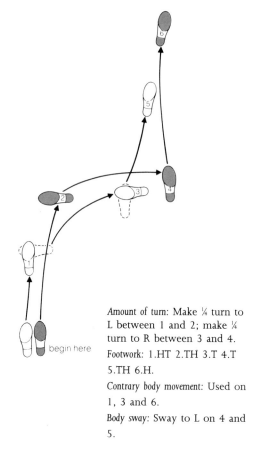

begin here

Amount of turn: Make ¼ turn to L between 1 and 2; make ¼ turn to R between 3 and 4.

Footwork: 1.HT 2.TH 3.T 4.T 5.TH 6.H.

Contrary body movement: Used on 1, 3 and 6.

Body sway: Sway to L on 4 and 5.

LADY

Begin and finish backing LOD.

Heel Turn { 1. Back RF   } Turning to L to face diag. to wall   S
2. Close LF to RF, turning from R heel on to LF   S

Running Finish { 3. Forward RF, OP, in CBMP   Q
4. Side LF   Q
5. Back RF, RS leading   S
6. Back LF in CBMP, PO   S

Amount of turn: Make ⅜ turn to L between 1 and 2; make ⅜ turn to R between 3 and 5.

Footwork: 1. TH 2.H 3.HT 4.T 5.TH 6.T.

Contrary body movement: Used on 1, 3, and 6.

Body sway: Sway to R on 4 and 5.

Note: Nos. 3, 4, 5 and 6 are known as the Running Finish.

This fig. may be preceded by:

(1) The Quarter Turns or any Heel Pivot.
(2) The Double Reverse Spin, ended on LOD.
(3) The Reverse Pivot Turn.

This fig. may be followed by:

(1) Any Natural fig.
(2) The Lock Step Forward.
(3) The Fish Tail.

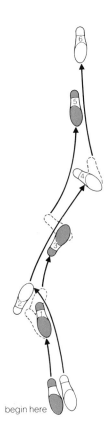

begin here

Lock Step Backward

MAN

Begin and finish backing diag. to wall.

1. Back LF, in CBMP, PO	S
2. Back RF	Q
3. Cross LF in front of RF	Q
4. Diag. back RF	S
5. Back LF, in CBMP, PO	S

Amount of turn: Nil.
Footwork: 1.HT 2.T 3.T 4.TH 5.T.
Contrary body movement: Used slightly on 1; used on 5.
Body sway: Nil.

LADY

Begin and finish facing diag. to wall.

1. Forward RF, OP, in CBMP	S
2. Diag. forward LF	Q
3. Cross RF behind LF	Q
4. Diag. forward LF	S
5. Forward RF, OP, in CBMP	S

Amount of turn: Nil.
Footwork: 1.HT 2.T 3.T 4.TH 5.H.
Contrary body movement: Used slightly on 1; used on 5.
Body sway: Nil.

This fig. may be preceded by:

(1) 1 and 2 of the Zig-Zig.
(2) Steps 2 to 5 danced after a Spin Turn.

This fig. may be followed by:

(1) A Heel Pull (man).
(2) The Running Finish (see the Running Zig-Zag note).
(3) The Impetus or the Open Impetus Turn.

Cross Swivel

MAN

Begin facing diag. to wall and finish facing diag. to centre.

1. Forward LF	Turning to L	S
2. Close RF to LF, slightly back, weight on LF	to face diag. to centre	
3. Forward RF, OP, in CBMP		S

Amount of turn: Make ¼ turn to L between 1 and 2.
Footwork: 1.H 2.Pressure on T of LF, foot flat and pressure on inside edge of T of RF 3.H.
Contrary body movement: Used on 1 and 3.
Body sway: Sway to L on 2.

Cross Swivel

LADY

Begin backing diag. to wall and finish backing diag. to centre.

1. Back RF	⎫ Turning to L	S
2. Close LF to RF, slightly forward, weight on RF	⎬ to back diag. to centre	
3. Back LF, in CBMP, PO	⎭	S

Amount of turn: Make ¼ turn to L between 1 and 2.
Footwork: 1.TH 2.H, then inside edge of T 3.T.
Contrary body movement: Used on 1 and 3.
Body sway: Sway to R on 2.

This fig. may be preceded by:

(1) Any Heel Pivot.
(2) The Double Reverse Spin.
(3) The Reverse Pivot.

This fig. may be followed by:

(1) The Running Finish.
(2) The Fish Tail.
(3) Any Natural Turn, or the Quarter Turns if ended diag. to wall at a corner.
(4) The Lock Step Forward.

Fish Tail

MAN

Begin facing diag. to centre and finish diag. to wall.

1. Forward RF, OP, in CBMP	⎫ Turning to R	S
2. Cross LF behind RF	⎬ to face diag.	Q
3. Forward RF and slightly to side (small step)	⎭ to wall	Q
4. Diag. forward LF, LS leading		Q
5. Cross RF behind LF		Q
6. Diag. forward LF		S
7. Forward RF, OP, in CBMP		S

Amount of turn: Make ¼ turn to R between 1 and 3.
Footwork: 1.HT 2.T 3.T 4.T 5.T 6.TH 7.H.
Contrary body movement: Used on 1 and 7.
Body sway: Sway to R on 2.
Note: This fig. may be danced diag. to wall with no turn.

LADY

Begin backing diag. to centre and finish backing diag. to wall.

1. Back LF in CBMP, PO	⎫	S
2. Cross RF in front of LF	⎬ Turning to R to back diag.	Q
3. Back LF and slightly to side (small step)	⎭ to wall	Q
4. Diag. back RF, RS leading		Q
5. Cross LF in front of RF		Q
6. Diag. back RF		S
7. Back LF, in CBMP, PO		S

Amount of turn: Make ¼ turn to R between 1 and 3.
Footwork: 1.T 2.T 3.T 4.T 5.T 6.TH 7.T.
Contrary body movement: Used on 1 and 7.
Body sway: Sway to L on 2.

This fig. may be preceded by:

(1) The Cross Swivel.
(2) Any fig. ended diag. to wall with RF (lady LF) outside lady (e.g., the Cross Chassé, the Progressive Chassé). (See note above.)

This fig. may be followed by:

(1) Any Natural Turn.
(2) The Quarter Turns.

This is another Quickstep Promenade Position. It could be followed by a Wing (see page 70 where it is described as a Waltz figure although today it is often presented in Quickstep) or the Tipple Chassé taken from Promenade Position (page 113).

Quick Open Reverse Turn

MAN

Begin facing LOD and finish according to which figure is to follow the Quick Open Reverse.

1. Forward LF	Turning to	s
2. Side RF	L to back	Q
3. Back LF in CBMP, PO	LOD	Q
4. Back RF (partner in front)		s

Amount of turn: Make ¼ turn to L between 1 and 3; make ⅜ or ½ turn on 4 if making it a Reverse Pivot.

Footwork: 1.HT 2.T 3.TH 4.T.

Contrary body movement: Used on 1 and 4.

Body sway: Sway L on 2 and 3.

LADY

Begin backing LOD and finish according to which figure is to follow the Quick Open Reverse.

1. Back RF		s
2. Side LF, slightly forward	Turning to L to	Q
3. Forward RF, OP, in CBMP	face LOD	Q
4. Forward LF (in front of partner)		s

Amount of turn: Make ½ turn to L between 1 and 2; make ⅜ or ½ turn on 4 if making it a Reverse Pivot.

Footwork: 1.TH 2.T 3.TH 4.H.

Contrary body movement: Used on 1 and 4.

Body sway: Sway to R on 2 and 3.

This fig. may be preceded by:

(1) Any Heel Pivot.

(2) The Double Reverse Spin.

(3) The Reverse Pivot.

(4) The Progressive Chassé ended diag. to centre or along LOD.

This fig. may be followed by:

(1) A Reverse Pivot on the fourth step into the Quick Open Reverse Turn, any Reverse Turn, the Zig-Zig, or the Running Zig-Zag.

(2) The Progressive Chassé, when fourth step will be the first of Progressive Chassé.

(3) The Heel Pivot.

(4) The Four Quick Run.

Check and Four Quick Run

MAN

At a corner, having danced a Progressive Chassé, you will be facing diag. to wall. Finish the Four Quick Run facing diag. to wall of 'new' LOD.

Check	1. Back LF, in CBMP, PO	Towards the	s
	2. Back RF (partner in front)	'new' centre	s
	3. Side LF, slightly forward (facing wall)		Q
	4. Forward RF, OP, in CBMP (diag. to		
Four	wall)		Q
Quick	5. Diag. forward LF		Q
Run	6. Cross RF behind LF		Q
	7. Diag. forward LF		s
	8. Forward RF, OP, in CBMP		s

Amount of turn: Make ¼ turn to L between the last step of the Progressive Chassé and step 4.

Footwork: 1.TH 2.THT 3.T 4.T 5.T 6.T 7.TH 8.H.

Contrary body movement: Used on 2 and 8.

Body sway: Nil.

Note: The Four Quick Run may be danced without the Check, when it could be preceded by the Quick Open Reverse Turn or the first four steps of the Chassé Reverse Turn. These are the two most popular amalgamations using the Four Quick Run.

LADY

At a corner, having danced a Progressive Chassé, you will be backing diag. to wall. Finish the Four Quick Run backing diag. to wall of 'new' LOD.

Check	1. Forward RF	Towards 'new'	s
	2. Forward LF	centre	s
	3. Side RF (backing to wall)		Q
Four	4. Back LF, in CBMP, PO (diag. to wall)		Q
Quick	5. Diag. back RF		Q
Run	6. Cross LF in front of RF		Q
	7. Diag. back RF		s
	8. Back LF, in CBMP, PO		s

Amount of turn: Make ¼ turn to L between last step of Progressive Chassé and step 4.

Footwork: 1.H 2.HT 3.T 4.T 5.T 6.T 7.TH 8.T.

Contrary body movement: Used on 2 and 8.

Body sway: Nil.

These figs. may be preceded by:

(1) Any Progressive Chassé ended at a corner.
(2) Any fig. ended OP on RF (lady: back LF, PO) (e.g. the Running Zig-Zag or the Running Right Turn).

These figs. may be followed by:

(1) Any Natural fig.
(2) The Forward Lock Step.
(3) The Fish Tail.

Running Right Turn

This figure is usually used across a corner as described below.

MAN

Begin facing diag. to wall and finish facing new LOD.

	1, 2, 3, 4. Dance the Natural Pivot Turn	SQQS
	5. Forward on to RF, in CBMP (still turning to R)	S
	6. Side LF (still turning to R)	S
	7. Back RF, preparing to lead PO, RS leading	S
Running Finish	8. Back LF, in CBMP, PO (turning to R)	Q
	9. Side RF, slightly forward	Q
	10. Forward LF, preparing to step OP, LS leading	S
	11. Forward RF, OP, in CBMP	S

Amount of turn: Across a corner made ⅜ turn to R on pivot of Natural Pivot Turn; make ½ turn to R between 5 and 7; make ⅜ turn to R between 8 and 9.

Footwork: 1.HT 2.T 3.TH 4.THT 5.HT 6.T 7.TH 8.T 9.T 10.TH 11.H.

Contrary body movement: Used on 1, 4, 5, 8 and 11.

Body sway: Sway to R on 2 and 3; sway to R on 6 and 7; sway to L on 9 and 10.

LADY

Begin backing diag. to wall and finish backing 'new' LOD

	1, 2, 3, 4. Dance the Natural Pivot Turn	SQQS
	5. Back on to LF (still turning to R)	S
Heel Turn	6. Close RF to LF (turning from L heel on to RF)	S
	7. Forward LF, preparing to step OP, LS leading	S
Running Finish	8. Forward RF, OP, in CBMP	Q
	9. Side LF	Q
	10. Back RF, RS leading	S
	11. Back LF, in CBMP, PO	Q

Amount of turn: Across a corner make ⅜ turn to R on pivot of Natural Pivot Turn; make ½ turn to R between 5 and 6; make ⅜ turn to R between 8 and 10.

Footwork: 1.TH 2.T 3.TH 4.HTH 5.TH 6.HT 7.TH 8.HT 9.T 10.TH 11.T.

Contrary body movement: Used on 1, 4, 5, 8 and 11.

Body sway: Sway to L on 2 and 3; sway to L on 6 and 7; sway to R on 9 and 10.

This fig. may be preceded by:

(1) Any fig. finished diag. to wall with RF free (lady LF).

This fig. may be followed by:

(1) Any Natural Turn commencing on LOD.
(2) The Quarter Turns.
(3) The Quick Open Reverse Turn (if Running Finish is ended diag. to new centre).
(4) The Fish Tail.

Change of Direction

MAN

Begin facing diag. to wall and finish facing diag. to centre.

1. Forward LF	s
2. Diag. forward RF, RS leading	s
3. Close LF to RF, slightly forward, without weight (relaxing both knees)	s
4. Forward LF, in CBMP	s

Turning to L to face diag. to centre (bracketing steps 1–3)

Amount of turn: Make ¼ turn to L between 1 and 3.

Footwork: 1.H 2.Inside edge of TH 3.Inside edge of T of LF 4.H.

Contrary body movement: Used on 1 and 4.

Body sway: Sway to L on 3, straightening on 4.

LADY

Begin backing diag. to wall and finish backing diag. to centre.

1. Back RF	s
2. Diag. back LF, LS leading	s
3. Close RF to LF, slightly back, without weight (relaxing both knees)	s
4. Back RF, in CBMP	s

Turning to L to face diag. to centre (bracketing steps 1–3)

Amount of turn: Make ¼ turn to L between 1 and 3.

Footwork: 1.TH 2.T, inside edge of TH 3.Inside edge of T of RF 4.T.

Contrary body movement: Used on 1 and 4.

Body sway: Sway to R on 3, straightening on 4.

This fig. may be preceded by:

(1) The Quarter Turns or any Heel Pivot.

(2) The Reverse Pivot Turn.

(3) The Double Reverse Spin.

This fig. may be followed by:

(1) Any Reverse fig.

Double Reverse Spin

Although called the Double Reverse Spin, this does not signify that it must be used twice. It is better to use it only once at a time.

Whilst the man does three steps the lady does four, that is why it is counted 'slow, slow, quick, quick'.

MAN

Begin facing LOD and finish facing diag. to wall.

1. Forward LF	s
2. Side RF	s
Toe Pivot { 3, 4. Close LF to RF (completing turn on RF)	QQ

Turning to L to back diag. to wall (bracketing steps 1–2)

Amount of turn: Make ⅜ turn to L between 1 and 2; make ½ turn to L between 2 and 3.

Footwork: 1.HT 2.T 3.T, LF, then TH of RF.

Contrary body movement: Used on 1.

Body sway: Nil.

LADY

Begin backing to LOD and finish backing diag. to wall.

Heel Turn { 1. Back RF	s
2. Close LF to RF, turning from R heel on to LF	s
3. Side RF, slightly back	Q
4. Cross LF in front of RF	Q

Turning to L to face LOD (bracketing steps 1–2)

Amount of turn: Make ½ turn to L between 1 and 2; make ⅜ turn to L between 2 and 4.

Footwork: 1.TH 2.HT 3.T 4.TH.

Contrary body movement: Used on 1.

Body sway: Nil.

This fig. may be preceded by:

(1) Any Heel Pivot.

(2) The Toe Pivot.

(3) The Reverse Pivot.

This fig. may be followed by:

(1) The Cross Chassé or the Cross Swivel.

(2) The Change of Direction.

(3) The Running Zig-Zig, or any Reverse fig.; if turned to end on LOD, more turn than above.

Quick Open Reverse Pivot Turn

Actually there are four steps in this figure, but a fifth step is described to enable readers to understand how this figure is linked to the figures following it.

MAN

Begin facing LOD and finish according to which figure is to follow the Reverse Pivot.

1, 2, 3. Dance 1, 2 and 3 of the Quick Open Reverse Turn .... SQQ

4. Back RF, pivoting to L .... S

5. Forward LF .... S or Q

Amount of turn: On 4 the amount of pivot should vary from ⅛ to ½ of a turn to L according to which figure you use after it. Also, 5 will be S or Q, according to which figure is to follow. If the Double Reverse Spin, make about ⅜ of a turn on 4, and 5 will be the first step of the Double Reverse Spin (S).

Footwork: 1.HT 2.T 3.TH 4.THT 5.H.

Contrary body movement: Used on 1, 4 and 5.

Body sway: 1, 2 and 3 as in the Quick Open Reverse Turn; no sway on 4 and 5.

LADY

Begin backing LOD and finish according to which figure is to follow the Reverse Pivot.

1, 2, 3. Do 1, 2 and 3 of the Quick Open Reverse Turn .... SQQ

4. Forward LF, pivoting to L .... S

5. Back RF .... S or Q

Amount of turn: See notes on man's steps.

Footwork: 1.TH 2.T 3.TH 4.HTH 5.T.

Contrary body movement: Used on 1, 4 and 5.

Body sway: 1, 2 and 3 as in the Quick Open Reverse Turn; no sway on 4 and 5.

This fig. may be preceded by:

(1) Any Heel Pivot or Toe Pivot.
(2) A Reverse Pivot ended along LOD.
(3) The Change of Direction.

This fig. may be followed by:

(1) The Cross Chassé.
(2) The Zig-Zag.
(3) The Running Zig-Zag or any Reverse fig.
(4) The Cross Swivel.

Natural Turn with Hesitation

This may be used at a corner or along side of room. Foot positions are similar to the Hesitation Change in the Waltz but step 5 is wider, and the LF (lady RF) brushes on step 6.

Footwork: Man: 4.TH 5.H, Inside edge of foot, whole foot 6.Inside edge of T (LF).
Lady: 4.HT 5.TH 6.Inside edge of T (RF).

Body sway: A sway to L (lady to R) on steps 5 and 6 is optional.

Rhythm: SQQSSS.

This fig. may be followed by:

A Reverse fig. or The Progressive Chassé to R.

The Tipple Chassé to Right

Preceded by steps 1, 2 and 3 of the Natural Turn.

MAN

Begin backing LOD and finish facing diag. to wall.

1. LF back
2. RF to side
3. LF closes to RF
4. RF to side and slightly forward
5. LF diag. forward, LS leading
6. RF crosses behind LF
7. LF diag. forward

Amount of turn: Make ¼ turn to R between 1 and 2; make ⅛ turn to R between 3 and 4.

Footwork: 1.TH 2.T 3.T 4.T 5.T 6.T 7.TH.

Contrary body movement: Used on 1.

Body sway: Nil.

Rhythm: SQQSQQS.

Note: A slight flexing of the knees may be used on step 4 straightening again as step 5 is taken. See also notes below.

LADY

Begin facing LOD and finish backing diag. to wall.

1. RF forward
2. LF to side
3. RF closes to LF
4. LF to side and slightly back
5. RF back, RS leading
6. LF cross in front of RF
7. RF diag. back

Amount of turn: Make ¼ turn to R between 1 and 2; make ⅛ turn to R between 3 and 4.

Footwork: 1.HT 2.T 3.T 4.T 5.T 6.T 7.TH.

Contrary body movement: Used on 1.

Body sway: Nil.

This fig. may be preceded by:

(1) Any fig. ended diag. to wall leaving RF free (lady LF).

(2) The Zig-Zag or the Running Zig-Zag (when commenced along LOD).

(3) The Running Right Turn.

This fig. may be followed by:

(1) The Quarter Turns.

(2) Any Natural Turn.

Note: If danced along the side of the room, end facing diag. to centre and follow with a Quick Open Reverse.

The Tipple Chassé to Right

Preceded by steps 1, 2, 3 and 4 of a Back Lock.

MAN

Begin backing diag. to wall and finish facing diag. to wall.

1. LF back in CBMP
2. RF to side
3. LF closes to RF
4. RF to side and slightly forward
5. LF diag. forward, LS leading
6. RF crosses behind LF
7. LF diag. forward

Amount of turn: Make ⅛ turn to R between 1 and 2; make ⅛ turn to R between 3 and 4.

Footwork: 1.TH 2.T 3.T 4.T 5.T 6.T 7.TH.

Contrary body movement: Used on 1.

Body sway: Nil.

Rhythm: SQQSQQS.

LADY

Begin facing diag. to wall and finish backing diag. to wall.

1. RF forward in CBMP, OP
2. LF to side
3. RF closes to LF
4. LF to side and slightly back
5. RF back, RS leading
6. LF crosses in front of RF
7. RF diag. back

Amount of turn: Make ¼ turn to R between 1 and 2; make ⅛ turn to R between 2 and 3; make ⅛ turn to R between 3 and 4.

Footwork: 1.HT 2.T 3.T 4.T 5.T 6.T 7.TH.

Contrary body movement: Used on 1.

Body sway: Nil.

Note: When sway is used (see note 3 below) the sway will be to the R (lady to L) on 4.

Special Notes:

1. When dancing the Tipple Chassé after 3 steps of a Natural Turn at a corner, less turn may be made on step 4 to end facing the new LOD. Step 4 will then be 'to side' (not side and slightly forward). Footwork on step 4 will be 'TH and inside edge of T (LF)' – knees will flex to check the turn. Continue with steps 2 to 5 of a Lock Step, moving diag. to centre of new LOD. Step 5 as lady (2 of the Lock Step) must be taken diag. back (not back) when this alignment is used. Use normal rise on the Lock Step. See No. 3 below. Follow with a Quick Open Reverse Turn.

2. The same amalgamation could be used along the side of room making ⅜ turn on the Chassé to end facing DC.

3. A sway to R, with head turned to R (lady to L) may be used on the Tipple Chassé.

The Zig-Zag, Back Lock and Running Finish

MAN

Begin and finish facing LOD.

1. LF forward
2. RF to side
3. LF back in CBMP
4. RF back
5. LF crosses in front of RF
6. RF diag. back
7. LF back in CBMP
8. RF to side and slightly forward
9. LF forward preparing to step OP, LS leading

Amount of turn: Make ¼ turn to L between 1 and 2; make ⅛ turn to L between 3 and 4; make ⅜ turn to R between 7 and 8.

Footwork: 1.HT 2.TH 3.TH 4.T 5.T 6.TH 7.T 8.T 9.TH.

Contrary body movement: Used on 1, 3 (slight) and 7.

Body sway: Sway to the L on 8 and 9.

Note: 'RS lead' is needed on steps 4 and 6 as the body is already in the correct position for the Back Lock when the 'Body turns less' between steps 2 and 3.

Rhythm: SSSQQSQQS.

LADY

Begin and finish backing LOD.

1. RF back
2. LF closes to RF (Heel Turn)
3. RF forward in CBMP OP
4. LF diag. forward
5. RF crosses behind LF
6. LF diag. forward
7. RF forward in CBMP OP
8. LF to side
9. RF back, RS leading

Amount of turn: Make ⅜ turn to L between 1 and 2; make ¼ turn to R between 7 and 8; make ⅛ turn to R between 8 and 9.

Footwork: 1.TH 2.H 3.HT 4.T 5.T 6.TH 7.HT 8.T 9.TH.

Contrary body movement: Used on 1, 3 (slight) and 7.

Body sway: Sway to the R on 8 and 9.

This fig. may be preceded by:

(1) Any Heel Pivot.
(2) Reverse Pivot.
(3) Double Reverse Spin.
(4) The last step of the Natural Turn and Change of Direction could be used.

This fig. may be followed by:

(1) Any Natural fig.
(2) Forward Lock Step.
(3) Fish Tail.

The Progressive Chassé to the Right

This figure is usually preceded by a Change of Direction.

MAN

Begin facing diag. to centre and finish backing diag. to wall.

1. LF forward
2. RF to side
3. LF closes to RF
4. RF to side and slightly back

Amount of turn: Make ⅛ turn to L between 1 and 2; make ⅛ turn to L between 2 and 3.

Footwork: 1.HT 2.T 3.T 4.TH.

Contrary body movement: Used on 1.

Body sway: Nil.

Rhythm: SQQS.

Note: The last step of the Change of Direction (which is the first step of the Chassé to R) will not be taken in CBMP.

LADY

Begin backing diag. to centre and finish facing diag. to wall.

1. RF back
2. LF to side
3. RF closes to LF
4. LF to side and slightly forward

Amount of turn: Make ¼ turn to L between 1 and 2.

Footwork: 1.TH 2.T 3.T 4.TH.

Contrary body movement: Used on 1.

Body sway: Nil.

Note: If a half turn is made on the Progressive Chassé the amounts of turn will be:

Man: ¼ between 1–2, ⅛ between 2–3, ⅛ between 4 and first step of following figure.

Lady: ⅜ between 1–2 (body turn less). Body completes turn on 3: ⅛ between 3–4 (body turns less).

This fig. may be preceded by:

(1) Change of Direction and a Natural Turn with an extra 'S'.

(2) A Heel Pivot, Reverse Pivot or Double Reverse Spin.

(3) Wing.

This fig. may be followed by:

A Back Lock and Running Finish or a Tipple Chassé to R are the best endings. See also the amalgamations below.

Amalgamations:

1. Quarter Turns; Change of Direction; Progressive Chassé to R; Back Lock; Running Finish.

2. Natural Turn with Hesitation (SQQSSS); LF forward into Progressive Chassé to R; Running Finish.

3. Open Impetus Turn into Wing (SQQSSS SQQ); LF forward, OP on L side, diag. to centre, into a Progressive Chassé to R, turning to L to back diag. centre. Follow with steps 5–8 of the V.6 (below), then a Forward Lock Step.

4. Spin Turn; RF back and pivot to L to face diag. centre (S); Progressive Chassé to R. End back diag. wall (SQQS); LF back into Back Fish Tail (SQQQQS); Running Finish (QQSS or SQQS).

This professional couple from Japan, Kosuke and Tomoko Ichimura, seems to be flying around the dance-floor at the Bournemouth International Centre. Both are barely touching the ground . . . definitely a figure for experts only!

The V.6

This figure is usually preceded by 1, 2 and 3 of a Natural Turn.

MAN

Begin backing diag. to centre and finish facing diag. to wall.

1. LF back
2. RF back, RS leading
3. LF crosses in front of RF
4. RF back
5. LF back in CBMP
6. RF back
7. LF to side and slightly forward

Amount of turn: Make ¼ turn to L between 6 and 7.

Footwork: 1.TH 2.T 3.T 4.TH 5.TH 6.T 7.TH.

Contrary body movement: Used on 1 and 6.

Body sway: Nil.

Rhythm: SQQSSQQ.

LADY

Begin facing diag. to centre and finish backing diag. to wall.

1. RF forward
2. LF forward, LS leading
3. RF crosses behind LF
4. LF forward, preparing to step OP
5. RF forward in CBMP OP
6. LF forward
7. RF to side and slightly back

Amount of turn: Make ¼ turn to L between 6 and 7.

Footwork: 1.HT 2.T 3.T 4.TH 5.HT 6.T 7.TH.

Contrary body movement: Used on 1 and 6.

Body sway: Nil.

Amalgamations:

1. Dance a Spin Turn. Follow with the V.6 commencing on step 2.

2. Progressive Chassé ended near a corner. Check back to the V.6 with lady outside on first step.

3. Overturn step 6 and 7 of the V.6 to end facing diag. centre (or LOD); RF forward OP, follow with Quick Open Reverse into Four Quick Run.

4. Dance step 1–7 of the V.6; RF forward OP, into a Fish Tail.

THESE FIGURES ARE COMMON TO SEVERAL DANCES
They can all precede or follow when used in the Quickstep.

Telemark

Rhythm: SSSSQQ or QQS (after a Reverse Pivot)

This fig. may be preceded by:

(1) Any Heel Pivot.
(2) The Reverse Pivot or Double Reverse Spin.
(3) The Wing.

This fig. may be followed by:

(1) Any Natural fig.
(2) The Lock Step.
(3) The Fish Tail.
(4) If ended diag. to centre follow with a Quick Open Reverse.

Impetus Turn

Rhythm: SQQSSS

This fig. may be preceded by:

(1) The Chassé Reverse Turn.
(2) The Cross Chassé.
(3) The Progressive Chassé or any fig. ended diag. to wall leaving RF free (lady LF).
(4) The Zig-Zag or Running Zig-Zag when commenced along LOD.
(5) The Natural Turn.
(6) The Natural Pivot Turn.
(7) The Running Right Turn.

This fig. may be followed by:

The same endings as given for the Natural Spin Turn, if taken at a corner. Or, if taken along the side of room, the Progressive Chassé to centre followed by a Quick Open Reverse is the normal ending. Steps 4, 5 and 6 could be used after a Foxtrot Natural Turn.

Open Impetus Turn

Rhythm: SQQSSS

This fig. may be preceded by:

(1) The Chassé Reverse Turn.
(2) The Cross Chassé.
(3) The Progressive Chassé or any fig. ended diag. to wall leaving RF free (lady LF).
(4) The Zig-Zag or Running Zig-Zag when commenced along LOD.
(5) The Natural Turn.
(6) The Natural Pivot Turn.
(7) The Running Right Turn.

This fig. may be followed by:

A Wing, which is the best ending in Quickstep, followed by a Closed Telemark and Fish Tail. Complete Rhythm: SQQSSS SQQ SSSS QQQQSS.

Outside Spin

Rhythm: SSS or QQS

This fig. may be preceded by:

Steps 1 to 4 of a Back Lock or steps 1 to 3 of a Foxtrot Natural Turn.

This fig. may be followed by:

Any Natural fig.

16

The Tango

The Tango in its basic form need not take up a lot of room and it is really a very simple dance for beginners to learn. The music is easy to follow as the beats are very well marked; it is written in 2/4 time (i.e., there are two beats to each bar of music). It is helpful to listen to the music and to pick out the beats by clapping hands in time with the music before learning the figures.

The Hold for the Tango differs slightly from that of the other dances. The lady is held slightly more towards the right side of the man; his right hand is placed a little farther round her, so that his right side, from head to foot, is slightly in advance of his left side; this position is characteristic of the Tango Walk Forward. The lady places her left hand a little higher on the man's right upper arm and slightly more towards the back of his arm. The man's left forearm and the lady's right forearm should be curved inwards a little more towards their bodies.

The Walk Forward is almost the same as that used in everyday life, and each step is of natural length. The foot is placed on the floor on the heel first, and then on to the whole foot. Each step takes up one beat of music and is counted 'slow'. (Note: A step in the Tango time 'quick' takes up half a beat only.) Each walking step should be bold and firm; this is very important.

As a result of the Tango hold, each forward walk with the left foot will be placed slightly across the body, and each forward walk with the right foot in an open position (i.e. not across the body). The way to obtain the correct position is: as the left foot moves forward, see that the back of the left knee brushes past the front of the right knee; as the right foot moves forward, see that the front of the right knee brushes past the back of the left knee. At the same time be careful to keep the feet in line, with the body pointing slightly to the left. These walking steps, when repeated, will curve slightly to the left.

The Backward Walk should also be as natural as possible. When the step is taken back, the toes should meet the floor first, then the ball of the foot; the heel should not be in contact with the floor until the other foot is brought back and passes it.

As a result of the Tango hold, each backward walk with the right foot will be placed slightly across the body, and each backward walk with the left foot will be in an open position. As in the forward walk, the easiest way to obtain the correct position is: as the right foot moves backward, see that the front of the right knee brushes past the back of the left knee. As the left foot moves backward, see that the back of the left knee brushes past the front of the right knee. Naturally the backward walks will also curve to the left if repeated.

The Knees should be more relaxed in the Tango because the steps are taken and the feet moved as in normal walking.

Other Characteristics of the Tango. In all figures that end with the feet closed (i.e., the Rock Turn, the Open Reverse Turn, the Closed Promenade, and the Back Corté), the feet should close, man's right foot slightly behind his left foot, lady's left foot slightly in advance of her right foot, if the close is danced facing partner. In Promenade Position, lady's left foot would close a little back.

On page 129 will be found a simple routine for the beginner.

Progressive Side Step

MAN

Begin facing diag. to wall.

1. Forward LF	Q
2. Side RF (almost closed to LF) slightly back	Q
3. Forward LF	S

Finish facing LOD, having curved slightly to L on 2, or finish facing diag. to wall.

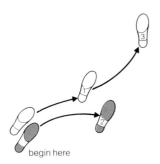

begin here

Amount of turn: A slight turn to L may be made.
Footwork: 1.H 2.Inside edge of foot 3.H.
Contrary body movement: Nil (CBMP on 1 and 3).

LADY

Begin backing diag. to wall.

1. Back RF	Q
2. Side LF (almost closed to RF) slightly forward	Q
3. Back RF	S

Finish backing LOD, having curved slightly to L on 2, or finish backing diag. to wall.

Amount of turn: A slight turn to L may be made.
Footwork: 1.BH 2.Inside edge of BH 3.B.
Contrary body movement: Nil (CBMP on 1 and 3).

This fig. may be preceded by:

(1) A walk on RF (lady LF).
(2) The Rock Turn.
(3) The Open Reverse Turn.
(4) The Closed Promenade.
(5) The Back Corté.

This fig. may be followed by:

(1) A walk on RF (lady LF).
(2) The Rock Turn.

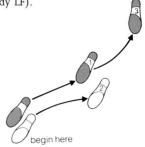

begin here

Kim and Cecilie Rygel of Norway, the 1992 World Amateur Ballroom Champions who are now professionals, are moving from the Progressive Link (page 133) into the Closed Promenade (page 124).

Rock Turn

MAN

Begin facing diag. to wall.

1. Forward RF		S
2. Side LF, slightly back	Make ¼	Q
3. Transfer weight forward to RF, RS leading	turn to R	Q
4. Back LF, small step, LS leading		S
5. Back RF		Q
6. Side LF, slightly forward	Make ¼	Q
7. Close RF to LF, slightly back	turn to L	S

Finish facing diag. to wall.

LADY

Begin backing diag. to wall.

1. Back LF	S
2. Forward RF and slightly to R	Q
3. Back LF and slightly to L, LS leading	Q
4. Forward RF, small step, RS leading	S
5. Forward LF	Q
6. Side RF, slightly back	Q
7. Close LF to RF, slightly forward	S

Finish backing diag. to wall.

Amount of turn: Make ¼ turn to R between 1 and 3; make ¼ turn to L between 4 and 6.

Footwork: 1.BH 2.H 3.Inside edge of BH 4.H 5.H 6.Inside edge of BH 7.Whole foot.

Contrary body movement: Used slightly on 1; used on 5 (CBMP on 5).

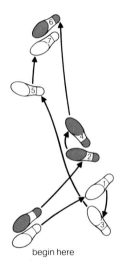

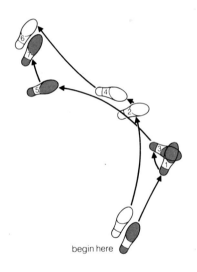

begin here

begin here

Amount of turn: Make ¼ turn to R between 1 and 3; make ¼ turn to L between 4 and 6.

Footwork: 1.H 2.Inside edge of BH 3.Inside edge of BH 4.Inside edge of BH 5.BH 6.Inside edge of foot 7.Whole foot.

Contrary body movement: Used slightly on 1; used on 5 (CBMP on 5).

This fig. may be preceded by:

(1) The Progressive Side Step.
(2) A walk on LF (lady RF).
(3) The Natural Promenade Turn, making the last step the first of the Rock Turn.

This fig. may be followed by:

(1) A walk on LF (lady RF).
(2) The Progressive Side Step.
(3) The Back Corté.

Open Reverse Turn

(With partner outside on 3, with closed ending.)

MAN

Begin facing diag. to centre.

1. Forward LF	Turning to L to back LOD	Q
2. Side RF		Q
3. Back LF, PO		S
4. Back RF	Turning to L to face diag. to wall	Q
5. Side LF, slightly forward		Q
6. Close RF to LF, slightly back		S

Finish facing diag. to wall.

LADY

Begin backing diag. to centre.

1. Back RF	Turning to L to face LOD	Q
2. Side LF and slightly forward		Q
3. Forward RF, OP		S
4. Forward LF	Turning to L to back diag. to wall	Q
5. Side RF, slightly back		Q
6. Close LF to RF, slightly forward		S

Finish backing diag. to wall.

Amount of turn: Make ¾ turn to L.

Footwork: 1.BH 2.Whole foot 3.H 4.H 5.Inside edge of BH 6.Whole foot.

Contrary body movement: Used on 1 and 4 (CBMP on 1, 3).

This fig. may be preceded by:

(1) A walk on RF (lady LF).

This fig. may be followed by:

(1) A walk on LF (lady RF).
(2) The Progressive Side Step.
(3) The Back Corté (at a corner).

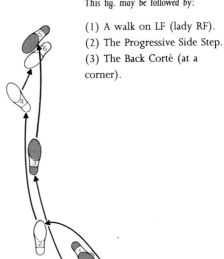

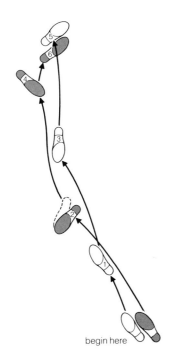

begin here

Amount of turn: Make ¾ turn to L.

Footwork: 1.H 2.BH 3.BH 4.BH 5.Inside edge of foot 6. Whole foot.

Contrary body movement: Used on 1 and 4 (CBMP on 1, 3).

Closed Promenade

MAN

Begin sideways on to LOD, with toes pointing diag. to wall (PP).

1. Side LF, in PP	S
2. Forward and across LF with RF, in PP	Q
3. Side LF, slightly forward	Q
4. Close RF to LF, slightly back	S

Finish facing diag. to wall, with partner facing square to you.

Amount of turn: Nil.

Footwork: 1.H 2.H 3.Inside edge of foot 4. Whole foot.

Contrary body movement: Nil (CBMP on 2).

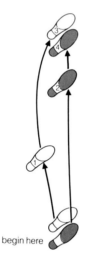

begin here

Amount of turn: Make ¼ turn to L between 2 and 3.

Footwork: 1.H 2.H 3.Inside edge of BH 4.Whole foot.

Contrary body movement: On 2, when lady turns square to partner (CBMP on 2).

This fig. may be preceded by:

(1) A walk on RF, brushing LF towards RF before moving it sideways for 1 of the Closed Promenade (lady brushing RF).

(2) The Natural Promenade Turn, brushing LF towards RF before moving it sideways for 1 of the Closed Promenade (lady brushing RF).

(3) The Progressive Link.

This fig. may be followed by:

(1) A walk on LF (lady RF).

(2) The Progressive Side Step.

(3) Another Closed Promenade if the lady is kept in PP instead of turning square to partner on 3 of the first Closed Promenade.

(4) The Back Corté.

(5) The Natural Promenade Turn if lady is kept in PP throughout the Closed Promenade (see 3 above).

(6) The Progressive Link.

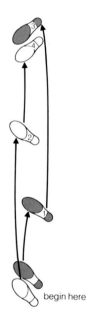

begin here

LADY

Begin sideways on to LOD, with toes pointing diag. to centre (PP).

1. Side RF, in PP	S
2. Forward and across RF with LF, in PP	Q
3. Side RF, slightly back, turning to L to face square to partner	Q
4. Close LF to RF, slightly forward	S

Finish backing diag. to wall.

In this attractive step to the side, taken in a Promenade Position in the Tango, note how the lady keeps her poise into her partner's right arm. This is essential in all Promenade figures and positions.

Back Corté

MAN

Begin backing down LOD, or 'new' LOD if used at a corner.

1. Back LF, LS leading		S
2. Back RF	⎫	Q
3. Side LF, slightly forward	⎬ Make ¼ turn to L	Q
4. Close RF to LF, slightly back	⎭	S

Finish facing diag. to wall (or 'new' wall).

Amount of turn: Make up to ¼ turn to L between 2 and 3.

Footwork: 1.Inside edge of BH 2.BH 3.Inside edge of foot 4.Whole foot.

Contrary body movement: Used on 2 (CBMP on 2).

begin here

LADY

Begin forward down LOD, or 'new' LOD if used at a corner.

1. Forward RF, RS leading		S
2. Forward LF	⎫	Q
3. Side RF, slightly back	⎬ Make ¼ turn to L	Q
4. Close LF to RF, slightly forward	⎭	S

Finish backing diag. to wall (or 'new' wall).

Amount of turn: Make up to ¼ turn to L between 2 and 3.

Footwork: 1.H 2.H 3.Inside edge of BH 4.Whole foot.

Contrary body movement: Used on 2 (CBMP on 2).

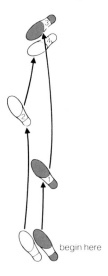

begin here

This fig. may be preceded by:

(1) The Rock Turn, used near a corner.

(2) The Open Reverse Turn, used near a corner.

(3) The Closed Promenade, used near a corner.

(4) Any of the above figures used on the sides of the ballroom if no turn is made on the Back Corté and it is commenced and finished facing diag. to wall (lady backing diag. to wall).

This fig. may be followed by:

(1) A walk on LF (lady RF).

(2) The Progressive Side Step.

(3) The Back Corté, repeated if no turn is used on it the first time it is danced.

Natural Promenade Turn

MAN

At a corner. Begin sideways on to LOD, with toes pointing diag. to wall (PP).

1. Side LF, in PP	S
2. Forward RF, in PP ⎫ Turning to R	Q
3. Side LF (slightly back) ⎬ to back LOD	Q
4. Forward RF (and then brush LF in towards RF if following with the Closed Promenade)	S

Finish facing diag. to wall of 'new' LOD.

Amount of turn: Make ¾ turn to R.

Footwork: 1.H 2.H 3.BHB 4.H, then inside of B of LF.

Contrary body movement: Used on 2 and 4 (CBMP on 2 and 4).

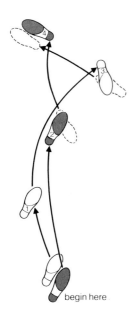

begin here

LADY

At a corner. Begin sideways on to LOD, with toes pointing diag. to centre (PP).

1. Side RF, in PP	S
2. Forward LF and across RF, in PP	Q
3. Forward RF (between partner's feet)	Q
4. Side LF (and slightly back from RF), and then brush RF towards LF if following with the Closed Promenade	S

Finish step 4, the side step with LF, backing diag. to 'new' wall, and continue to turn (as you brush RF towards LF) into PP sideways on to 'new' LOD, with toes pointing diag. to 'new' centre.

Amount of turn: Make ¾ turn to R.

Footwork: 1.H 2.H 3.H 4.BH, then inside edge of B of RF.

Contrary body movement: Used on 3 only (CBMP on 2).

This fig. may be preceded by:

(1) A walk on RF (lady LF), opening to PP as for the Closed Promenade.
(2) The Closed Promenade, when lady is kept in PP and *not* turned square to partner.
(3) The Progressive Link.

This fig. may be followed by:

(1) The Closed Promenade.
(2) The Rock Turn, when the last step of the Promenade Turn will become the first step of the Rock Turn.

begin here

Simple Routine for Practising the Tango

(For men)

Two walks, LF, RF; Progressive Side Step; Rock Turn; *then*

Two walks, LF, RF; Progressive Side Step; one walk, RF; Open Reverse Turn; *then*

Two walks, LF, RF; Progressive Side Step; one walk, RF, opening into PP; Closed Promenade (turning partner square); *then*

Two walks, LF, RF; Progressive Side Step; one walk, RF, opening into PP; Natural Promenade Turn if at a corner; Closed Promenade.

To introduce the Back Corté, dance it after any figure in the above sequences which ended with the feet closed (e.g. the Open Reverse Turn, the Closed Promenade (partner square), the Rock Turn). Following the Back Corté, go into the two walks, LF, RF.

Note: It is not necessary for ladies to study this routine; it is for men who have difficulty in making up their minds what to do next. These amalgamations need not be danced in the order given above; it depends largely on where you are in the room. (For instance, the fourth one including the Natural Promenade Turn could be danced first if you were commencing fairly near a corner.)

I have found this routine and variations of it most useful for classes; especially for pupils who wish to learn the Tango in a short time. Having mastered the figures above the pupil can pass on to those which follow.

The Basic Reverse Turn

MAN

Begin diag. to centre and finish facing diag. to wall.

	1. Forward LF, in CBMP	Q
	2. Side RF, slightly back (backing LOD)	Q
	3. Cross LF in front of RF	S
Closed Ending	4. Back RF	Q
	5. Side LF, slightly forward	Q
	6. Close RF to LF, slightly back	S

Amount of turn: Make ⅜ turn to L between 1 and 2; make ⅛ turn to L between 4 and 6 (or no turn on 4, 5 and 6).

Footwork: 1.H 2.BH 3.Whole foot 4.BH 5.Inside edge of foot 6.Whole foot.

Contrary body movement: Used on 1 and 4.

LADY

Begin backing diag. to centre and finish in PP facing diag. to centre, or square to partner backing diag. to wall.

	1. Back RF, in CBMP	Q
	2. Side LF, slightly forward	Q
	3. Close RF to LF, slightly back (facing LOD)	S
Closed Ending	4. Forward LF	Q
	5. Side RF, slightly back	Q
	6. Close LF to RF, slightly forward	S

Amount of turn: Make ⅜ turn to L between 1 and 3; make ⅛ turn to L between 4 and 6 (or no turn on 4, 5 and 6).

Footwork: 1.BH 2.Whole foot 3.Whole foot 4.H 5.Inside edge of BH 6.Whole foot.

Contrary body movement: Used on 1 and 4.

This fig. may be preceded by:

A walk on RF (lady LF).

This fig. may be followed by:

(1) A walk on LF (lady RF).

(2) Any Promenade fig. if man opens partner to PP on the Closed Ending.

(3) The Progressive Side Step.

(4) The Rock Back on LF or Back Corté at a corner, or if the Closed Ending is danced without any turn.

(5) The Progressive Link.

(6) The Four Step.

(7) The Promenade Link or the Fallaway Promenade, if man opens lady to PP on the Closed Ending.

From whatever angle The Drag in the Tango is viewed, you can see how the lady's poise is held into the man's right arm. Although she has extended her head-line away from her partner, she has maintained superb contact through her body, or middle-line.

Open Promenade

This figure is taken sideways to the line of dance.

MAN

Begin in PP, facing diag. to wall, and finish between wall and diag. to wall.

1, 2. Dance 1 and 2 of the Closed Promenade	SQ
3. Side LF, slightly forward (turning partner square)	Q
4. Forward RF, OP, in CBMP	S

Amount of turn: Make slight turn to R between 2 and 3.
Contrary body movement: Nil.

LADY

Begin in PP, facing diag. to centre, and finish backing between wall and diag. to wall.

1, 2. Dance 1 and 2 of the Closed Promenade	SQ
3. Side RF, slightly back (turning square to partner)	Q
4. Back with LF, in CBMP, PO	S

Amount of turn: Make nearly ¼ turn to L between 2 and 3.
Contrary body movement: Used on 2.

This fig. may be preceded by:

(1) A walk on RF, brushing LF to RF without weight, opening to PP.
(2) Any Closed Ending, when lady is opened to PP.
(3) The Back Corté, opening lady to PP.
(4) The Natural Twist Turn.
(5) The Natural Promenade Turn, brushing LF to RF without weight, opening to PP.
(6) The Progressive Link.
(7) The Four Step.

This fig. may be followed by:

(1) A walk on LF.
(2) The Progressive Side Step.
(3) The Back Corté, commenced with PO on first step.
(4) The Rock Back on LF and the Closed Ending.
(5) The Progressive Link.
(6) The Four Step.

Open Reverse Turn

(Lady in front on 3)

This figure can be danced in two ways. The more popular way is to do 1, 2 and 3 (described below), and then finish with 4, 5 and 6 of the Basic Reverse Turn, the Closed Ending.

The Open Ending given below may be used as an ending instead of the Closed Ending for any Reverse Turn.

MAN

Begin facing diag. to centre and finish almost facing diag. to wall.

	1. Forward LF, in CBMP	Q
	2. Side RF, slightly back	Q
	3. Back LF, LS leading (down LOD)	S
Open Ending	4. Back RF	Q
	5. Side LF, slightly forward	Q
	6. Forward RF, OP, in CBMP	S

Amount of turn: Make just under ¾ turn to L on this fig.
Footwork: 1.H 2.BH 3.Inside edge of BH 4.BH 5.Inside edge of foot 6.H.
Contrary body movement: Used on 1 and 4.

LADY

Begin backing diag. to centre and finish almost backing diag. to wall.

	1. Back RF, in CBMP	Q
	2. Close L heel to R heel	Q
	3. Forward RF, RS leading (down LOD)	S
Open Ending	4. Forward LF	Q
	5. Side RF, slightly back	Q
	6. Back LF, in CBMP, PP	S

Amount of turn: Make just under ¾ of a turn to L on this fig.
Contrary body movement: Used on 1 and 4.

This fig may be preceded by:

(1) A walk on RF (lady LF).

This fig. may be followed by:

(1) A walk on LF.
(2) The Progressive Side Step.
(3) The Progressive Link.

(4) The Back Corté, danced with lady outside on 1.

(5) The Four Step.

Natural Twist Turn

MAN

Begin and finish in PP, feet facing diag. to wall, or finish backing diag. to centre, when the Back Corté is to follow.

1.	Side LF, in PP	S
2.	Forward RF and across in PP and CBMP	Q
3.	Side LF (backing diag. to centre)	Q
4.	Cross RF behind LF, with feet apart (back to LOD)	S
5. }	Twist just over ½ turn to R (on L heel and ball of RF), finishing with weight on RF (finish	
6. }	with feet almost closed together)	QQ

Amount of turn: Make ⅜ of a turn to R between 2 and 4. (Make just over ¼ of a turn on 5 and 6 when the Back Corté is to follow.)

Footwork: 1.H 2.H 3.BH 4.B 5, 6.Begin on B of RF and H of LF. End on whole foot RF and inside edge of B of LF.

Contrary body movement: Used on 2.

LADY

Begin and finish in PP, facing diag. to centre.

1. Side RF, in PP	S
2. Forward LF and across in PP and CBMP	Q
3. Forward RF (between partner's feet, down LOD)	Q
4. Forward LF, preparing to step OP, LS leading	S
5. Forward RF, OP, in CBMP (to wall)	Q
6. Close LF to RF (facing diag. to centre)	Q

Amount of turn: Make a complete turn to R.

Footwork: 1.H 2.H 3.H 4.H 5.HB 6.BH.

Contrary body movement: Used on 3 and 5.

This fig. may be preceded by:

(1) Any Promenade fig. except the Open Promenade.

(2) A walk on RF, opening lady to PP.

(3) Any Closed Finish, opening lady to PP.

(4) The Progressive Link.

(5) The Four Step.

(6) The Fallaway Promenade.

This fig. may be followed by:

(1) Any Promenade fig.

(2) The Back Corté.

(3) The Rock Back on LF and the Closed Ending.

(4) The Promenade Link.

(5) The Fallaway Promenade.

Progressive Side Step Reverse Turn

(With the Rock Back on LF and Closed Ending)

MAN

Begin facing diag. to centre and finish facing diag. to wall.

Progressive Side Step {	1. Forward LF, in CBMP	} Turning to L ⅛ turn	Q
	2. Side RF, slightly back		Q
	3. Forward LF, in CBMP		S
	4. Forward RF, RS leading		S
Rock No. 1 {	5. Transfer weight back to LF, LS leading	} No turn	Q
	6. Transfer weight forward to RF, RS leading		Q
	7. Back LF, LS leading, small step		S
Close Ending {	8. Back RF, in CBMP	} Turning to L	Q
	9. Side LF, slightly forward		Q
	10. Close RF to LF, slightly back		S

Amount of turn: Make ⅜ turn to L.

Footwork: 1.H 2.Inside edge of foot 3.H 4.H 5.Inside edge of BH 6.H 7.Inside edge of BH 8.BH 9.Inside edge of foot 10.Whole foot.

Contrary body movement: Used on 1, 3 and 8.

Progressive Side Step Reverse Turn

LADY

Begin backing diag. to centre and finish backing diag. to wall.

Progressive Side Step	1. Back RF, in CBMP	Turning to L ⅜ turn	Q
	2. Side LF, slightly forward		Q
	3. Back RF, in CBMP		S
	4. Back LF, LS leading		S
Rock No. 1	5. Transfer weight forward to RF, RS leading	No turn	Q
	6. Transfer weight back to LF, LS leading		Q
	7. Forward RF, RS leading, small step		S
Closed Ending	8. Forward LF, in CBMP	Turning to L	Q
	9. Side RF, slightly back		Q
	10. Close LF to RF, slightly forward		S

Amount of turn: Make ⅜ turn to L.

Footwork: 1.BH 2.Inside edge of foot 3.BH 4.Inside edge of BH 5.H 6.Inside edge of BH 7.H 8.H 9.Inside edge of BH 10.Whole foot.

Contrary body movement: Used on 1, 3 and 8.

This fig. may be preceded by:

(1) A walk on RF (lady LF).

This fig. may be followed by:

(1) A walk on LF (lady RF).
(2) Any Promenade fig. if lady is opened to PP on the Closed Ending.
(3) The Progressive Side Step.
(4) The Progressive Link.
(5) The Four Step.
(6) The Promenade Link or Fallaway Promenade if lady is opened to PP on the Closed Ending.
(7) (a) The Back Corté
(b) The Rock Back on LF and the Rock Back on RF into the Back Corté.
(c) The Rock Back on LF, Walk RF back slow and then forward LF, in CBMP, into a Progressive Side Step, turning to end diag. to wall.

} After the first four steps of the Progressive Side Step Reverse Turn

The Rock Back on LF

MAN

Begin and finish down LOD, moving backwards.

1. Back LF, LS leading (down LOD) Q
2. Transfer weight forward to RF, RS leading (against LOD) Q
3. Back LF, LS leading, small step (down LOD) S

Amount of turn: Nil.

Footwork: 1.Inside edge of BH 2.H 3. Inside edge of BH.

Contrary body movement: Nil.

LADY

Begin and finish down LOD, moving forward.

1. Forward RF, RS leading (down LOD) Q
2. Transfer weight back to LF, LS leading (against LOD) Q
3. Forward RF, RS leading, small step (down LOD) S

Amount of turn: Nil.

Footwork: 1.H 2.Inside edge of BH 3.H.

Contrary body movement: Nil.

This fig. may be preceded by:

(1) Any Closed Ending ended back LOD.
(2) The Open Promenade at a corner, when the Rock will be danced PO throughout.
(3) The Rock Back on RF.
(4) 1, 2, 3 and 4 (as part of Progressive Side Step Reverse Turn).
(5) The Natural Twist Turn, when the Rock will be danced diag. to centre.

This fig. may be followed by:

(1) The Rock Back on RF.
(2) The Closed Ending.
(3) The Open Ending.
(4) 4, 5 and 6 of the Closed Reverse Turn, or step forward RF into the Progressive Side Step.

The Rock Back on RF

MAN

Begin and finish down LOD, moving backwards.

1. Back RF, in CBMP (down LOD)	Q
2. Transfer weight forward to LF, in CBMP (against LOD)	Q
3. Back RF, small step in CBMP (down LOD)	S

Amount of turn: Nil.
Footwork: 1.BH 2.H 3.BH.
Contrary body movement: Nil.

LADY

Begin and finish down LOD, moving forward.

1. Forward LF, in CBMP (down LOD)	Q
2. Transfer weight back to RF, in CBMP (against LOD)	Q
3. Forward LF, small step in CBMP (down LOD)	S

Amount of turn: Nil.
Footwork: 1.H 2.BH 3.H.
Contrary body movement: Nil.

This fig. may be preceded by:

(1) The Rock Back on LF.
(2) The first step of Back Corté.

This fig. may be followed by:

(1) The Back Corté.
(2) The Rock Back on LF.

Progressive Link

MAN

Begin diag. to wall and finish in PP diag. to wall.

1. Forward LF, in CBMP	Q
2. Side RF, slightly back, in PP	Q

Amount of turn: The body turns slightly to R on 2.
Footwork: 1.H 2.Inside edge of foot and inside edge of B of LF.
Contrary body movement: Nil.

LADY

Begin backing diag. to wall and finish in PP facing diag. to centre.

1. Back RF, in CBMP	Q
2. Side LF, slightly back, in PP	Q

Amount of turn: Make ¼ turn to R between 1 and 2.
Footwork: 1.BH 2.Inside edge of BH and inside edge of B of RF.
Contrary body movement: Nil.

This fig. may be preceded by:

(1) A walk on RF (lady LF).
(2) Any Closed Ending.
(3) The Back Corté.
(4) The Open Promenade.
(5) The Open Ending.
(6) The Promenade Link.

This fig. may be followed by:

(1) Any fig. commenced in PP (e.g. the Natural Twist Turn, the Natural Promenade Turn, or the Promenades, etc.).

Promenade Link

MAN

Begin in PP and finish facing the wall.

1. Side LF, in PP	S
2. Forward RF and across in PP and CBMP	Q
3. Close LF to RF, keeping weight on RF, turning slightly to R (to face wall)	Q

Amount of turn: Make ⅛ turn to R on 3.
Footwork: 1.H 2.HB (foot flat) 3.Inside edge of B.
Contrary body movement: Used on 2.

LADY

Begin in PP and finish backing wall.

1. Side RF, in PP	S
2. Forward LF and across in PP and CBMP	Q
3. Close RF to LF, keeping weight on LF, turning slightly to L (to back wall)	Q

Amount of turn: Make ⅛ turn to L on 3.

Footwork: 1.H 2.HB (foot flat) 3.Inside edge of B.

Contrary body movement: Used on 2.

This fig. may be preceded by:

(1) A walk on RF (lady LF).
(2) Any Closed Finish, danced opening lady to PP.
(3) The Back Corté, danced opening lady to PP.
(4) The Natural Twist Turn.
(5) The Natural Promenade Turn, danced brushing LF in to RF after Promenade Turn and opening lady to PP.
(6) The Progressive Link.
(7) The Four Step.
(8) The Fallaway Promenade.

This fig. may be followed by:

(1) The Progressive Side Step.
(2) The Progressive Link.
(3) The Four Step.
(4) The walk on LF (lady RF).
(5) The Promenade Link, danced with man and lady turning to L, when it will be commenced facing LOD and travel diag. to centre. To follow, dance any Reverse fig.

Four Step

MAN

Begin facing the wall and finish in PP facing diag. to wall.

1. Forward LF in CBMP	Q
2. Side RF, slightly back	Q
3. Back LF, in CBMP, PO	Q
4. Close RF to LF, slightly back, in PP	Q

Amount of turn: Make ⅛ turn to L between 1 and 2, or no turn.

Footwork: 1.H. 2.BH 3.BH 4.BH.

Contrary body movement: Used on 1.

LADY

Begin backing to wall and finish in PP facing diag. to centre.

1. Back RF, in CBMP	Q
2. Side LF, slightly forward	Q
3. Forward RF, in CBMP, OP	Q
4. Close LF to RF, slightly back, in PP	Q

Amount of turn: Make ⅛ turn to L between 1 and 2; make ¼ turn to R between 3 and 4.

Footwork: 1.BH 2.Whole foot 3.HB (foot flat) 4.BH.

This fig. may be preceded by:

(1) Any Closed Ending.
(2) The Back Corté.
(3) The Open Promenade.
(4) The Open Ending.
(5) The Promenade Link.

This fig. may be followed by:

(1) Any Promenade fig. (e.g. the Natural Twist Turn, the Natural Promenade Turn, the Fallaway Promenade, the Closed or Open Promenade).

Fallaway Promenade

MAN

Begin in PP along LOD and finish in PP facing wall.

1. Side LF, in PP	S
2. Forward RF and across in PP and CBMP	Q
3. Side LF still in PP (backing almost diag. to centre)	Q
4. Back RF, in FAP, RS leading (to centre, backing diag. to centre)	S
5. Back LF, in FAP and CBMP	Q
6. Close RF to LF, slightly back, in PP	Q

Amount of turn: Make ¼ turn to R between 1 and 4; make ⅛ turn to L between 4 and 5.

Footwork: 1.H 2.H 3.BH 4.Inside edge of BH 5.BH 6.BH.

Contrary body movement: Used on 2.

The Progressive Link (page 133) is here seen side-on, danced by Alan Shingler and Donna Reeve of England with superb contact. The lady has not turned too far out and away from her partner. Compact and powerful . . . that's Tango today.

Fallaway Promenade

LADY

Begin in PP along LOD and finish in PP facing LOD.

1. Side RF, in PP	S
2. Forward LF and across in PP and CBMP	Q
3. Forward RF, in PP and CBMP	Q
4. Back LF, in FAP, LS leading	S
5. Back RF, in FAP and CBMP	Q
6. Close LF to RF, slightly back in PP	Q

Amount of turn: Make ¼ turn to R between 1 and 4; make ⅛ turn to L between 5 and 6.

Footwork: 1.H 2.H 3.H 4.Inside edge of BH 5.BH 6.Whole foot.

Contrary body movement: Used on 3 and 5.

This fig. may be preceded by:

(1) A walk on RF (lady LF), lady opened to PP.
(2) The Four Step.
(3) The Progressive Link.
(4) The Natural Twist Turn.

This fig. may be followed by:

(1) Any Promenade fig. danced diag. to wall (i.e. the Natural Twist Turn, or the Natural Promenade Turn).

The Outside Swivel (1)

This figure is usually preceded by an Open Promenade and followed by a Promenade Link.

MAN

Begin between centre and diag. to centre against the LOD and finish facing diag. to wall.

1. LF back in CBMP, RF crosses in front of LF without weight. End in PP	S
2. RF forward and across in PP and CBMP	Q
3. LF to side, almost closed to RF without weight	Q

Amount of turn: Make just under ⅛ turn to R on 1; make ⅛ turn to L between 1 and 2.

Footwork: 1.BH with pressure on B of RF 2.H 3.Inside edge of B.

Contrary body movement: Used on 1.

Note: Most advanced dancers do not cross the RF in front on step 1, but leave it forward and then move it slightly leftwards on step 2.

LADY

Begin between centre and diag. to centre against the LOD and finish backing diag. to wall.

1. RF forward in CBMP, OP, LF closes, slightly back, without weight. End in PP	S
2. LF forward and across in PP and CBMP	Q
3. RF to side, almost closed to LF, without weight	Q

Amount of turn: Make just over ¼ turn to R on 1; make ⅜ turn to L between 2 and 3.

Footwork: 1.HB (foot flat) and inside edge of B of LF 2.HB (foot flat) 3. Inside edge of B.

Contrary body movement: Used on 1 and 2.

Note. Advanced dancers often lift the LF from the floor on step 1, making sure to keep the knees in contact while this 'flick' of the foot is danced.

This fig. may be preceded by:

(1) The Open Promenade.
(2) Any Open Finish.
(3) The Closed Promenade or any Closed Finish by stepping back LF, lady outside.
(4) 2 steps of Open Reverse or 2 steps of Four Step.

This fig. may be followed by:

(1) Steps 2, 3 and 4 of a Closed or Open Promenade after step 1.
(2) The Promenade Link as described above is the normal ending, and is usually followed by the Brush Tap.

The Outside Swivel (2)

This figure is usually preceded by a turning to left after an Open Promenade, ended diag. to wall.

MAN

Begin against LOD and finish facing diag. to centre.

1. LF back in CBMP. RF moves leftwards in front of LF without weight. End in PP	S
2. RF forward and across in PP and CBMP	Q
3. LF side, almost closed, without weight	Q

Amount of turn: Make ¼ turn to L.

Footwork: 1.BH with pressure on B of RH 2.H 3. Inside edge of B.

Contrary body movement: Nil.

LADY

Begin against LOD and finish backing diag. to centre.

1. RF forward in CBMP, OP, LF closes, slightly back, without weight. End in PP — S
2. LF forward and across in PP and CBMP — Q
3. RF to side, almost closed, without weight — Q

Follow with a Reverse Turn.

Amount of turn: Make ⅛ turn to L between the preceding step and 1; make ¼ turn to R on 1; make ⅜ turn to L between 2 and 3.

Footwork: 1.HB (foot flat) and inside edge of B of LF 2.HB (foot flat) 3.Inside edge of B.

Contrary body movement: Used on 1 and 2.

The Outside Swivel (3)

This figure is usually preceded by 1 and 2 of a Reverse Turn.

MAN

Begin facing diag. to centre and finish facing wall.

1. LF forward in CBMP — Q
2. RF to side — Q
3. LF back in CBMP, RF moves leftwards in front of LF without weight in PP — S
4. RF forward and across in PP and CBMP — Q
5. LF to side, almost closed, without weight — Q

Amount of turn: Make ½ turn to L between 1 and 3; make ⅛ turn between 3 and 4.

Footwork: 1.H 2.BH 3.BH with pressure on B of RF 4.H 5.Inside edge of B.

Contrary body movement: Used on 1.

LADY

Begin facing diag. to centre and finish backing diag. to wall.

1. RF back in CBMP — Q
2. LF to side and slightly forward — Q
3. RF forward in CBMP, OP. LF closes, slightly back without weight in PP — S
4. LF forward and across in PP and CBMP — Q
5. RF to side, almost closed, without weight — Q

Amount of turn: Make ½ turn to L between 1 and 3; make ¼ turn to R on 3; make ⅜ to L between 4 and 5.

Footwork: 1.BH (whole foot) 2.Whole foot 3.HB (foot flat) and inside edge of ball of LF 4.HB (foot flat) 5.Inside edge of B.

Contrary body movement: Used on 1, 3 and 4.

This fig. may be followed by:

The Four Step.
Note: There is a sharp Foot Swivel on RF as the LF moves diag. to centre on step 3.

The Brush Tap

This figure is usually preceded by a Promenade Link.

MAN

Begin facing diag. to wall and finish facing LOD.

1. LF forward in CBMP
2. RF to side
3. LF brushes to RF without weight
4. LF to side, small step, without weight

Amount of turn: Make ⅛ turn to L between 1 and 2.
Footwork: 1.H 2.BH 3.Foot slightly off the floor 4.Inside edge of B.

Contrary body movement: Used on 1.

Note: When the LF is placed on step 4, the L knee should veer inwards.

Kim and Cecilie Rygel of Norway (above) show absolute togetherness . . . absolute control.
Similarly, their fellow countrymen, Kai Lillebo and Monica Rotvold dancing a Progressive Link
in the Tango (right) make an excellent couple, revealing their understanding and constant
training.

LADY

Begin facing diag. to wall and finish backing LOD.

1. RF back in CBMP
2. LF to side
3. RF brushes to LF without weight
4. RF to side, small step, without weight

Amount of turn: Make ⅛ turn to L between 1 and 2.

Footwork: 1.BH 2.Whole foot 3.Foot slightly off the floor 4.Inside edge of B.

Contrary body movement: Used on 1.

Note: The Brush Tap is normally used after a Promenade Link ended facing diag. to wall.

This fig. may be preceded by:

(1) Walk on RF.
(2) The Closed Promenade or any Closed Finish.
(3) The Open Promenade or any Open Finish.
(4) The Promenade Link.

This fig. may be followed by:

(1) Walk on LF.
(2) The Progressive Side Step.
(3) Turn PP for any Promenade figure.
(4) The Progressive Link.
(5) The Four Step.

If used near a corner a Back Corté or LF Rock could follow.

17

The Viennese Waltz

Viennese or quick waltzes are popular in many ballrooms. The ideal tempo is 60 bars to the minute, but the figures may be danced to any waltz played between 44 and 64 bars per minute. Figures 1, 2, 3 and 4 are the only figures necessary to enjoy dancing to this rhythm, and the two Fleckerl figures are for advanced dancers.

Natural Right Turn

MAN

Begin facing diag. to centre and finish facing diag. to centre.

1. Forward RF, strong step ⎫
2. Side LF, long step ⎬ Turning to R to backing diag. to centre
3. Close RF to LF ⎭

4. Back LF, slightly to side
5. Side RF, short step
6. Close LF to RF, slightly back

Amount of turn: Make ⅜ turn to R between 1 and 2; make ⅛ turn to R between 2 and 3; make ⅛ turn to R between 3 and 4; make ⅜ turn to R between 4 and 5.

Footwork: 1.HT 2.T 3.TH 4.TH 5.T 6.Foot flat.

Contrary body movement: Used on 1 and 4.

Body sway: Sway to R on 2 and 3. Sway to L on 5 and 6.

Note: The man may hold the preceding sway slightly at the beginning of steps 1 and 4.

LADY

Dances man's 4, 5, 6   1, 2, 3.

This fig. may be preceded by:

(1) The Forward Change Reverse to Natural.
(2) The Natural Turn.
(3) The Natural Fleckerl.

This fig. may be followed by:

(1) The Natural Turn.
(2) The Forward Change Natural to Reverse.
(3) The Natural Fleckerl.

Note: Travelling round the ballroom (on the outside), dance eight or sixteen bars of the Natural Turns before changing to another fig.

Reverse Turn

MAN

Begin facing LOD and finish facing LOD.

1. Forward LF, strong step ⎫
2. Side RF, long step ⎬ Turning to L to backing LOD
3. Cross LF in front of RF ⎭

4. Back RF, slightly to side
5. Side LF, short step
6. Close RF to LF, slightly back

Amount of turn: Make ¼ turn to L between 1 and 2; make ¼ turn to L between 2 and 3; make ⅛ turn to L between 3 and 4; make nearly ⅜ turn to L between 4 and 5. Complete the turn between 5 and 6.

Footwork: 1.HT 2.T 3.TH 4.TH 5.T 6.Foot flat.

Contrary body movement: Used on 1 and 4.

Body sway: Sway to L on 2 and 3; sway to R on 5 and 6.

Note: Between 5 and 6 the man will dance a small foot swivel to L on LF. The lady will dance a small foot swivel to L between 2 and 3.

LADY

Dances man's 4, 5, 6   1, 2, 3.

This fig. may be preceded by:

(1) The Reverse Turn.
(2) The Forward Change from the Natural to Reverse.
(3) The Reverse Fleckerl.

This fig. may be followed by:

(1) The Reverse Turn.
(2) The Forward Change from the Reverse to Natural.
(3) The Reverse Fleckerl.

Note: Travelling round the ballroom, dance eight or sixteen bars of the Reverse Turns before changing to another fig.

Forward Change (Natural to Reverse)

MAN

Begin facing diag. to centre and finish facing LOD.

1. Forward RF
2. Forward LF, curving
3. Close RF to LF

Amount of turn: Make ⅛ turn to R between 1 and 3.
Footwork: 1.HT 2.T 3.TH.
Contrary body movement: Used on 1.
Body sway: Sway to R on 2 and 3.

LADY

Dances normal opposite movements.

This fig. may be preceded by:

(1) The Natural Turn.

This fig. may be followed by:

(1) The Reverse Turn.

Forward Change (Reverse to Natural)

MAN

Begin facing LOD and finish facing diag. to centre.

1. Forward LF
2. Forward RF, curving
3. Close LF to RF

Amount of turn: Make ⅛ turn to L between 1 and 3.
Footwork: 1.HT 2.T 3.TH.
Contrary body movement: Used on 1.
Body sway: Sway to L on 2 and 3.

LADY

Dances normal opposite movements.

This fig. may be preceded by:

(1) The Reverse Turn.

This fig. may be followed by:

(1) The Natural Turn.

Note: Changes from Natural to Reverse, and vice versa, should be made on the musical phrasing. Do not change in the middle of an eight-bar phrase, always change at the end, or continue one of the turns and change at the end of the sixteen-bar phrase.

General note: The change steps may be danced forward or back by man or lady.

Natural Fleckerl

MAN

Begin facing LOD and finish facing LOD.

1. Diag. forward RF between lady's feet (facing diag. to wall)
2. Side LF, half weight on it (backing LOD)
3. Turn to R on RF (facing LOD)
4. Side LF (facing LOD)
5. Cross RF well behind LF, turn to R, weight still over LF (backing LOD)
6. Turn to R on LF, uncrossing the feet (facing LOD)

Amount of turn: Make ⅛ turn to R between preceding step and 1; make ½ turn to R between 1 and 2; make ⅜ turn to R between 2 and 3; make ⅛ turn to R between 3 and 4; make ½ turn to R between 4 and 5; make ⅜ turn to right between 5 and 6.

Footwork: 1.HT 2.T 3.TH 4.HT 5.T 6.TH.

Contrary body movement: Used on 1.

Body sway: Nil.

Note: There is no Rise and Fall and no Sway in the Fleckerls.

LADY

Dances man's 4, 5, 6   1, 2, 3.

Note: The Fleckerl is a fast turn on one spot. Partner is held firmly and in a close hold. When dancing the Natural Fleckerl, dance Natural Turns to the centre of the room, and dance eight or sixteen bars of Natural Fleckerls, then dance to the outside of the ballroom again with Natural Turns.

Reverse Fleckerl

MAN

Begin facing LOD and finish facing LOD.

1. Turn to L on L heel (pointing to centre)
2. Swing RF round, ending RF to side (backing LOD)
3. Turn on RF to L and cross LF loosely in front of RF (facing LOD)
4. Side RF, slightly back (backing diag. to wall against LOD)
5. Cross LF well behind RF (a type of twist turn, half weight), turn to L
6. Turning to L on LF uncross the feet (facing LOD), and change weight on to RF

Amount of turn: Make ¼ turn to L between preceding step and step 1; make ⅜ turn to L between 1 and 2; make ⅜ turn to L between 2 and 3; make ⅛ turn to L between 3 and 4; make ½ turn to L between 4 and 5; make ⅜ turn to L between 5 and 6.

Footwork: 1.HT 2.T 3.TH 4.THT 5.T 6.TH of RF, 'and' H of LF.

Contrary body movement: Used on 1.

Body sway: Nil.

LADY

Dances man's 4, 5, 6   1, 2, 3.

Note: The Fleckerl is a fast turn on one spot. When dancing the Reverse Fleckerl, dance Reverse Turns to the centre of the ballroom, and dance eight or sixteen bars of Reverse Fleckerl, then dance Reverse Turns to the outside of the ballroom again.

This type of Oversway position is favoured by many experienced dancers. Like all advanced actions and picture steps, this position can only be achieved once you have mastered all the techniques in this book.

18

The Rumba

The Rumba has a fascinating rhythm, and the figures in their simple form are not difficult to learn.

The Music is written in 2⁄4 or 4⁄4 time, but for practical purposes it is best to consider 4⁄4, which gives 4 counts to each bar of music, 1, 2, 3, 4.

The Beat Values are as follows:

Count:	2	3	4–1
OR	Q	Q	S
Beat Values:	1	1	2

The Cuban Rumba dancer normally makes the actual foot movements only on beats 2, 3, 4, with a controlled and very slight lateral hip action on beat 1.

The best method of Starting to Dance is to stand with the feet very slightly apart and the weight on the LF (as man); very narrow side step on RF on count 1, then move forward with LF into the Basic Movement on count 2 – lady normal opposite. From there it is not difficult to retain the rhythm, having started the dance on the first beat of a bar of music. A simple way of counting the dance for the beginner is to start on the correct beat as described above, then use the 'quick, quick, slow' count instead of 2, 3, 4–1. Both methods of counting are given with each figure.

The Hold is the same as for the Samba (page 165), and the body is held naturally upright with the shoulders relaxed. The weight of the body is kept over the balls of the feet. 'Open Hold' is a position in which the lady and man are apart and facing each other, man holding lady's right hand in his left hand, with arms just above waist level and not quite straight at the elbow. The lady's arm should remain relaxed and her left hand should not be lower than waist level; her left, or 'free' hand is then in a position to return comfortably to man's right shoulder when he wishes to regain normal hold. 'Fan Position' is a position where the lady and man are apart, holding as in Open Hold. The lady is on the left side and slightly in front of the man, at right-angles to him with her LF back. Man has his feet apart with his weight on RF.

Footwork. All the steps are danced on the ball of the foot first, immediately lowering softly on to the flat of the foot. Heel leads are never used.

Tempo. The dance can be performed over a wide range of tempi. The tempo laid down for competitions is 27 bars per minute.

Leading. The man should lead the lady firmly but lightly, and only when changing from one figure to another. The lady, having received the lead into a figure, should dance the remainder on her own, particularly in movements where she is in Open Hold.

Hip Movement. There is a very slight lateral movement of the hips on the 4–1 counts of most basic figures which occurs only because the full weight of the body is not immediately transferred through the foot on count 4 and the step is taken on a relaxed knee; as full weight is taken into the leg on count 1 the knee straightens and the other knee relaxes. This results in a very slight lateral swing of the hips, but it should be stressed that this must not be obvious, and is mostly a feeling the dancer experiences through the relaxing and straightening of the knees. The straightening should be soft and the knees must never be fully braced.

Basic Movement

MAN

Begin and end in Normal Hold; a gradual turn to L is made on each step.

Note: The normal amount of turn is approximately ¼ to L over the six steps, but slightly more turn can be made. The width of the side step is approximately the length of one's own foot.

			Count
1. Forward LF, releasing R heel	Forward Half Basic Movement		2 (or Q)
2. Replace weight on RF			3 (or Q)
3. Side LF			4–1 (or s)
4. Back RF, releasing L heel	Backward Half Basic Movement		2 (or Q)
5. Replace weight on LF			3 (or Q)
6. Side RF			4–1 (or s)

Repeat ad lib.

LADY

Begin and end in Normal Hold; a gradual turn to L is made on each step.

			Count
1. Back RF releasing L heel	Backward Half Basic Movement		2 (or Q)
2. Replace weight on LF			3 (or Q)
3. Side RF			4–1 (or s)
4. Forward LF, releasing R heel	Forward Half Basic Movement		2 (or Q)
5. Replace weight on RF			3 (or Q)
6. Side LF			4–1 (or s)

Repeat ad lib.

This fig. may be preceded by:

(1) The Basic Movement.
(2) The Progressive Walk Forward.
(3) The Progressive Walk Back, into Back Basic.
(4) The Opening Out from Natural Top, into Back Basic.
(5) The Alemana.
(6) The Side Step.
(7) The Cucaracha (to man's R).
(8) The Hockey Stick, regaining normal hold on Forward Basic.
(9) The Reverse Top.
(10) The Natural Top.

This fig. may be followed by:

(1) The Basic Movement.
(2) The Progressive Walk Back (after two steps of Forward Basic, back on man's third step).
(3) The Progressive Walk Forward (after two steps of Back Basic, forward on man's third step).
(4) The Natural Top: after steps 1–2 Forward Basic without the turn normally made to L, man side and slightly back LF on step 3, lady forward RF between his feet.
(5) The Fan.
(6) The Side Step: man brushes LF to RF (without weight) on count 1 of Back Basic; lady RF to LF (without weight) on count 1 of Forward Basic.
(7) The Cucaracha (to man's L) brushing without weight as in No. 6 above.

This is a static display (opposite) before the Open Facing Position is regained in the Rumba. In contrast, the atmosphere of the Paso Doble is caught by Michael Hull and Linda Pettersen of Germany (above). The lady is in a Spanish Line, which is sometimes referred to as the Press Line.

Progressive Walk Forward

MAN

Begin and end in Normal Hold, usually facing LOD.

	Count
1. Forward LF	2 (or Q)
2. Forward RF	3 (or Q)
3. Forward LF	4—1 (or s)
4. Forward RF	2 (or Q)
5. Forward LF	3 (or Q)
6. Forward RF	4—1 (or s)

Note: The Progressive Walk Forward may be danced without turn or curved slightly to L or R for approximately ¼ turn; e.g. begin diag. to wall and curve to L, or begin diag. to centre and curve to R.

LADY

Begin and end in Normal Hold, usually backing LOD.

	Count
1. Back RF	2 (or Q)
2. Back LF	3 (or Q)
3. Back RF	4—1 (or s)
4. Back LF	2 (or Q)
5. Back RF	3 (or Q)
6. Back LF	4—1 (or s)

This fig. may be preceded by:

(1) The Basic Movement (after two steps Back Basic, forward on man's third step).

This fig. may be followed by:

(1) The Basic Movement.
(2) The Fan.
(3) The Side Step (if Walks are ended at a corner).

Progressive Walk Back

MAN

Begin and end in Normal Hold, usually backing LOD.

	Count
1. Back RF	2 (or Q)
2. Back LF	3 (or Q)
3. Back RF	4–1 (or S)
4. Back LF	2 (or Q)
5. Back RF	3 (or Q)
6. Back LF	4–1 (or S)

Note: The Progressive Walk Back may be danced without turn or curved slightly to L or R for approximately ¼ turn; e.g. begin back diag. to wall and curve to L, or begin back diag. to centre and curve to R.

LADY

Begin and end in Normal Hold, usually facing LOD.

	Count
1. Forward LF	2 (or Q)
2. Forward RF	3 (or Q)
3. Forward LF	4–1 (or S)
4. Forward RF	2 (or Q)
5. Forward LF	3 (or Q)
6. Forward RF	4–1 (or S)

This fig. may be preceded by:

(1) The Basic Movement (after two steps Forward Basic back on man's third step).

This fig. may be followed by:

(1) The Basic Movement (Backward Half).

(2) The Natural Top (man side and slightly back LF on sixth Backward Walk, lady forward RF between his feet).

(3) The Fan (steps 4–6).

Notes on Progressive Walks

Man dances the Forward Walks, whilst lady dances the Backward Walks, and vice versa. The action of the legs and feet during the Walks is most important.

Description (Forward Walks): Step forward (foot not quite in contact with the floor) with a relaxed knee, and 'push' the ball of the foot into the floor at the end of the movement, immediately lowering to flat of foot. The knee is softly straightened (not braced) as the weight of the body is taken into the leg, and at the same time the heel of the other foot is released and the knee relaxed. At the end of each Forward Walk the weight of the body should be over the front leg, with the forward knee straight and the back knee relaxed.

Description (Backward Walks): Step back with a relaxed knee (foot not quite in contact with the floor until extent of the step is reached) on ball of foot, immediately dropping to flat of foot and softly straightening the knee. The forward knee remains relaxed. The weight of the body is kept well over the moving foot and although pressure should be released from the heel of the front foot, the foot must not be lifted off the floor.

The Natural Top

MAN

Begin and end in Normal Hold, and make a continuous turn to R.

	Count
1. Cross RF behind LF (R toe turned out)	2 (or Q)
2. Side and slightly forward LF (L toe turned in)	3 (or Q)
3. Cross RF behind LF (toe turned out)	4–1 (or S)
4. Side and slightly forward LF (toe turned in)	2 (or Q)
5. Cross RF behind LF (toe turned out)	3 (or Q)
6. Side and slightly forward LF (toe turned in)	4–1 (or S)
7. Cross RF behind LF (toe turned out)	2 (or Q)
8. Side and slightly forward LF (toe turned in)	3 (or Q)
9. Close RF to LF	4–1 (or S)

Note: The man should not exaggerate the crossing movement of his RF, but place his R toe near to, or just past, the L heel. The lady and man face square to each other during this figure, and describe a circle around a common centre which is midway between them. The feet must be placed in position without swivelling. The heel of the man's RF should lower towards the floor, but actual contact with the floor is optional. The amount of turn made on this figure is variable, particularly according to the speed of the music; an approximate guide is 1½ turns to R.

LADY

Begin and end in Normal Hold, and make a continuous turn to R.

	Count
1. Side and slightly back LF (L toe turned in)	2 (or Q)
2. Cross RF in front of LF (R toe turned out)	3 (or Q)
3. Side and slightly back LF (toe turned in)	4–1 (or S)
4. Cross RF in front of LF (toe turned out)	2 (or Q)
5. Side and slightly back LF (toe turned in)	3 (or Q)
6. Cross RF in front of LF (toe turned out)	4–1 (or S)
7. Side and slightly back LF (toe turned in)	2 (or Q)
8. Cross RF in front of LF (toe turned out)	3 (or Q)
9. Side and slightly back LF (toe turned in)	4–1 (or S)

Note: The lady's feet must also be placed in position without swivelling; she should not exaggerate the crossing movement of her RF, but place her R heel close to, or just past her L toe.

This fig. may be preceded by:

(1) The Forward Half Basic (steps 1–2 but without the turn normally made to L), man side and slightly back LF on step 3; lady forward RF between his feet.
(2) The Progressive Walk Back: on sixth step man's LF and lady's RF as No. (1) above.
(3) The Basic from Hockey Stick: third step as No. (1) above and regain normal hold.
(4) The Fan, man making ¼ turn L to face lady between steps 5–6, continuing with No. (1) above.

This fig. may be followed by:

(1) The Opening Out from Natural Top into Back Basic.
(2) The Closed Hip Twist.
(3) The Opening Out Movement into Reverse Top.
(4) The Cucarachas (to man's L on first).
(5) The Basic Movement.

Opening Out from Natural Top

MAN

Begin and end in Normal Hold.

	Count
1. Side LF, lowering L arm and leading lady to open out to R side	2 (or Q)
2. Replace weight on RF, commencing to turn lady to her L	3 (or Q)
3. Close LF to RF, continuing to turn lady to normal position	4–1 (or s)

LADY

Begin and end in Normal Hold

		Count
1. Turning strongly to R on ball of LF, step back RF releasing L heel	} Up to ½ turn R	2 (or Q)
2. Commencing to turn L, replace weight forward on LF	} Up to ½	3 (or Q)
3. Continuing to turn L to face man side RF (small step)	} turn L	4–1 (or s)

Man: Lead lady into Close Hold and turn body and feet ⅛ turn L, placing L heel to R toe with LF turned out.

Lady: Continuing to turn strongly to L (an extra ⅛ turn) to face man, step back and slightly to side on RF (toe of RF facing toe of man's LF) with R toe turned in.

(b) The man may step forward LF (short step) on step 1, with an overturn of the body to R. Replace weight on RF turning body slightly to L on step 2; step 3 as above.

This fig. may be preceded by:

(1) The Natural Top.
(2) The Alemana (overturned as lady, then make up to ¼ turn R on step 1 of Opening out).

This fig. may be followed by:

(1) The Backward Half Basic Movement (as man).
(2) If step 3 is overturned, Reverse Top.
(3) The Closed Hip Twist (steps 4–6).
(4) The Fan (steps 4–6).

This Rumba position is popular today. The lady has to retain a very stretched ankle and leg-line.

The Fan

MAN

Begin in Normal Hold, end in Fan Position (described at the beginning of the chapter).

		Count
1. Forward LF releasing R heel	Forward Half Basic Movement, making normal turn L	2 (or Q)
2. Replace weight on RF		3 (or Q)
3. Side LF		4–1 (or s)
4. Back RF (leading lady forward in line), releasing L heel		2 (or Q)
5. Replace weight on LF, leading lady with R hand to move back and to man's L side, then releasing R hand		3 (or Q)
6. Side RF, extending L arm sideways		4–1 (or s)

Note: The end of this figure, with the lady in Open Hold on L side of man and at right-angles to him, is known as 'Fan Position'.

LADY

Begin in Normal Hold, end in Fan Position (described at the beginning of the chapter).

		Count
1. Back RF releasing L heel	Backward Half Basic Movement, making normal turn L	2 (or Q)
2. Replace weight on LF		3 (or Q)
3. Side RF		4–1 (or s)
4. Forward LF towards man, releasing L heel		2 (or Q)
5. Back and slightly to side RF, turning to L and releasing L hand	¼ turn L	
		3 (or Q)
6. Back LF, still turning slightly		4–1 (or s)

Note: The man may turn ¼ to L on steps 5–6 to finish facing lady in Open Hold, the following figures are then the same as those given for Hockey Stick, but lady must close RF to LF on first step. After Hockey Stick lady's first step is always back RF. *For examination purposes, the Fan is described as having three steps (nos. 4–6) with an entry, which is usually the Forward Half Basic.*

This fig. may be preceded by:

(1) The Basic Movement.
(2) The Back Progressive Walks (into steps 4–6 of Fan).
(3) The Forward Progressive Walks.
(4) The Alemana.
(5) The Side Step.
(6) The Cucarachas (last one to man's R).
(7) The Hockey Stick (regaining normal hold on first part Fan).
(8) The Reverse Top.
(9) The Natural Top.

This fig. may be followed by:

(1) The Alemana.
(2) The Hockey Stick, or (if man turns) any of the figures which follow Hockey Stick.

The Closed Hip Twist

MAN

Begin in Normal Hold, end in Fan Position.

	Count
1. Side LF, lowering L arm and leading lady to open out to R side	2 (or Q)
2. Replace weight on RF, commencing to turn lady to her L	3 (or Q)
3. Close LF to RF, continuing to turn lady square, keeping L arm just above waist level	4–1 (or s)
4. Back RF, leading lady with pressure on base of R hand to swing her L hip forward	2 (or Q)
5. Replace weight forward on LF, leading lady to turn to her L, then release hold with R hand	3 (or Q)
6. Side RF, extending L arm sideways	4–1 (or s)

LADY

Begin in Normal Hold, end in Fan Position.

		Count
1. Turning strong to R on ball of LF, step back RF releasing L heel	Up to ½ turn R	2 (or Q)
2. Commencing to turn L, replace weight forward on LF	Up to ½	3 (or Q)
3. Continuing to turn L to face man, side RF (small step)	turn L	4–1 (or s)
4. Turning to R on RF, brush LF forward (small step) swinging L hip forward for the Hip Twist	⅜ turn R in the feet, but very little turn in shoulders	2 (or Q)
5. Turning to L on LF, step back and slightly to side on RF	½ turn L	3 (or Q)
6. Still turning slightly, back LF	⅛ turn L	4–1 (or s)

Note: The man may turn ¼ to L on steps 5–6 to finish facing lady in Open Hold; the following figures are then the same as those for Hockey Stick, but lady must close RF to LF on first step. After Hockey Stick lady's first step is always back RF. *For examination purposes the Closed Hip Twist is described as having three steps (nos. 4–6) with an entry, which is usually the Opening Out from Natural Top.*

Begin in Normal Hold, end in Fan Position (described at the beginning of the chapter).

This fig. may be preceded by:

(1) The Natural Top.
(2) The Alemana (overturned as lady, then make up to ¼ turn R on step 1 of Opening Out).

This fig. may be followed by:

(1) The Alemana.
(2) The Hockey Stick.
(3) The Reverse Top (steps 4–9): retain Close Hold and turn strongly to L on sixth step. Closed Hip Twist (man, side and slightly forward RF, lady, cross LF behind RF, toe turned out).

The *Alemana*

MAN

Begin in Fan Position, end in Normal Hold.

	Count
1. Forward LF, releasing R heel (L arm sideways to allow lady to close RF back to LF)	2 (or Q)
2. Replace weight on RF, leading lady to move forward	3 (or Q)
3. Close LF to RF, raising L arm, commencing to turn lady to her R	4–1 (or S)
4. Back RF, releasing L heel	2 (or Q)
5. Replace weight on LF	3 (or Q)
6. Close RF to LF	4–1 (or S)

(Steps 4–6 bracketed:) Turning lady to her R under L arm, then resume Normal Hold

Note: The man does not turn when dancing the Alemana. When lady overturns the Alemana, on the first step of the following figure the man may step forward LF (short step) with an overturn of the body to R.

LADY

Begin in Fan Position, end in Normal Hold.

		Count
1. Close RF back to LF		2 (or Q)
2. Forward LF (Progressive Walk)		3 (or Q)
3. Forward RF (Progressive Walk) raising R arm, turning slightly R towards man	⅛ turn R	4–1 (or S)
4. Forward LF		2 (or Q)
5. Forward RF		3 (or Q)
6. Forward LF		4–1 (or S)

(Steps 4–6 bracketed:) Three Progressive Walks on the spot, turning 1⅛ turns to R under man's L arm to face him. Resume Normal Hold

Note: The lady may overturn steps 4–6 of the Alemana, making 1⅜ turn R on these three steps to end at right-angles to man on his R side. The sixth step should still be placed forward into position, but owing to the extra turn on this step her LF will end side and slightly back. The lady may also overturn steps 4–6, making 1⅝ turn R on these three steps to end facing the same way as man on his R side. The sixth step is still forward LF, but owing to the extra ½ turn her LF will end almost back.

This fig. may be preceded by:

(1) The Fan.

(2) The Closed Hip Twist.

(3) The Cucaracha to L for man, followed by (a) steps 4–6 of Alemana, lady then makes 1 turn R; or (b) Cucaracha to R.

(4) The Hockey Stick (Alemana is then danced facing partner. Lady makes 1 turn).

(Continued on next page.)

This dramatic Paso Doble position conjures up an image of a matador draping a cape (his partner) around his shoulders.

This fig. may be followed by:

(1) The Basic Movement.
(2) The Cucarachas first on man's L.   } After normal amount
(3) The Fan.   of turn: 1¼ total

(4) The Closed Hip Twist (lady up to ¼ turn R on first step).

(5) The Opening Out Movement (lady up to ¼ R first step) into Back Basic for man.
(6) The Opening Out, man stepping side and slightly back LF on step 3, } After overturned
turning to R, continuing with Natural Top (lady's RF forward between his feet).   amount: 1½ total

(7) The Closed Hip Twist, lady making only slight body turn R on first step.
(8) The Opening out Movement (lady only slight body turn on first step) } After overturned
into Back Basic for man.   amount: 1¾ total

The Side Step

MAN

Begin and end in Normal Hold, facing wall.

	Count
1. Side LF	2 (or Q)
2. Close RF to LF	3 (or Q)
3. Side LF	4–1 (or S)
4. Close RF to LF	2 (or Q)
5. Side LF	3 (or Q)
6. Close RF to LF	4–1 (or S)

LADY

Begin and end in Normal Hold, backing wall.

	Count
1. Side RF	2 (or Q)
2. Close LF to RF	3 (or Q)
3. Side RF	4–1 (or S)
4. Close LF to RF	2 (or Q)
5. Side RF	3 (or Q)
6. Close LF to RF	4–1 (or S)

This fig. may be preceded by:

(1) The Basic Movement: man brushes LF to RF (without weight) on count 1 Backward Half, lady RF to LF (without weight) Forward Half.
(2) The Cucarachas (last one to man's R) if facing wall.

This fig. may be followed by:

(1) The Basic Movement.
(2) The Cucaracha(s) – first to man's L.
(3) The Cucaracha to L then steps 4–6 of Alemana (lady makes one turn R).

The Cucarachas

(Pressure Steps)

MAN

Begin and end in Normal Hold.

		Count
1. Side LF, pushing ball of foot into the floor, leaving part of weight on RF	Cucaracha to Left	2 (or Q)
2. Replace full weight on RF		3 (or Q)
3. Close LF to RF		4–1 (or S)
4. Side RF, pushing ball of foot into the floor, leaving part of weight on LF	Cucaracha to Right	2 (or Q)
5. Replace full weight on LF		3 (or Q)
6. Close RF to LF		4–1 (or S)

Repeat steps 1–6 if desired.

LADY

Begin and end in Normal Hold.

		Count
1. Side RF, pushing ball of foot into the floor, leaving part of weight on LF	Cucaracha to Right	2 (or Q)
2. Replace full weight on LF		3 (or Q)
3. Close RF to LF		4–1 (or S)
4. Side LF, pushing ball of foot into the floor, leaving part of weight on RF	Cucaracha to Left	2 (or Q)
5. Replace full weight on RF		3 (or Q)
6. Close LF to RF		4–1 (or S)

Repeat steps 1–6 if desired.

Note: The heel of the moving foot should make light contact with the floor on the pressure steps, and half weight or more should be transferred. The heel of the supporting foot should remain on the floor.

General Note on Cucarachas: They are usually danced sideways (as above description) but may also be danced forward, back, or turning in more advanced figures.

This fig. may be preceded by:

(1) The Basic Movement: man brushes LF to RF (without weight) on count 1 Backward Half, lady RF to LR (without weight) Forward Half.

(2) The Side Step.

(3) The Natural Top (man leads lady to close her LF to RF on step 9).

(4) The Alemana (normal amount of turn for lady).

This fig. may be followed by:

(1) The Basic Movement.

(2) The Fan.

(3) Steps 4–6 of Alemana (after Cucaracha Left as man) lady making one turn.

(4) The Progressive Walk Forward (lady back) curved to L.

The Hockey Stick

MAN

Begin in Fan Position, end in Open Hold.

	Count

1. Forward LF, releasing R heel (L arm sideways to allow lady to close RF back to LF) — 2 (or Q)
2. Replace weight on RF, leading lady to move forward — 3 (or Q)
3. Close (or nearly close) LF to RF, raising L arm — 4–1 (or S)
4. Back RF, commencing to turn lady to L under L arm — 2 (or Q)
5. Replace weight on LF, turning lady under L arm, commencing to turn slightly R towards her — ⅛ turn R — 3 (or Q)
6. Forward RF towards lady, still turning slightly, lowering L arm — 4–1 (or S)

Note: The fourth step should be small, as the lady is commencing to travel away from the man. The length of the sixth step can be adjusted according to whether the man wishes to resume Normal Hold on the following figure. The man should 'follow' the lady on this step, so that he finishes in a fairly close position.

LADY

Begin in Fan Position, end in Open Hold.

	Count

1. Close RF back to LF ⎫ Progressive Walks — 2 (or Q)
2. Forward LF ⎭ — 3 (or Q)
3. Forward RF, raising R arm — 4–1 (or S)
4. Forward LF (Prog. Walk) commencing to turn L under man's L arm — ⅛ turn L — 2 (or Q)
5. Continuing to turn L, step back and slightly to side on RF — ⅜ turn L — 3 (or Q)
6. Still turning slightly, back LF (now facing man) lowering R arm — ⅛ turn L — 4–1 (or S)

Note: The man has 'followed' the lady on the last step of Hockey Stick and ends rather close to her, therefore the lady must step *back* RF on first step of any following figure.

This fig. may be preceded by:

(1) The Fan.
(2) The Closed Hip Twist.

This fig. may be followed by:

(1) The Basic Movement, regaining Normal Hold between steps 2 and 3.

(2) The Basic Movement into Natural Top: after two steps Basic, without turning L, regain Normal Hold. Man side and slightly back LF on step 3, lady forward RF between his feet.

(3) The Alemana facing partner (lady makes one turn).

This Rumba Walk action looks very similar to an Opening Out movement.

The Reverse Top

MAN

Begin and end in Normal Hold, but rather close – man holding lady firmly with R hand not more than 1 or 2 inches (2.5–5cm) away – and make a continuous turn to the Left.

	Count
1. Side and slightly forward RF (R toe slightly turned in)	2 (or Q)
2. Pivot on toe of LF (in place) until heel of LF is opposite toe of RF	3 (or Q)
3. Side and slightly forward RF (as in step 1)	4–1 (or s)
4. Pivot on toe of LF (as in step 2)	2 (or Q)
5. Side and slightly forward RF (as in step 1)	3 (or Q)
6. Pivot on toe of LF (as in step 2)	4–1 (or s)
7. Side and slightly forward RF (as in step 1)	2 (or Q)
8. Pivot on toe of LF (as in step 2)	3 (or Q)
9. Side and slightly forward RF (as in step 1)	4–1 (or s)

Note: The amount of turn made on this figure is variable, but an approximate guide is 1½ to 1¾ turns to the Left.

LADY

Begin and end in Normal Hold, but rather close, and make a continuous turn to the Left.

	Count
1. Cross LF behind RF (L toe turned out)	2 (or Q)
2. Back and slightly to side RF (R toe turned in)	3 (or Q)
3. Cross LF behind RF (toe turned out)	4–1 (or s)
4. Back and slightly to side RF (toe turned in)	2 (or Q)
5. Cross LF behind RF (toe turned out)	3 (or Q)
6. Back and slightly to side RF (toe turned in)	4–1 (or s)
7. Cross LF behind RF (toe turned out)	2 (or Q)
8. Back and slightly to side RF (toe turned in)	3 (or Q)
9. Cross LF behind RF (toe turned out)	4–1 (or s)

General Notes on Reverse Top: The lady and man should face square to each other during this figure. The man's L toe should be kept on one spot, this being the centre around which his RF makes a circle. The lady dances Backward Progressive Walks turned strongly to left; her RF makes a larger circle than man's RF, and her LF (on the outside of the turn) describes a larger circle than her RF. Both lady and man maintain a naturally upright position throughout the Reverse Top, his weight being centralized over the toe of his LF.

The lady must lower her heels into the floor on each step, as in Backward Progressive Walks.

This fig. may be preceded by:

(1) The Opening Out from Natural Top, if turned to L on step 3 (see Note which follows description of this fig.).

(2) The Closed Hip Twist: retain Close Hold and turn strongly to L on last step Closed Hip Twist. Sixth step is then: man, side and slightly forward RF; lady, cross LF behind RF (toe turned out). Continue with steps 4–9 of Reverse Top.

This fig. may be followed by:

(1) The Basic Movement.

(2) First two steps Basic Movement: then (man) back LF leading lady outside on R side, swivelling her through into step 4–6 Closed Hip Twist; (lady) forward RF OP on R side, swivel LF forward turning strongly to R into steps 4–6 Closed Hip Twist.

(3) Steps 1–2 Basic Movement (without the turn L) into Natural Top; step 3 man side and slightly back LF, lady forward RF between his feet.

The Opening Out From Reverse Top

MAN

	Count
1, 2, 3, 4, 5 and 6. Dance the first 6 steps of the normal Reverse Top	2, 3, 4—1 (or QQS) 2, 3, 4—1 (or QQS)
7. Side RF, slightly forward, releasing lady with R hand	2 (or Q)
8. Close L heel to R instep	3 (or Q)
9. Side RF, extending L hand sideways	4—1 (or s)

LADY

	Count
1, 2, 3, 4, 5 and 6. Dance the first 6 steps of the normal Reverse Top	2, 3, 4—1 (or QQS) 2, 3, 4—1 (or QQS)
7. Back LF ⎫	2 (or Q)
8. Back RF ⎬ Curving to L to end in Fan Position	3 (or Q)
9. Back LF ⎭	4—1 (or s)

This fig. may be preceded by:

(1) The Opening Out Movement for Reverse Top (see Reverse Top).

This fig. may be followed by:

(1) The Alemana.
(2) The Hockey Stick.
(3) Steps 1, 2 and 3 of Alemana, then Natural Top.

The Open Hip Twist

MAN

	Count
1. Forward LF, raising R Heel	2 (or Q)
2. Replace weight to RF	3 (or Q)
3. Almost close LF to RF, bracing the L arm, leading lady to move closer	4—1 (or s)
4. Back RF, raising L heel	2 (or Q)
5. Replace weight to LF	3 (or Q)
6. Almost close RF to LF, turning to L slightly	4—1 (or s)

LADY

	Count
1. Back RF, raising L heel	2 (or Q)
2. Replace weight to LF	3 (or Q)
3. Forward RF, commencing to turn R on count 1	4—1 (or s)
4. Forward LF, turning ⅜ to R	2 (or Q)
5. Back RF, slightly to side ⎫ Turning ⅝	3 (or Q)
6. Back LF, end in Fan position ⎬ to L between 5 and 6	4—1 (or s)

This fig. may be preceded by:

(1) The Hockey Stick.
(2) The Spiral.

This fig. may be followed by:

(1) The Alemana.
(2) The Hockey Stick.
(3) Steps 1, 2 and 3 of the Alemana, then Natural Top.

The Spiral

MAN

	Count
1. Side LF, leading lady to open out to R side	2 (or Q)
2. Replace weight to RF	3 (or Q)
3. Close LF to RF, turning the lady to her L, raising L arm	4–1 (or S)
4. Back RF, small step, raising L heel	2 (or Q)
5. Replace weight to LF	3 (or Q)
6. Forward RF, slightly to side, turning to L to face partner	4–1 (or S)

Note: Steps 1, 2 and 3 are the Opening Out Movement.

LADY

	Count
1. Step back RF, making up to ½ turn to R	2 (or Q)
2. Replace weight to LF (small step), commencing to turn L	3 (or Q)
3. Side RF, turning to L to face partner, the pivot on R toe ½ turn to L, keeping L leg across front of R leg (the turn is made under partner's L arm)	4–1 (or S)
4. Forward LF, turning ⅛ to L	2 (or Q)
5. Back RF, slightly side	3 (or Q)
6. Back LF, facing partner	4–1 (or S)

(Turning ½ to L between steps 5 and 6)

Note: Steps 1, 2 and 3 are the Opening Out Movement.

This fig. may be preceded by:

(1) The Basic Movement.
(2) The Side Step.
(3) The Natural Top.

This fig. may be followed by:

(1) The Open Hip Twist.
(2) The Alemana (from facing partner in open position).

Hand to Hand

MAN

Begin in Closed Facing Position in Double Hold and finish in Closed Facing Position.

	Count
1. LF back in R Side-by-Side Position	2 (or Q)
2. Replace weight to RF	3 (or Q)
3. LF to side	4–1 (or S)
4. RF back in L Side-by-Side Position	2 (or Q)
5. Replace weight to LF	3 (or Q)
6. RF to side	4–1 (or S)
7–9. Repeat steps 1–3	2, 3, 4–1

Note: Take Double Hold at end of preceding step. Lead lady to turn by holding arms steady as turn is made. Release with L hand on steps 1 and 7, regain Double Hold on 3 and 6, release with R hand on step 4.

LADY

Begin in Closed Facing Position in Double Hold and finish in Closed Facing Position.

	Count
1. RF back in R Side-by-Side Position	2 (or Q)
2. Replace weight to LF	3 (or Q)
3. RF to side	4–1 (or S)
4. LF back in L Side-by-Side Position	2 (or Q)
5. Replace weight to RF	3 (or Q)
6. LF to side	4–1 (or S)
7–9. Repeat steps 1–3	2, 3, 4–1

Note: From the time man takes Double Hold at end of preceding step both arms should be held steady.

This fig. may be preceded by:

(1) The Alemana (stepping to side on 6).
(2) The Spot Turn to L.

(Continued on next page.)

Rick Valenzuela and Melissa Dexter of the USA demonstrate a Forward Walk action with dramatic gestures.

This fig. may be followed by:

From steps 3 or 9

(1) The Spot Turn to L.

(2) 4–6 Closed Hip Twist (leading lady with R hand to turn R, changing her R hand into man's L to complete the figure). Lady will turn ¼ to R and ½ to L on her Closed Hip Twist.

(3) 4–6 of Basic Movement or Fan.

(4) 4–6 Alemana.

Man may close LF to RF on step 9 and lead lady into a Spiral Turn continuing with 4–6 of Spiral.

From step 6

(1) The Basic Movement.

(2) The Spot Turn to R.

(3) The Fan.

Spot Turns

These are three forward walks danced solo by man or lady circling to the L or R, or a solo turn in which one foot may remain on a spot around which the circle is made. A complete turn is normally used.

Spot Turn to Left

Normally commenced with RF–RLR.

This fig. may be preceded by:

(1) The Hand to Hand.

(2) The Spot Turn to R.

This fig. may be followed by:

(1) The Basic Movement.

(2) The Fan.

(3) The Spot Turn to R.

(4) The Side Step.

Spot Turn to Right

Normally commenced with LF–LRL.

This fig. may be preceded by:

(1) The Spot Turn to L.

(2) 1–6 of Hand to Hand.

This fig. may be followed by:

(1) 4–6 Basic Movement.

(2) The Progressive Walks Backward.

(3) The Spot Turn to L.

19

The Samba

The Samba is a gay and lively dance in which there are figures to suit all grades of dancers.

The Music is usually written in 2/4 time (i.e. two beats to each bar of music), but is also sometimes written in 4/4 time.

The Tempo varies considerably, from 45 up to 65 bars per minute, but a good average speed is 50 bars per minute.

Rhythms. There are three main rhythms used in the basic figures: 1, 2 (or SS); 1 & 2 (or S a S); and SQQ; another rhythm of QQQQ is used, but only in one figure – the Corta Jaca.

The Beat Values of the above counts are (in 2/4 time) '1, 2' – 1 beat, 1 beat; '1 a 2'–3/4, 1/4, 1 beat; 'SQQ' – 1 beat 1/2 , 1/2. In 4/4 time the beat values would be doubled, i.e., '1 a 2' becomes 1 1/2, 1/2 and 2 beats etc. The figures are really quite simple to learn, but changing from one rhythm to another requires practice.

The Hold. The man's left arm is held a little higher than in the standard ballroom dances; the left hand should be about on a level with the top of his left ear. The lady places her left hand on the man's right shoulder and the couple dance slightly apart in most basic figures. Where a closer hold is used this is mentioned at the beginning of the description of the figure.

The Basic Movements of the Samba, that is, all the movements which are counted 1,2 or 1 a 2, are danced with slight downward bouncing or dropping action which is characteristic of the Samba. This action is obtained through the flexing and straightening of the knees as the weight is taken on to the foot, co-ordinated with the lowering of the feet on to the floor. In figures with 1 a 2 count, the knees will straighten slightly on the 'a' count, and the dropping action will be used on the counts of 1, 2. When the timing of a figure is SQQ, or QQQQ, the dropping action is not used. A full description of the dropping action is on page 170.

Footwork. Each forward step should be taken on to the ball of the foot, going immediately on to the flat of the foot. An exception to this is the strong heel lead used on the first step of the Corta Jaca. When a step is counted 'a', it is taken on the ball of the foot.

Leading the figures in the Samba may present difficulty at first. The man should remember that it is necessary to lead by using both arms, often with tension in the arms to initiate a lead. The lady responds by keeping her arms ready to tauten immediately she receives his lead, relaxing them when her partner has indicated which figure he intends to dance.

Rhythm Dancing. The figures on the following pages may be danced either in a spacious ballroom, or in a crowded room by using the close hold all the time and very small steps.

Natural Basic Movement

MAN

Begin and end in Normal Hold. Count

1. Forward RF, bending then straightening the knees — 1 (or s)
2. Close LF to RF without weight on LF, bending then straightening the knees — 2 (or s)
3. Back LF, bending then straightening the knees — 1 (or s)
4. Close RF to LF without weight on RF, bending then straightening the knees — 2 (or s)

Gradual turn R of up to ¼ on four steps

Repeat *ad lib.*

LADY

Begin and end in Normal Hold. Count

1. Back LF, bending then straightening the knees — 1 (or s)
2. Close RF to LF without weight on RF, bending then straightening the knees — 2 (or s)
3. Forward RF, bending then straightening the knees — 1 (or s)
4. Close LF to RF without weight on LF, bending then straightening the knees — 2 (or s)

Gradual turn R of up to ¼ on four steps

Repeat *ad lib.*

This fig. may be preceded by:

(1) The Reverse Basic (steps 1, 2).
(2) The Outside Basic.
(3) The Whisk (to man's L).
(4) The Progressive Basic.
(5) The Rock (on man's LRL).
(6) The Corta Jaca (into steps 3, 4 of Natural Basic).

This fig. may be followed by:

(1) The Reverse Basic (after steps 1, 2 of Natural Basic).
(2) The Whisk (to man's R).
(3) The Outside Basic Movement (if facing wall).
(4) The Progressive Basic (if facing diag. wall).
(5) The Corta Jaca (if facing wall).
(6) The Rocks (if facing LOD).

*Modern Samba contains many rhythmic actions done on the spot. Here, Neil Dewer and
Lorraine Kuznik of England show confidence and flair.*

Reverse Basic Movement

MAN

Begin and end in Normal Hold.

Count

1. Forward LF, bending then straightening the knees — 1 (or s)
2. Close RF to LF without weight on RF, bending then straightening the knees — Gradual turn L of — 2 (or s)
3. Back RF, bending then straightening the knees — up to ¼ on four steps — 1 (or s)
4. Close LF to RF, without weight on LF, bending then straightening the knees — 2 (or s)

Repeat *ad lib.*

LADY

Begin and end in Normal Hold.

Count

1. Back RF, bending then straightening the knees — 1 (or s)
2. Close LF to RF without weight on LF, bending then straightening the knees — Gradual turn L of — 2 (or s)
3. Forward LF, bending then straightening the knees — up to ¼ on four steps — 1 (or s)
4. Close RF to LF, without weight on RF, bending then straightening the knees — 2 (or s)

Repeat *ad lib.*

This fig. may be preceded by:

(1) The Reverse Basic (steps 1, 2).
(2) The Whisk (to man's R).
(4) The Outside Basic (steps 1–6).
(6) The Rock (on man's RLR).

This fig. may be followed by:

(1) The Natural Basic (after steps 1, 2 of Reverse Basic).
(2) The Whisk (to man's L).
(3) The Progressive Basic (after steps 1, 2 of Reverse Basic if facing diag. wall).
(4) The Outside Basic (after steps 1, 2 of Reverse Basic if facing wall).
(5) The Rocks (after steps 1, 2 of Reverse Basic or after complete Reverse Basic continue with steps 4–6 of Rocks).
(6) The Bota Fogo in Promenade (if facing wall).
(7) The Travelling Bota Fogo (if facing LOD).
(8) The Bow (leading lady into Close Hold at end of Reverse Basic).

Outside Basic Movement

MAN

Begin and end facing wall in Normal Hold, and on each count use the same bending and straightening action as described in Natural and Reverse Basic Movements.

		Count
1. Forward RF		1 (or s)
2. Close LF to RF, without weight on LF, turning L to face diag. wall	⅛ turn L	2 (or s)
3. Back LF, lady outside on R side		1 (or s)
4. Close RF to LF, without weight on RF, lady on R side		2 (or s)
5. Forward RF, outside lady		1 (or s)
6. Close LF to RF, without weight on LF, turning R to face wall	⅛ turn R	2 (or s)
7. Back LF (lady in line)		1 (or s)
8. Close RF to LF, without weight on RF		2 (or s)

LADY

Begin and end backing wall in Normal Hold, and on each count use the same bending and straightening action as described in Natural and Reverse Basic Movements.

		Count
1. Back LF		1 (or s)
2. Close RF to LF, without weight on RF, turning L to back diag. wall	⅛ turn L	2 (or s)
3. Forward RF, outside man on R side		1 (or s)
4. Close LF to RF, without weight on LF, man on R side		2 (or s)
5. Back LF, man outside on R side		1 (or s)
6. Close RF to LF, without weight on RF, turning R to back wall	⅛ turn R	2 (or s)
7. Forward RF (facing man)		1 (or s)
8. Close LF to RF, without weight on LF		2 (or s)

Note: The Outside Basic is based on two Natural Basic Movements, turning the first to L and the second to R. The closing steps in Natural, Reverse, Outside, and Progressive Basics must be firm closes of the feet, with the heels in light contact with the floor and a certain amount of pressure in the whole of the foot at the end of each closing step.

This fig. may be preceded by:

(1) The Natural Basic (turned to face wall).

(2) The Reverse Basic (steps 1–2) if facing wall.

(3) The Outside Basic.

(4) The Whisk (to man's L).

(5) The Progressive Basic, then Outside Basic beginning diag. wall and turned to face LOD.

(6) The Travelling Bota Fogo (on man's LRL), then steps 5–8 of Outside Basic beginning diag. centre and ending diag. wall. Man turns square to lady on step 6 or step 8.

This fig. may be followed by:

(1) The Natural Basic.

(2) The Reverse Basic (after steps 1–6 of Outside Basic).

(3) The Whisk (to man's R).

(4) The Corta Jaca.

(5) The Travelling Bota Fogo commenced with man's RF (OP) facing LOD (after steps 1–4 Outside Basic turning ¼ L on step 2).

(6) The Samba Walks in PP. Man turns lady to PP on steps 3–4 of Outside Basic, continuing with Walk on RF. Lady dances 1–2 of Outside Basic, then Bota Fogo on RLR, continuing with Walk on LF.

Natural Basic Movement

(Alternative method)

MAN

	Count
1. Forward RF, bending knees at end of step	1 (or s)
2. Close LF to RF, part of weight on LF, straightening the knees	'a'
3. Transfer full weight to RF, bending then straightening the knees	2 (or s)
4. Back LF, bending knees at end of step	1 (or s)
5. Close RF to LF, part of weight on RF, straightening the knees	'a'
6. Transfer full weight to LF, bending then straightening the knees	2 (or s)

LADY

		Count
1.		1 (or s)
2.	Dance steps 4, 5, 6	'a'
3.		2 (or s)
4.		1 (or s)
5.	Dance steps 1, 2, 3	'a'
6.		2 (or s)

Note: The method of dancing the Basic Movements with this alternative count is a natural interpretation if the Samba music is played at a medium to fast tempo. It is perfectly permissible for the lady to dance 1 'a' 2 (three steps) to each bar of music whilst the man is dancing 1, 2 (two steps) or vice versa. Dancing two steps only to each bar of music is, however, less tiring.

Also note that the bending and straightening of the knees on each of the 1, 2 counts gives the characteristic 'dropping' action in these figures. A more detailed description of the action used is as follows:

MAN

	Count
1. Forward RF on ball of foot, lowering immediately to flat of foot; as weight is taken on to RF bend both knees	1

	Count
2. Begin to close LF towards RF and straighten both knees; as LF closes to RF (firmly, on ball then flat of foot but without weight) bend both knees	2
3. Begin to move LF back and straighten both knees; as weight is taken on to LF bend both knees	1
4. Begin to close RF towards LF and straighten both knees; as RF closes to LF (firmly, on ball then flat of foot but without weight) bend both knees	2

Straighten both knees as RF begins to move forward into repeat of step 1

Progressive Basic Movement

MAN

Begin and end facing diag. wall in Normal Hold.

	Count
1. Forward RF	1 (or s)
2. Close LF to RF, firmly, but without weight	2 (or s)
3. Side LF	1 (or s)
4. Close RF to LF, firmly, but without weight	2 (or s)

Repeat *ad lib.* to obtain progression along LOD.

LADY

Begin and end backing diag. wall in Normal Hold.

	Count
1. Back LF	1 (or s)
2. Close RF to LF, firmly, but without weight	2 (or s)
3. Side RF	1 (or s)
4. Close RF to LF, firmly, but without weight	2 (or s)

Repeat *ad lib.* to obtain progression along LOD.

Note: There is only a very slight lilt in this figure, as opposed to the deliberate bending and straightening of the knees which give the downward bounce in the other Basic Movements. The action of closing the feet on steps 2 and 4 of Progressive Basic is delayed to get a much sharper feeling as the feet are brought together.

(Continued on next page.)

Samba Walks are frequently taken in the Shadow Position when the couple dance together in perfect synchronization.

The Progressive Basic Movement may be preceded by:

(1) The Natural Basic (turned to diag. wall).
(2) The Reverse Basic (steps 1–2) if facing diag. wall.
(3) The Progressive Basic.
(4) The Whisk (on man's L) if turned to diag. wall.

The Progressive Basic Movement may be preceded by:

(1) The Natural Basic.
(2) The Reverse Basic (after steps 1–2 of Progressive Basic).
(3) The Corta Jaca (turned to face wall).
(4) The Bow (after steps 1–2 Progressive Basic).

Samba Whisks

Normally, both man and lady begin and end facing wall in Normal Hold. As in Basic Movements, there is a dropping action, occurring on the count of 1 and on the count of 2.

MAN

		Count
1. Side RF (small step)		1 (or s)
2. Cross L toe behind RF (approximately toe to heel) with toe lightly turned out	Whisk to R	'a'
3. Replace weight on RF in place		2 (or s)
4. Side LF (small step)		1 (or s)
5. Cross R toe behind LF (approximately toe to heel) with toe lightly turned out	Whisk to L	'a'
6. Replace weight on LF in place		2 (or s)

LADY

		Count
1. Side LF (small step)		1 (or s).
2. Cross R toe behind LF (approximately toe to heel) with toe lightly turned out	Whisk to L	'a'
3. Replace weight on LF in place		2 (or s)
4. Side RF (small step)		1 (or s)
5. Cross L toe behind RF (approximately toe to heel) with toe lightly turned out	Whisk to R	'a'
6. Replace weight on RF in place		2 (or s)

Note: The Whisks may be turned gradually to R or L, but it is more usual to dance them facing wall as described above. The lady and man face square to each other; the hips do not turn.

The Whisk to R may be preceded by:

(1) The Natural Basic.
(2) The Outside Basic.
(3) Steps 1-3 of Bow.
(4) The Whisk to L.

The Whisk to R may be followed by:

(1) The Reverse Basic.
(2) The Whisk to L.
(3) The Promenade Bota Fogo.
(4) The Promenade Samba Walk, having turned on man's R. Whisk approx. ¼ to L.

The Whisk to L may be preceded by:

(1) The Reverse Basic.
(2) The Bow.
(3) The Promenade Samba Walk on man's RF, turning L. Whisk approx. ¼ to R to face wall.
(4) The Whisk to R.

The Whisk to L may be followed by:

(1) The Natural Basic.
(2) The Whisk to R.
(3) The Outside Basic.
(4) The Corta Jaca.
(5) The Progressive Basic (if L Whisk is turned to diag. wall).

Promenade Samba Walks

MAN

Begin and end facing LOD in PP and Normal Hold.

	Count
1. Forward LF relaxing knees and moving hips slightly forward	1 (or s)
2. Back RF, very small step on toe with part weight, commencing to straighten knees and hips to normal position	'a'
3. Transfer full weight to LF drawing it slightly back, regaining normal position in hips and knees	2 (or s)
4. Forward RF relaxing knees and moving hips slightly forward	1 (or s)
5. Back LF, very small step on toe with part weight, commencing to straighten knees and hips to normal position	'a'
6. Transfer full weight to RF drawing it slightly back, regaining normal position in hips and knees	2 (or s)

Repeat ad lib., progressing gradually along LOD.

LADY

Begin and end facing LOD in PP and Normal Hold.

	Count
1. Forward RF relaxing knees and moving hips slightly forward	1 (or s)
2. Back LF, very small step on toe with part weight, commencing to straighten knees and hips to normal position	'a'
3. Transfer full weight to RF drawing it slightly back, regaining normal position in hips and knees	2 (or s)
4. Forward LF relaxing knees and moving hips slightly forward	1 (or s)
5. Back RF, very small step on toe with part weight, commencing to straighten knees and hips to normal position	'a'
6. Transfer full weight to LF drawing it slightly back, regaining normal position in hips and knees	2 (or s)

Repeat ad lib., progressing gradually along LOD.

Note: The shoulders must be kept level and steady throughout this movement. To achieve this, be sure to take the full weight of the body into steps 1 and 4.

This fig. may be preceded by:

(1) The Whisk (to man's R turned approx. ¼ L to PP).

(2) The Promenade Bota Fogo (on man's LRL) then steps 4–6 Samba Walks.

(3) The Outside Basic (steps 1–4) turning lady to PP on fourth step, continue with steps 4–6 Samba Walks.

Note: Lady dances steps 1–2 of Outside Movement, then Promenade Bota Fogo on RLR, continuing with steps 4–6 Samba Walks.

This fig. may be followed by:

(1) The Whisk (to man's L turned approx. ¼ R to face wall).

(2) The Promenade Bota Fogo (on man's RLR turning into Counter PP) after steps 1–3 of Samba Walks.

(3) The Natural Basic Movement (commenced in PP turning R to face lady on step 2), taken after steps 1–3 of Samba Walks.

Corta Jaca

MAN

Begin and end facing wall in Normal Hold.

	Count
1. Strong step forward RF with heel lead (no dropping action) leading lady with a slight push of the arms	S
2. Forward and very slightly leftwards on LF on heel (do not lower to flat foot) keeping L knee straight	Q
3. Slide RF leftwards, keeping foot flat and knee very slightly relaxed	Q
4. Back and very slightly leftwards on toe of LF (do not lower to flat foot) relaxing L knee	Q
5. Slide RF leftwards, keeping foot flat and knee very slightly relaxed	Q

Repeat steps 2, 3, 4, 5 ad lib., and end with steps 2, 3.

Note: The RF should not move forward or back, only sideways, progressing gradually along LOD, and should move level with (but not crossed behind or in front of) the LF. On step 1, man lowers his L arm and tenses both arms to lead the lady to move back.

LADY

Begin and end backing wall in Normal Hold.

	Count
1. Strong step back LF (no dropping action) keeping arms firm for man's lead	S
2. Back and very slightly rightwards on RF on toe (do not lower to flat foot) keeping R knee straight	Q
3. Slide LF rightwards, keeping foot flat and knee very slightly relaxed	Q
4. Forward and very slightly rightwards on RF on heel (do not lower to flat foot) keeping R knee straight	Q
5. Slide LF rightwards, keeping foot flat and knee very slightly relaxed	Q

Repeat steps 2, 3, 4, 5 ad lib. and end with steps 2, 3.

Note: The LF should not move forward or back, only sideways, progressing gradually along LOD and should move level with (but not crossed behind or in front of) the RF.

This fig. may be preceded by:

(1) The Natural Basic (turned to face wall).
(2) The Reverse Basic, steps 1–2 (turned to face wall).
(3) The Whisk (to man's L).
(4) The Outside Basic.
(5) The Progressive Basic (followed by Corta Jaca turned to face wall).
(6) The Rock (on man's LRL at a corner).

This fig. may be followed by:

(1) The Natural Basic (steps 3–4 with or without turn).
(2) The Whisk (to man's L).

This is a Promenade Movement in Samba, a Rocks figure to the right, arms open, and performed with exuberance.

The Rocks

MAN

Begin and end facing LOD in Normal Hold.

	Count
1. Forward RF, lowering left arm slightly and preparing lady to receive his lead by tension in his arms	S
2. Rock forward on LF	Q
3. Rock back on RF	Q
4. Forward LF	S
5. Rock forward on RF	Q
6. Rock back on LF	Q

Repeat ad lib.

Note: The man should dance the Rocks without turning his feet. Both feet should face LOD throughout this figure. It is optional whether the 'slow' steps are (a) ball, flat of foot, or (b) heel, flat.

LADY

Begin and end backing LOD in Normal Hold.

	Count
1. Back LF, foot straight and backing LOD	S
2. Swing RF back with a circular movement from the knee, and place R toe behind L heel (toe turned out)	Q
3. Replace weight forward on LF	Q
4. Back RF, straightening the foot to back LOD	S
5. Swing LF back with a circular movement from the knee, and place L toe behind R heel (toe turned out)	Q
6. Replace weight forward on RF	Q

Repeat ad lib.

Note: There is a slight turning out movement in the hips as the feet are swung into position on steps 2 and 5.

This fig. may be preceded by:

(1) The Natural Basic.

(2) The Reverse Basic (steps 1–2).

(3) The Reverse Basic (steps 1–4, continuing with steps 4–6 of Rocks).

(4) The Bow (without the leaning action on steps 4–6), continuing with steps 4–6 of Rocks.

This fig. may be followed by:

(1) The Natural Basic.

(2) The Reverse Basic (after steps 1–3 of Rocks).

(3) The Bow (after steps 1–3 of Rocks).

(4) The Outside Basic (at a corner).

(5) The Corta Jaca (at a corner).

Bota Fogo

(In Promenade)

Both man and lady begin in Normal Hold facing wall, end in PP. Use dropping action on counts of 1, 2, straightening on 'a' counts.

MAN

		Count
1. Forward LF		1 (or s)
2. Side RF commencing to turn L, leading lady to PP	⅛ turn L	'a'
3. Replace weight on LF, still turning slightly, now in PP		2 (or s)
4. Forward and across on RF in PP		1 (or s)
5. Side LF commencing to turn right, leading lady to Counter PP	¼ turn R	'a'
6. Replace weight on RF, still turning slightly, now in Counter PP		2 (or s)
7. Forward and across on LF in Counter PP		1 (or s)
8. Side RF commencing to turn left, leading lady to PP	¼ turn L	'a'
9. Replace weight on LF, still turning slightly, now in PP		2 (or s)

Repeat steps 4—9 if desired.

Note: The hold with man's right hand should be kept fairly loose to enable him to dance comfortably when in Counter PP.
The weight of the body should be kept central during this figure, therefore some weight should be retained on the supporting foot when stepping to side on the 'a' counts.

LADY

		Count
1. Back RF		1 (or s)
2. Side LF commencing to turn R	⅛ turn R	'a'
3. Replace weight on RF, still turning slightly, now in PP		2 (or s)
4. Forward and across on LF in PP		1 (or s)
5. Side RF commencing to turn L		'a'
6. Replace weight on LF, still turning slightly, now in Counter PP	¼ turn L	2 (or s)
7. Forward and across on RF in Counter PP		1 (or s)
8. Side LF commencing to turn R		'a'
9. Replace weight on RF, still turning slightly, now in PP	¼ turn R	2 (or s)

Repeat steps 4—9 if desired.

Note: The weight of the body should be kept central during this figure, therefore some weight should be retained on the supporting foot when stepping to side on the 'a' counts. This figure (unlike the Travelling Bota Fogo) is not danced in sQQ rhythm.

This fig. may be preceded by:

(1) The Natural Basic.

(2) The Whisk (to man's R).

(3) The Bow (if facing wall).

(4) The Promenade Samba Walk (on man's LRL), commencing with steps 4—6 of Bota Fogo.

This fig. may be followed by:

(1) The Samba Walk on PP (on man's RLR).

(2) The Natural Basic commenced in PP (man turns R to face lady on step 2).

(3) The Natural Basic as above for steps 1—2, continuing forward LF (as man) into Reverse Basic.

Bota Fogo

(Travelling)

MAN

Begin facing LOD in Normal Hold, end facing diag. to centre, lady on R side. Use dropping action on counts of 1, 2, straightening on 'a' counts.

		Count
1. Forward LF in line with lady		1 (or s)
2. Side RF commencing to turn to L, leading lady to turn L	⅛ turn L	'a'
3. Replace weight on LF, still turning slightly		2 (or s)
4. Forward RF, outside lady on her R side		1 (or s)
5. Side LF, commencing to turn R	¼ turn R	'a'
6. Replace weight on RF, still turning slightly		2 (or s)
7. Forward LF outside lady on her L side		1 (or s)
8. Side RF, commencing to turn L	¼ turn L	'a'
9. Replace weight on LF, still turning slightly		2 (or s)

Repeat steps 4–9 if desired.

Note: The weight of the body should be kept central during this figure, as in Promenade Bota Fogo.

LADY

Begin backing LOD in Normal Hold, end backing diag. to centre, man on R side. Use dropping action on counts of 1, 2, straightening on 'a' counts.

		Count
1. Back RF		1 (or s)
2. Side LF, commencing to turn L	¼ turn L	'a'
3. Replace weight on RF, still turning slightly		2 (or s)
4. Back LF		1 (or s)
5. Side RF, commencing to turn R	¼ turn R	'a'
6. Replace weight on LF, still turning slightly		2 (or s)
7. Back RF		1 (or s)
8. Side LF, commencing to turn L	¼ turn L	'a'
9. Replace weight on RF, still turning slightly		2 (or s)

Repeat steps 4–9 if desired.

Note: When danced to slow or medium tempo, the figure may be timed SQQ. The dropping and straightening action will not then be used and slightly less turn will be made.

This fig. may be preceded by:

(1) The Reverse Basic (turned to face LOD).

(2) The Bow (turned to face LOD).

(3) The Outside Movement (steps 1–4, man turning ¼ L to face LOD) then commence Travelling Bota Fogo OP from step 4, making ⅛ turn R on steps 5–6.

This fig. may be followed by:

(1) The Outside Movement (steps 5–8) man turning square to lady either on step 6 or step 8.

(2) The Bow (commenced OP) after steps 4–6 of Travelling Bota Fogo, preferably in SQQ timing. Man turns square to lady on step 2 of Bow.

Note on Promenade and Travelling Bota Fogos

MAN AND LADY

On counts of 'a 2' the toes should be as near as possible on a parallel line with the foot which has stepped on counts '1'.

The Bota Fogo may be danced with man or lady moving back. The steps are the same as given for the lady in the Bota Fogo (Travelling) starting from step 4 and ending with step 9. These six steps may be repeated.

This fig. may be preceded by:

(1) The Steps 1–2 of Outside Basic Movement commenced facing against LOD.
(2) The Reverse Basic (steps 1.2). Commenced with partner in line.
(3) The Reverse Turn (steps 1, 2, 3).

This fig. may be followed by:

(1) The Outside Basic Movement (steps 3–8).

This figure may be danced in Normal Hold or in PP.

The Bow

MAN

Begin in any direction, leading lady into Close Hold at end of preceding figure. No dropping action.

		Count
1. Forward LF, leaning forward very slightly from the waist		S
2. Side RF, retaining slight lean	Approx. ¼ turn L	Q
3. Close LF to RF, retaining slight lean		Q
4. Back RF, leaning back very slightly from the waist		S
5. Side LF, retaining slight lean	Approx. ¼ turn L	Q
6. Close RF to LF, retaining slight lean		Q

Repeat ad lib.

LADY

Begin in any direction, according to previous figure, in Close Hold. No dropping action.

	Count
1. Back RF, leaning back very slightly from the waist	S
2. Side LF, retaining slight lean	Q
3. Close RF to LF retaining slight lean	Q
4. Forward LF leaning forward very slightly from the waist	S
5. Side RF, retaining slight lean	Q
6. Close LF to RF, retaining slight lean	Q

This fig. may be preceded by:

(1) The Reverse Basic.
(2) The Natural Basic (steps 1–2).
(3) The Outside Basic (steps 1–6).
(4) The Whisk (to man's R).
(5) The Progressive Basic (steps 1–2).
(6) The Rocks (steps 1–3).
(7) The Travelling Bota Fogo, after step 6 continue with Bow (taking step 1 OP).

This fig. may be followed by:

(1) The Reverse Basic.
(2) The Travelling Bota Fogo (if facing LOD).
(3) The Promenade Bota Fogo (if facing wall).
(4) The Whisk to man's L (if facing wall).
(5) The Whisk to man's R (after steps 1–3 of Bow, if facing wall).

The Volta

(From Samba Whisks)

MAN

Dance 1 and 2 of the Natural Right Basic, followed by the Whisk to L and the Whisk to R, ending with weight on RF.

	Count
1. Place L heel to R toe, turning to L	1 (or s)
2. Move RF slightly to R	'a'
3. Draw L heel to R toe, turning to L	2 (or s)
4. Move RF slightly to R	'a'
5. Draw L heel to R toe, turning to L	1 (or s)
6. Move RF slightly to R	'a'
7. Draw L heel to R toe, turning to L	2 (or s)

Dance the Whisk to R and the Whisk to L, ending with weight on LF, and follow with the Volta, turning to R.

	Count
1. Draw R heel to L toe, turning to R	1 (or s)
2. Move LF slightly to L	'a'
3. Draw R heel to L toe, turning to R	2 (or s)
4. Move LF slightly to L	'a'
5. Draw R heel to L toe, turning to R	1 (or s)
6. Move LF slightly to L	'a'
7. Draw R heel to L toe, turning to R	2 (or s)

Dance the Whisk to L and follow with the Natural Right Basic.

LADY

Dances normal opposite movements.

Reverse Turn

MAN

Begin in Normal Hold facing LOD and end in Normal Hold facing diag. to wall.

		Count
1. Forward LF	} ⅛ turn L	1 (or s)
2. Side and slightly back RF		'a' (or s)
3. Cross LF in front of RF		2 (or Q)
4. Back RF	} ½ turn L	1 (or s)
5. Side LF almost closed to RF		'a' (or Q)
6. Close RF to LF		2 (or Q)

Note: If following with another Reverse Turn make ½ turn to L over 1–3. There may be a slight inclination of the body to the L on steps 2 and 3 and to the R on steps 5 and 6.

LADY

		Count
1.	} Dances steps 4, 5, 6	1 (or s)
2.		'a' (or Q)
3.		2 (or Q)
4.	} Dances steps 1, 2, 3	1 (or s)
5.		'a' (or Q)
6.		2 (or Q)

Note: There may be a slight inclination of the body to the R on steps 2 and 3 and to the L on steps 5 and 6.

This fig. may be preceded by:

(1) First half of Natural Basic Movement.
(2) The Reverse Basic Movement.
(3) The Reverse Turn.
(4) First half of The Rocks.

This fig. may be followed by:

(1) The Reverse Basic Movement.
(2) The Whisk to L.
(3) The Bota Fogo commencing LF forward.
(4) The Bota Fogo commencing LF back.
(5) Reverse Turn.

20

The Cha-Cha-Cha

The Cha-Cha-Cha is still the most popular of all the Latin-American dances.

The Music is easily distinguishable. The melodic notes are invariably played short or staccato. The music is usually in 4/4 time, sometimes 2/4, and the ideal tempo is 32 bars per minute, although the Cha-Cha-Cha is often played quicker than this.

Timing. The Cha-Cha-Cha is a Cuban dance, based on the Rumba, and (as in Rumba) the Cuban dancers take the forward or leading step off the second beat of the bar of music.

Starting the Dance. The correct way is to stand with the feet slightly apart and the weight on the LF as man: step side on RF (very narrow step) *on the first beat of the bar of music* (lady normal opposite), then forward LF (lady back RF) into the Basic Movement counting 'Step, Step, Cha-Cha-Cha'. All the figures can then be counted in this way.

Some dancers in the ballrooms in England step forward LF into the first step of Basic Movement, using the first beat of the bar of music and counting 1, 2, Cha-Cha-Cha, and this method is quite good for the beginner. However, the 2, 3, 4 & 1 count explained above is the only timing accepted in any of the medal tests, examinations or competitions organized by leading Societies of Teachers of Dancing, and is simplicity itself if the dancer uses the starting method given and then continues counting the phonetically rhythmic 'Step, Step, Cha-Cha-Cha'.

The Hold is the same as for the Samba (see page 165); refer to the chapter on Rumba for descriptions of Open Hold and Fan Position.

Footwork is the same as in Rumba, steps being taken on the ball of the foot immediately lowering to the flat foot. Heel leads are not used.

The *Beat Values* are:

Count:	Step	Step	Cha	Cha	Cha
OR	2	3	4	&	1
OR	Slow	Slow	Quick	Quick	Slow
Beat Values:	1	1	½	½	1

Basic Movement

MAN

Begin and end in Normal Hold; a gradual turn to L is made on each step. Make about a ¼ turn L over the 10 steps.

		Count
1. Forward LF releasing R heel		Step
2. Replace weight on RF	Forward	Step
3. Side LF	Half Basic	Cha
4. Move RF towards LF	Movement	Cha
5. Side LF, small step		Cha
6. Back RF releasing L heel		Step
7. Replace weight on LF	Backward	Step
8. Side RF	Half Basic	Cha
9. Move LF towards RF	Movement	Cha
10. Side RF, small step		Cha

Repeat ad lib.

LADY

Begin and end in Normal Hold; a gradual turn to L is made on each step. Make about a ¼ turn L over the 10 steps.

		Count
1. Back RF releasing L heel		Step
2. Replace weight on LF	Backward	Step
3. Side RF	Half Basic	Cha
4. Move LF towards RF	Movement	Cha
5. Side RF, small step		Cha
6. Forward LF releasing R heel		Step
7. Replace weight on RF	Forward	Step
8. Side LF	Half Basic	Cha
9. Move RF towards LF	Movement	Cha
10. Side LF, small step		Cha

Repeat ad lib.

This fig. may be preceded by:

(1) The Alemana.

(2) The Hand to Hand.

(3) The Hockey Stick, regaining Normal Hold for Basic.

(4) The Time Step, to man's R. ⎫ regaining Normal
(5) The Spot Turn, to man's L. ⎭ Hold for Basic.

(6) The Natural Top.

(7) The Opening Out from Natural Top; continue with Backward Half Basic.

(8) The Cross Basic.

This fig. may be followed by:

(1) The Cross Basic.

(2) The Fan.

(3) The Time Step (to man's L) releasing hold at end of Backward Half Basic.

(4) The Hand to Hand: on steps 3–5 of Forward Half Basic man turns ¼ R releasing hold with R hand; continue with steps 6–10 of Hand to Hand. Lady normal opposite.

(5) The Spot Turn (to man's R) releasing hold at end of Backward Half Basic.

(6) The Spot Turn (to man's L) releasing hold at end of Forward Half Basic.

(7) The Natural Top. On steps 3–5 Forward Half Basic leading lady to step forward between man's feet.

Bophuthatswana couple Neille Matjie and Salome Sechele are captured by the camera in a rhythmic action in the Cha-Cha-Cha, using hip rhythm on the spot.

The Fan

MAN

Begin in Normal Hold, end in Fan Position.

		Count
1. Forward LF, releasing R heel	} Forward Half Basic Movement, making slight turn L	Step
2. Replace weight on RF		Step
3. Side LF, turning slightly to L		Cha
4. Move RF towards LF		Cha
5. Side LF, small step		Cha
6. Back RF (leading lady forward in line) releasing L heel		Step
7. Replace weight on LF, leading lady with R hand to move back and to man's left side, then releasing R hand		Step
8. Side RF	} Extending L arm sideways, to finish with lady on L side of man	Cha
9. Move LF towards RF		Cha
10. Side RF, small step		Cha

LADY

Begin in Normal Hold, end in Fan Position.

		Count
1. Back RF, releasing L heel	} Backward Half Basic Movement, making slight turn L	Step
2. Replace weight on LF		Step
3. Side RF		Cha
4. Move LF towards RF		Cha
5. Side RF, small step		Cha
6. Forward LF towards man, releasing R heel		Step
7. Back and slightly to side RF turning to L and releasing L hand	} ¼ turn L	Step
8. Back LF still turning slightly		Cha
9. Move RF back towards LF		Cha
10. Back LF, small step		Cha

Note: For examination purposes the Fan is described as having five steps (Nos. 6–10), with an entry, which is usually the Forward Half Basic.

This fig. may be preceded by:

(1) The Basic Movement.
(2) The Alemana.
(3) The Hand to Hand (man turns square to lady and resumes Normal Hold).
(4) The Time Step (resuming Normal Hold).
(5) The Spot Turns (resuming Normal Hold).
(6) The Natural Top.
(7) The Hockey Stick (resuming Normal Hold).
(8) The Cross Basic.

This fig. may be followed by:

(1) The Alemana.
(2) The Hockey Stick.
(3) If man turns L (approx. ¼ on steps 8–10 of the Fan to face lady), Forward Half Basic Movement (regaining Normal Hold) into Natural Top; or Forward Half Basic into steps 6–10 of Alemana.

Alemana

MAN

Begin in Fan Position, end in Normal Hold.

	Count
1. Forward LF, releasing R heel (L arm sideways to allow lady to close RF to LF)	Step
2. Replace weight on RF, leading lady to move forward	Step
3. Side LF ⎫	Cha
4. Move RF towards LF ⎬ raising L arm, commencing to turn lady to her R	Cha
5. Side LF, small step	Cha
6. Back RF releasing L heel ⎫	Step
7. Replace weight on LF ⎪	Step
8. Side RF ⎬ turning lady to her R under left arm, then resume Normal Hold	Cha
9. Move LF towards RF ⎪	Cha
10. Side RF, small step ⎭	Cha

Note: The man does not turn when dancing the Alemana.

LADY

Begin in Fan Position, end in Normal Hold.

	Count
1. Close RF back to LF	Step
2. Forward LF	Step
3. Forward RF ⎫	Cha
4. Move RF towards LF ⎬ raising R arm and turning ⅛ R towards man	Cha
5. Side LF, small step ⎭	Cha
6. Forward LF ⎫	Step
7. Forward RF ⎪	Step
8. Forward LF ⎬ turning 1⅛ turns to R under man's L arm to face him. Resume Normal Hold	Cha
9. Move RF towards LF ⎪	Cha
10. Forward LF, small step ⎭	Cha

This fig. may be preceded by:

(1) The Fan.
(2) The Closed Hip Twist.
(3) The Hockey Stick (Alemana is then danced facing partner. Lady makes 1 turn).

This fig. may be followed by:

(1) The Basic Movement.
(2) The Cross Basic.

(3) The Fan.
(4) The Hand to Hand (on last part of Alemana man takes lady's L hand in his R hand and turns approx. ¼ to L, releasing hold with L hand).
(5) The Closed Hip Twist.

Note: The lady may overturn the Alemana: see chapter on Rumba for descriptions of following movements to this figure.

Hand to Hand

MAN

Begin with lady's L hand in man's R hand, normally both facing LOD. Lady on right side of man.   Count

1. Back LF against LOD, releasing R heel		Step
2. Replace weight on RF		Step
3. Side LF	turning approx. ½ turn R. to face against LOD, releasing hold with R hand	Cha
4. Move RF towards LF	and taking lady's R hand in man's L	Cha
5. Side LF, small step		Cha
6. Back RF, releasing L heel (lady on L side of man)		Step
7. Replace weight on LF		Step
8. Side RF	turning approx. ½ turn L to face LOD, releasing hold with L hand and	Cha
9. Move LF towards RF	taking lady's L hand in man's R	Cha
10. Side RF, small step		Cha

Both man and lady repeat steps 1–10 if desired.

LADY

Begin facing LOD on man's right side.   Count

1. Back RF against LOD, releasing heel		Step
2. Replace weight on LF		Step
3. Side RF	turning approx. ½ turn L to face against LOD	Cha
4. Move LF towards RF		Cha
5. Side RF, small step		Cha
6. Back LF, releasing R heel		Step
7. Replace weight on RF		Step
8. Side LF	turning approx. ½ turn R to face LOD	Cha
9. Move RF towards LF		Cha
10. Side LF, small step		Cha

This fig. may be preceded by:

(1) The Forward Half Basic Movement, man turning ¼ R on steps 3–5 and releasing hold with R hand. Continue with steps 6–10 of Hand to Hand.

(2) The Alemana, man turning ¼ L on steps 8–10 taking lady's L hand in R hand and releasing hold with L hand (lady overturns her Alemana).

(3) The Opening Out from Natural Top, man turning slightly R on steps 3–5 and releasing hold with R hand. Continue with steps 6–10 of Hand to Hand.

(4) After steps 1–5 of Hand to Hand (but retaining hold of lady with R hand) lead lady into steps 6 and 7 of Hip Twist, changing lady's R hand to man's L on steps 8–10. End in Fan Position.

Note: Lady makes only ¼ turn to R for the Hip Twist on step 6, and ½ to L between steps 7–10.

This fig. may be followed by:

(1) Forward Half Basic Movement, man turning only ¼ L to face lady on steps 7–10 of Hand to Hand, and resuming Normal Hold.

(2) Left Time Step (man) turning only ¼ L to face lady on steps 7–10 of Hand to Hand, and releasing hold.

(3) Backward Half Basic Movement, man turning only ¼ R to face lady on steps 2–5 of Hand to Hand, and resuming Normal Hold.

Swivel actions are very popular in competitions.

Hockey Stick

MAN

Begin in Fan Position, end in Open Hold.

	Count
1. Forward LF, releasing R heel (L arm sideways to allow lady to close RF to LF)	Step
2. Replace weight on RF, leading lady to move forward	Step
3. Side LF	Cha
4. Move RF towards LF ⎫ raising L arm	Cha
5. Side LF, small step ⎭	Cha
6. Back RF (small step), commencing to turn lady to L under L arm	Step
7. Replace weight on LF ⎫ ⅛ turn R between	Step
8. Forward RF ⎪ steps 7–10, turning	Cha
9. Move LF towards RF ⎬ lady underneath	Cha
10. Forward RF towards lady, lowering L arm ⎭ L arm	Cha

Note: The length of the last three steps can be adjusted, according to whether the man wishes to resume Normal Hold on the following figure. The man should 'follow' the lady so that he finishes in a fairly close position.

LADY

Begin in Fan Position, end in Open Hold.

	Count
1. Close RF to LF	Step
2. Forward LF	Step
3. Forward RF ⎫	Cha
4. Move LF towards RF ⎬ raising R arm	Cha
5. Forward RF, small step ⎭	Cha
6. Forward LF commencing to turn L under man's L arm ⅛ turn L	Step
7. Back and slightly to side RF ⎫ continuing to turn	Step
8. Back LF ⎪ another ½ turn L	Cha
9. Move RF towards LF ⎬ to finish facing man, lowering	Cha
10. Back LF, small step ⎭ arm at end	Cha

This fig. may be preceded by:

(1) The Fan.

(2) The Closed Hip Twist.

This fig. may be followed by:

(1) The Basic Movement (regaining Normal Hold between steps 2–3).

(2) The Basic Movement into Natural Top: after two steps Basic, regain Normal Hold. Man side and slightly back LF on step 3, lady forward RF between his feet.

(3) The Alemana facing partner (lady makes one turn; her first step is back RF).

Time Step

MAN

Begin and end facing lady, about two feet (half a metre) away and not holding.

		Count
1. Cross LF behind RF	⎫	Step
2. Replace weight on RF	⎪	Step
3. Side LF	⎬ Left Time Step	Cha
4. Move RF towards LF	⎪	Cha
5. Side LF, small step	⎭	Cha
6. Cross RF behind LF	⎫	Step
7. Replace weight on LF	⎪	Step
8. Side RF	⎬ Right Time Step	Cha
9. Move LF towards RF	⎪	Cha
10. Side RF, small step	⎭	Cha

Repeat *ad lib.* in groups of 5 steps.

LADY

Begin and end facing man, about two feet (half a metre) away and not holding.

		Count
1. Cross RF behind LF	⎫	Step
2. Replace weight on LF	⎪	Step
3. Side RF	⎬ Right Time Step	Cha
4. Move LF towards RF	⎪	Cha
5. Side RF, small step	⎭	Cha
6. Cross LF behind RF	⎫	Step
7. Replace weight on RF	⎪	Step
8. Side LF	⎬ Left Time Step	Cha
9. Move RF towards LF	⎪	Cha
10. Side LF, small step	⎭	Cha

Repeat *ad lib.* in groups of 5 steps.

This fig. may be preceded by:

(1) The Basic Movement, man releasing hold at end of Backward Half.

(2) The Hockey Stick, releasing hold at end.

(3) The Spot Turn to Left into Left Time Step.

(4) The Spot Turn to Right into Right Time Step.

(5) The Cross Basic, man releasing hold at end of Backward Half.

(6) The Alemana, releasing hold at end.

(7) The Natural Top, releasing hold at end.

(8) The Hand to Hand, man turning to face lady (only ¼ L) on steps 7–10, releasing hold.

This fig. may be followed by:

(1) The Basic Movement, regaining Normal Hold.

(2) The Fan, regaining Normal Hold.

(3) The Hand to Hand, man turning ¼ L on steps 8–10 of Right Time Step taking lady's L hand in his R hand.

(4) The Spot Turn to Right, after Right Time Step.

(5) The Spot Turn to Left, after Left Time Step.

(6) The Cross Basic, regaining Normal Hold.

Spot Turns

MAN

Begin and end facing lady, about two feet (half a metre) away and not holding.

Count

1. Forward LF turning to right	Approx.			Step
2. Forward RF continuing to turn	¾ turn R			Step
3. Side LF			Spot Turn to Right	Cha
4. Move RF towards LF	continuing to turn approx. ¼ turn R to face			Cha
5. Side LF, small step	lady			Cha
6.				Step
7.				Step
8	Right Time Step whilst lady dances her Spot Turn to Right			Cha
9.				Cha
10.				Cha

Repeat these 10 steps if desired, or dance *Left Time Step* facing lady as usual
(lady dances Right Time Step), then:

1. Forward RF turning to left	Approx.			Step
2. Forward LF continuing to turn	¾ turn L			Step
3. Side RF			Spot Turn to Left	Cha
4. Move LF towards RF	continuing to turn approx. ¼ turn L to face lady			Cha
5. Side RF, small step				Cha
6.				Step
7.				Step
8.	Dance Left Time Step whilst lady dances her Spot Turn to Left			Cha
9.				Cha
10.				Cha

Repeat these 10 steps if desired, or dance *Right Time Step* facing lady as usual (lady dances Left Time Step).

Note: Man may assist lady by leading her into Spot Turns with his hand on the back of her shoulder, releasing hold as lady dances solo turn.

Pelvic Rolls in the Shadow Position are performed in many of the Latin American dances. The arms, bodies and legs should all be matching throughout the action.

Spot Turns

LADY

Begin and end facing man, about two feet (half a metre) away and not holding.

			Count
1.			Step
2.			Step
3.	Dance Right Time Step whilst man dances his Spot Turn to Right		Cha
4.			Cha
5.			Cha
6. Forward LF turning to right	Approx. ¾ turn R		Step
7. Forward RF continuing to turn		Spot Turn to Right	Step
8. Side LF			Cha
9. Move RF towards LF	continuing to turn approx. ¼ turn R to face man		Cha
10. Side LF, small step			Cha

Repeat these 10 steps if desired, or dance *Right Time Step* facing man as usual
(man dances Left Time Step), then:

1.			Step
2.			Step
3.	Dance Left Time Step whilst man dances his Spot Turn to Left		Cha
4.			Cha
5.			Cha
6. Forward RF turning to left	Approx. ¾ turn L		Step
7. Forward LF continuing to turn		Spot Turn to Left	Step
8. Side RF			Cha
9. Move LF towards RF	continuing to turn approx. ¼ turn L to face man		Cha
10. Side RF, small step			Cha

Repeat these 10 steps if desired, or dance *Left Time Step* facing man as usual (man dances Right Time Step).

The Spot Turn to Right may be preceded by:

(1) The Basic Movement, man releasing hold at end of Backward Half.
(2) The Hockey Stick, releasing hold at end.
(3) The Right Time Step.
(4) The Alemana, releasing hold at end.

The Spot Turn to Right (10 steps) may be followed by:

(1) The Basic Movement, regaining Normal Hold.
(2) The Fan, regaining Normal Hold.
(3) The Hand to Hand, turning ¼ L on steps 8–10 of R Time Step and taking lady's L hand in R hand.
(4) The Left Time Step into Spot Turn L.
(5) The Cross Basic, regaining Normal Hold.
(6) The Hand to Hand, turning to face LOD.

The Spot Turn to Left may be preceded by:

(1) The Forward Half Basic, releasing hold at end.
(2) The Left Time Step.

The Spot Turn to Left (10 steps) may be followed by:

(1) The Backward Half Basic, regaining Normal Hold.
(2) The Right Time Step into Spot Turn R.
(3) The Backward Half Cross Basic, regaining Normal Hold.
(4) The Hand to Hand (steps 6–10).

The Natural Top

MAN

Begin and end in Normal Hold, and make a continuous turn R throughout this figure.

	Count
1. Cross RF behind LF (R toe turned out)	Step
2. Side and slightly forward LF (L toe turned in)	Step
3. Move R toe towards L heel (toe turned out)	Cha
4. Side and slightly forward LF (toe turned in)	Cha
5. Move R toe towards L heel (toe turned out)	Cha
6. Side and slightly forward LF (toe turned in)	Step
7. Cross RF behind LF (toe turned out)	Step
8. Side and slightly forward LF (toe turned in)	Cha
9. Move R toe towards L heel (toe turned out)	Cha
10. Side and slightly forward LF (toe turned in)	Cha
11. Cross RF behind LF (toe turned out)	Step
12. Side and slightly forward LF (toe turned in)	Step
13. Close RF to LF	Cha
14. } Hesitate with weight on RF	Cha
15. }	Cha

Note: For examination purposes the first Cha-Cha-Cha count is described as a very small chassé.

Man may also dance the following alternative on steps 13–15.

13. Move R toe towards L heel (toe turned out)	Cha
14. Side and slightly forward LF (toe turned in)	Cha
15. Close RF to LF	Cha

Turn approximately 1½ to 1¾ turns to the right on the complete figure.

LADY

Begin and end in Normal Hold, and make a continuous turn R throughout the figure.

	Count
1. Side and slightly back LF (L toe turned in)	Step
2. Cross RF in front of LF (R toe turned out)	Step
3. Side and slightly back LF (toe turned in)	Cha
4. Cross RF in front of LF (heel to toe, toe turned out)	Cha
5. Side and slightly back LF (toe turned in)	Cha
6. Cross RF in front of LF (toe turned out)	Step
7. Side and slightly back LF (toe turned in)	Step
8. Cross RF in front of LF (heel to toe, toe turned out)	Cha
9. Side and slightly back LF (toe turned out)	Cha
10. Cross RF in front of LF (heel to toe, toe turned out)	Cha
11. }	Step
12. }	Step
13. } Repeat steps 1–5	Cha
14. }	Cha
15. }	Cha

Turn approximately 1½ to 1¾ turns to the right on the complete figure.

Note: During the Natural Top the lady and man describe a circle around a common centre midway between them.

This fig. may be preceded by:

(1) The Forward Half Basic (steps 1–2), man side and slightly back LF for Cha-Cha-Cha, lady forward RF between his feet.

(2) The Fan, making ¼ turn L to face lady between steps 7–10, continue with No. (1) above and into Natural Top, resuming Normal Hold.

(3) The Hockey Stick, continue with No. (1) and Natural Top, resuming Normal Hold.

This fig. may be followed by:

(1) The Basic Movement.

(2) The Opening Out from Natural Top into Backward Half Basic for man.

(3) The Closed Hip Twist.

(4) The Hand to Hand, man turns ¼ L at end of Natural Top, releases hold with L hand and dances steps 1–2 with lady in crook of R arm.

(5) The Time Step, releasing hold.

Opening Out from the Natural Top

MAN

Begin and end in Normal Hold.

	Count
1. Forward LF, turning slightly towards lady (lowering L arm to lead her to open out to R side)	Step
2. Replace weight on RF, turning slightly to L (commencing to turn lady to her L)	Step
3. Side LF (continuing to turn lady to normal position)	Cha
4. Move RF towards LF	Cha
5. Side LF, small step	Cha

Note: Man may dance the following alternative on steps 1–5:

1. LF to side (Step)

2. Replace weight on RF (Step)

3. Close LF to RF and hesitate or mark time on the spot with RF and LF (Cha-Cha-Cha)

LADY

Begin and end in Normal Hold.

		Count
1. Back RF	Up to ½ turn R	Step
2. Replace weight on LF commencing to turn L		Step
3. Side RF, small step, continuing to turn to face man	Up to ½ turn L	Cha
4. Move LF towards RF		Cha
5. Side RF, small step		Cha

This fig. may be preceded by:

(1) The Natural Top.

(2) The Alemana.

This fig. may be followed by:

(1) The Basic Movement (steps 6–10).

(2) The Closed Hip Twist (steps 6–10).

(3) The Fan (steps 6–10).

(4) The Hand to Hand (steps 6–10), man turns slightly R on steps 3–5 of Opening Out from Natural Top releasing hold with R hand.

Three Cha-Cha-Chas

Three Cha-Cha-Cha Chassés may be danced consecutively, forward or backward. They would be counted '4 and 1, 2 and 3, 4 and 1'.

Forward. After 1–7 of Basic Movement. No turn can be made or a gradual turn to the L over the 9 steps. Follow with the Basic Movement.

Forward. After 1–7 of Hockey Stick. No turn can be made or a gradual turn to the L over the 9 steps. Follow with the Basic Movement, regaining Normal Hold.

Forward in R Side-by-Side Position. Taken after step 2 or step 12 of the Hand to Hand. No turn can be made or ⅛ to L and ⅛ to R on alternate chassé. Follow with a Spot Turn (man to L, lady to R).

Forward in L Side-by-Side Position. Taken after step 7 of the Hand to Hand. No turn can be made or ⅛ to L and ⅛ to R on alternate chassé. Follow with a Spot Turn (man to R, lady to L).

Backward. May be danced in Closed Facing Position or in Open Facing Position. Taken after step 2 of the Basic Movement. No turn can be made or a gradual turn to the R or L. Follow with steps 6–10 of the Basic Movement when no turn has been made or with steps 6–10 of the Fan when curving to the L or the Natural Top when curving to the R.

Note: The Three Cha-Cha-Chas may be danced in Normal Hold, in Double Hold or without Hold, in Closed or Open Facing Position.

Closed Hip Twist

MAN

	Count
Begin in Normal Hold, end in Fan Position.	
1. Forward LF, turning slightly towards lady (lowering L arm to lead her to open out to R side)	Step
2. Replace weight on RF, turning slightly to L (commencing to turn lady to her L)	Step
3. Side LF (continuing to turn lady to normal position)	Cha
4. Move RF towards LF	Cha
5. Side LF, small step	Cha
6. Back RF, releasing L heel (leading lady with pressure on base of R hand to swing her L hip forward)	Step
7. Replace weight on LF (leading lady to turn to her L then release hold with R hand)	Step
8. Side RF	Cha
9. Move LF towards RF } Extending L arm sideways	Cha
10. Side RF, small step	Cha

Note: The first three steps are the Opening Out from Natural Top – see description which follows that figure of alternative way of dancing steps 1–5.

LADY

		Count
Begin in Normal Hold, end in Fan Position.		
1. Back RF	Up to ½ turn R	Step
2. Replace weight on LF commencing to turn L		Step
3. Side RF, small step, continuing to turn to face man	Up to ½ turn L	Cha
4. Move LF towards RF		Cha
5. Side RF, small step		Cha
6. Turning to R on RF, brush LF forward (small step) swinging L hip forward for the Hip Twist	⅜ turn R in the feet, but very little turn in shoulders	Step
7. Turning to L on LF, step back and slightly to side on RF	½ turn L	Step
8. Back LF		Cha
9. Move RF back towards LF	continuing to turn ⅛ L	Cha
10. Back LF, small step		Cha

This fig. may be preceded by:

(1) The Natural Top.

(2) The Alemana (overturned as lady, then make up to ¼ turn R on step 1 of Opening Out).

This fig. may be followed by:

(1) The Alemana.

(2) The Hockey Stick.

Note: For examination purposes the Closed Hip Twist is described as having five steps (Nos. 6–10), with an entry, which is usually the Opening Out from Natural Top.

New York

MAN

Begin and end in Normal Hold.	Count
1. Forward LF making ¼ turn to R to side by side position	Step
2. Replace weight on RF and begin turning slightly to L	Step
3, 4, 5. Short step to side with LF to chassé RF, LF and completing ¼ turn to L	Cha-Cha-Cha
6. Forward RF making ¼ turn to L to side by side position	Step
7. Replace weight on LF and begin turning slightly to R	Step
8, 9, 10. Short step to side with RF to chassé LF, RF and completing ¼ turn to R	Cha-Cha-Cha

Method of leading into this figure.

Release hold with man's R hand on the Cha-Cha-Cha count of the preceding figure leading lady to L side by side position so that inside hands (man's L, lady's R) are joined for step 1 described above. Release hold with man's L hand and take lady's L hand in man's R hand while turning to facing position over steps 3, 4, 5. Then lead lady to R side by side position with inside hands (man's R, lady's L) on step 6. Release hold with man's R hand and take lady's R hand in man's L hand while turning to facing position over steps 8, 9, 10.

LADY

Begin and end in Normal Hold.	Count
1. Forward RF making ¼ turn to L side by side position	Step
2. Replace weight on LF and begin turning slightly to R	Step
3, 4, 5. Short step to side with RF to chassé LF, RF and completing ¼ turn to R	Cha-Cha-Cha
6. Forward LF making ¼ turn to R to side by side position	Step
7. Replace weight on RF	Step
8, 9, 10. Short step to side with LF to chassé RF, LF and completing ¼ turn to L	Cha-Cha-Cha

This fig. may be preceded by:

(1) The Basic Movement.
(2) The Alemana.
(3) The Hockey Stick.

This fig. may be followed by:

(1) The Basic Movement.
(2) The Fan.
(3) The Spot Turn to R.
(4) The Spot Turn L, following step no. 5

The Cross Basic

MAN

Begin and end in Normal Hold.		Count
1. Cross LF rather tightly in front of RF		Step
2. Back RF	Step	
3. Side LF	Cha	
4. Move RF towards LF	Turning up to	Cha
5. Side LF, small step	¼ turn L	Cha
6. Cross RF rather tightly behind LF		Step
7. Forward LF		Step
8. Side RF		Cha
9. Move LF towards RF	Turning up to	Cha
10. Side RF, small step	¼ turn L	Cha

LADY

Normal opposite. The lady dances steps 6–10, whilst man dances 1–5, and continues with steps 1–5 as man dances 6–10.

Note: The Cross Basic can be substituted for the ordinary Basic Movement, therefore this figure can be preceded and followed by the same figures as those given for Basic Movement.

A slight sway is permissible: to the Left on steps 1, 2; to the Right on steps 6, 7.

This Samba Walk is also danced in the Shadow Position.

21

The Paso Doble

The Paso Doble has gained in popularity in this country since many promoters included this dance in ballroom competitions. It is rarely danced by the general public, however, although the simple basic movements are very suitable for crowded ballrooms and restaurants, and the dance has been popular for many years on the Continent, particularly in France. It is a Spanish dance and the movements danced by the man are symbolic of those made by the torero (or matador) in the bullring. The lady represents the cape and her movements suggest the cape passes made during a bull-fight.

The Music is very stirring and is usually played in 2/4 or 6/8 – which is March time. Some Paso Dobles are written in 3/4 time, but 2/4 is exclusively used for medal tests and competitions. The tempo is 62 bars per minute.

Beat Values are

2/4 – normally one step for each beat of music;
3/4 – normally one step for each beat of music;
6/8 – normally one step for each three beats of music.

The counts given in all the following descriptions assume 2/4 time signature.

The Hold for this dance is similar to the Hold for English style dances, except that the arms are held rather higher, resulting in a closer top position. When figures are danced in Promenade or Counter Promenade Position, the body contact is lost and the lady is led to a position 12–18 inches (30–45 cm) away from the man. The normal dancing position cannot then be maintained as the man often uses both arms to lead his partner, consequently arm movements are introduced. They should not be exaggerated. When the partners are moving in Promenade or Counter Promenade Position the man's left and the lady's right arms should be lowered to just above waist level, and the arms held in a soft curve; the man should also loosen the hold with his right hand to allow freedom of movement.

Footwork. The Basic Movement, Sur Place and Chassés are danced with the weight over the balls of the feet and the heels just off (or lightly touching) the floor. Forward marching steps are normally taken with a heel lead.

The Basic Movement

MAN OR LADY

Normally begin with RF as man and LF as lady on the first beat of the bar of music. Dance a series of small steps forward or back (straight, or curved either to R or L), changing weight from one foot to the other (on the ball of each foot) with the knees very slightly relaxed. The steps are taken with pressure into the floor.

Count 1, 2, 1, 2, etc.

Sur Place

MAN OR LADY

This movement is danced on the spot and is a series of weight changes from one foot to the other, keeping the legs, feet and ankles close together. It may be danced without turn, or turned gradually to R or to L. If turn is used, the feet and ankles sometimes part slightly.

The Sur Place is a fundamental movement of the Paso Doble and may be used to precede and follow all figures.

As the weight is changed from the ball of one foot to the other, there is a slight movement from the ankles and the knees must be kept slightly relaxed. The steps are taken with pressure into the floor.

Begin on RF (normally RF as man, LF as lady),

Count 1

and as weight is changed to the other foot

Count 2 etc.

Chassés to the Left

MAN

Begin facing wall.	Count
1. Take weight on to RF in place (Sur Place)	1
2. Side on LF, small step	2
3. Close RF to LF	1
4. Side on LF, small step	2

Repeat steps 3–4 *ad lib*.

Note: The Chassés to Left may be danced travelling along LOD facing wall, or curved to left round a corner to new LOD.

LADY

Begin backing wall.	Count
1. Take weight on to LF in place (Sur Place)	1
2. Side on RF, small step	2
3. Close LF to RF	1
4. Side on RF, small step	2

Repeat steps 3–4 *ad lib*.

Note: The Chassés to Left may be danced travelling along LOD backing wall, or curved to left round a corner to new LOD.

This fig. *may be preceded by*:

(1) The Basic Movement.
(2) The Sur Place.

This fig. *may be followed by*:

(1) The Basic Movement.
(2) The Sur Place.

Chassés to the Right

MAN

Begin facing centre.	Count
1. Side RF, small step	1
2. Close LF to RF	2
3. Side RF, small step	1
4. Close LF to RF	2

Repeat *ad lib*.

Note: The Chassés to Right may be danced travelling along LOD backing wall, or curved to left round a corner to new LOD.

LADY

Begin backing centre.	Count
1. Side LF, small step	1
2. Close RF to LF	2
3. Side LF, small step	1
4. Close RF to LF	2

Repeat *ad lib*.

Note: The Chassés to Right may be danced travelling along LOD facing wall, or curved to left round a corner to new LOD.

This fig. *may be preceded by*:

(1) The Basic Movement.
(2) The Sur Place.
(3) The Promenade Link.

This fig. *may be followed by*:

(1) The Basic Movement.
(2) The Sur Place.

The Elevations

This movement (which can take the form of side chassés to left or right) is a stretching upwards, bracing the body and knees and rising high on toes, followed by a lowering to flat foot with heels touching the floor and knees relaxing slightly. The most popular form of Elevation is as follows:

Elevation with Side Chassés to Left

MAN

Begin facing wall. | Count

	Count
1. Take weight on to RF in place (Sur Place or Appel)	1
2. Side LF, small step, stretching up	2
3. Close RF to LF, remaining up	1
4. Side LF, small step, remaining up	2
5. Close RF to LF, remaining up	1
6. Side LF, small step, immediately lowering to flat foot	2
7. Close RF to LF, remaining down	1
8. Side LF, small step, remaining down	2
9. Close RF to LF, remaining down	1
10, 11, 12, 13 – Repeat steps 2, 3, 4, 5	2, 1, 2, 1

Note: Continue with Sur Place on LF lowering to normal position for this figure, or this popular ending:

14. Side LF, lowering slightly, turning lady to PP	2
15. Forward and across RF (heel lead) in PP	1
16. Close LF to RF, turning lady square and rising slightly to level of Sur Place	2

LADY

Begin backing wall. | Count

	Count
1. Take weight on to LF in place (Sur Place or Appel)	1
2. Side RF, small step, stretching up	2
3. Close LF to RF, remaining up	1
4. Side RF, small step, remaining up	2
5. Close LF to RF, remaining up	1
6. Side RF, small step, immediately lowering to flat foot	2
7. Close LF to RF, remaining down	1
8. Side RF, small step, remaining down	2
9. Close LF to RF, remaining down	1
10, 11, 12, 13 – Repeat steps 2, 3, 4, 5	2, 1, 2, 1

Note: Continue with Sur Place on RF, lowering to normal position for this figure, or this popular ending:

14. Side RF, lowering slightly, turning to PP	2
15. Forward and across LF (heel lead) in PP	1
16. Close RF to LF, turning left to face man and rising slightly to level of Sur Place	2

This fig. may be preceded by:

(1) The Sur Place.
(2) The Appel.
(3) The Basic Movement Forward (if facing wall).

This fig. may be followed by:

(1) The Sur Place.
(2) The Promenade ending described as steps 14–16.
(3) The Sur Place (LF as man) turning to PP followed by Huit.

Richard and Els Porter of England are very accomplished Paso Doble dancers. They illustrate their excellent body-tone and style in this strongly presented position.

Alternative Ways of Dancing the Elevations

MAN

Count

(1) Begin facing wall and after Sur Place or
Appel on RF dance one chassé up, LF, RF   1
(side, close),

one chassé down, LF, RF (side, close),   2, 1, 2, 1
repeating *ad lib*. The stretching up and
lowering occurs on the *side steps* in this case,
and the figure progresses leftwards.

(2) Begin facing wall and after Sur Place or   1
Appel on RF dance 1½ chassés up, LF, RF,
LF (side, close, side), followed by: 2, 1, 2

RF, LF, RF, LF down (close, side, close,
side), followed by: 1, 2, 1, 2

RF, LF, RF, LF up (close, side, close, side).   1, 2, 1, 2

The stretching up and lowering occurs on
the *closing steps* in this case, and the figure
progresses leftwards.

(3) Begin facing centre and (after Sur Place
or Appel on LF, count 2) dance chassés to
right: two chassés up (1, 2, 1, 2), two
down (1, 2, 1, 2); *or* one chassé up (1, 2), one
down (1, 2); *or* one step (side) up, count 1,
one down (close), count 2. If facing centre
follow only with Sur Place or Basic Movement.

LADY

Normal opposite.

Deplacement

MAN

Begin facing LOD, diag. to centre, or diag. to wall.

Count

1. Forward RF (heel lead)	1
2. Forward LF (heel lead)	2
3. Side RF (ball of foot) − ¼ turn L	1
4. Close LF to RF, with pressure on ball of LF	2

Note: To lead this figure successfully, man must *incline
his body forward* on the preceding Sur Place on his LF.
A sharp lowering of the left (and lady's right) arms
on step 3 is popular, gradually returning the arms to
Normal Hold in approximately the next four counts
of following Sur Place.

LADY

Begin backing LOD, backing diag. to centre, or
backing diag. to wall.

Count

1. Back LF	1
2. Back RF	2
3. Side LF (ball of foot) − ¼ turn L	1
4. Close RF to LF with pressure on ball of RF	2

This fig. may be preceded and followed only by Sur
Place.

Alternative Ways of Dancing Deplacement

MAN

(1) Three steps forward (RLR) on heels, then close
LF to RF rising to level of Sur Place. No turn.

(2) Three steps forward (RLR) on heels, then close
LF to RF turning ¼ to L, rising to level of Sur Place.

(3) The Attack. Dance the Appel on RF on step 1
then continue with steps 2, 3 and 4.

LADY

Normal opposite.

The Huit (Or Eight)

MAN

Begin in PP (normally diag. to wall) having taken the preceding step to side on LF (small step) on ball of foot. End Normal Hold.

	Count
1. Forward and across on RF (heel lead) in PP, lowering arms and leading lady slightly away	1
2. Close LF to RF, turning to face wall, leading lady to L side ⅛ turn R	2
3. Step in place on RF (as in Sur Place), lady on L side	1
4. Step in place on LF, leading lady across to R side	2
5. Step in place on RF, lady on R side	1
6. Step in place on LF, lady on R side	2
7. Step in place on RF, leading lady leftwards and towards you	1
8. Step in place on LF (with pressure on ball of foot), bringing lady to Close Hold	2

Notes: The man may make ⅛ turn L on step 8. Move the arms to left and right as if moving a cape, leading lady, mostly with R hand on the side of her back but also keep the muscles of L arm braced to assist lead.

Footwork: As in Sur Place it is optional whether the heels make contact with or are off the floor on steps 2–7, but in the latter case the man must not dance the Huit with elevation in the body, as there is no rise.

LADY

Begin in PP (normally facing diag. to centre) having taken the preceding step to side on RF (small step) on ball of foot. End in Normal Hold.

	Count
1. Forward and across on LF (heel lead) in PP	1
2. Side on RF on L side of man, with pressure on ball of foot and retaining some weight on LF. Commence to turn L } ¼ turn L	2
3. Replace full weight on LF still turning	1
4. Forward and across on RF (heel lead) to man's R side	2
5. Side on LF on R side of man, with pressure on ball of foot and retaining some weight on RF. Commence to turn R } ¼ turn R	1
6. Replace full weight on RF still turning	2
7. Forward and across on LF (heel lead) towards man. Commence to turn L slightly } ⅛ turn L	1
8. Close RF to LF (with pressure on ball of RF) turning square to man	2

Note: If the man has made ⅛ turn L on step 8, the lady will make ¼ turn L to face him between steps 7 and 8. There is no rise in the body. The lady should turn her hips as little as possible during this figure in order not to pull away from the man.

This fig. may be preceded by:

(1) The Sur Place.
(2) The Basic Movement Forward. } Turning to Promenade Position on last step.
(3) The Side Chassés to L.
(4) The Elevations to L.

This fig. may be followed by:

(1) The Sur Place.
(2) The Basic Movement.

The Appel

MAN OR LADY

The Appel is a preparatory step used as an indication to the lady that a moving figure is to follow. It is one step only (usually on man's RF and lady's LF); a sharp movement, lowering strongly to the flat of the foot (keeping it close to the other foot) accompanied by the appropriate lead for the figure which is to follow.

The Sixteen

MAN

Begin facing wall. End facing centre.

Step		Count
1. Step on RF in place (Appel)		1
2. Side on LF (heel lead) in PP, moving along LOD, lowering arms and leading lady slightly away	¼ turn L	2
3. Forward and across on RF in PP (heel lead) commencing to turn R		1
4. Side and slightly back on LF, continuing to turn R	⅜ turn R	2
5. Back RF, preparing to lead lady outside on R side, still turning, to back LOD		1
6. Back LF, lady outside on R side		2
7. Turning on LF, close RF to LF to face centre, leading lady to R side	¼ turn R	1
8. Step in place on LF, lady on R side		2
9. Step in place on RF, leading lady across to L side		1
10. Step in place on LF, lady on L side		2
11. Step in place on RF, lady on L side		1
12. Step in place on LF, leading lady across to R side		2
13. Step in place on RF, lady on R side		1
14. Step in place on LF, lady on R side		2
15. Step in place on RF, leading lady leftwards and towards you		1
16. Step in place on LF (with pressure on ball of foot), bringing lady to Close Hold		2

Note: The man may make ⅛ turn L on step 16. The last eight steps are similar to those of the Huit, but without the PP forward step on RF which occurs on step 1 of that figure for the man.

LADY

Begin backing wall. End facing centre.

Step		Count
1. Step on LF in place (Appel)		1
2. Side on RF (heel lead) in PP, moving along LOD, commencing to turn R	⅛ turn R	2
3. Forward and across on LF in PP (heel lead) continuing to turn R		1
4. Forward RF (heel lead) between man's feet, now facing LOD	⅛ turn R	2
5. Forward LF (heel lead) facing LOD, preparing to step outside man on his R side		1
6. Forward RF (heel lead) facing LOD on man's R side		2
7. Side on LF, on R side of man, with pressure on ball of foot and retaining some weight on RF. Commence to turn R	⅜ turn R	1
8. Replace full weight on RF, still turning		2

(Continued overleaf.)

Kenny McKechnie and Manuella Faller of Scotland capture the atmosphere of the Paso Doble — with superb balance, body-tone and presentation.

LADY: THE SIXTEEN (*Continued.*)

		Count
9. Forward and across on LF (heel lead) to man's L side		1
10. Side on RF, on L side of man, with pressure on ball of foot and retaining some weight on LF. Commence to turn L	¼ turn L	2
11. Replace full weight on LF, still turning		1
12. Forward and across on RF (heel lead) to man's R side		2
13. Side on LF, on R side of man, with pressure on ball of foot and retaining some weight on RF. Commence to turn R	¼ turn R	1
14. Replace full weight on RF, still turning		2
15. Forward and across on LF (heel lead) towards man. Commence to turn L slightly	⅛ turn L	1
16. Close RF to LF (with pressure on ball RF), turning square to man		2

Note: If the man has made ⅛ turn L on step 8, the lady will make ¼ turn L to face him between steps 7 and 8. There is no rise in the body on steps 9–16 which are those of the Huit.

This fig. may be preceded by:

(1) The Sur Place.
(2) The Basic Movement Forward (if facing wall).

This fig. may be followed by:

(1) The Sur Place.

The Separation

MAN

Begin and end facing LOD.

	Count
1. Step on RF in place (Appel)	1
2. Forward LF (heel lead) rising at end of step, lowering arms and leading lady to step farther back	2
3. Close RF to LF (on balls of feet) extending L arm forward, releasing hold with R hand	1
4. Step on LF in place (still up)	2
5. Continue to step in place, on RF, LF, RF, LF, 6. gradually lowering through the feet to normal 7. position, leading lady forward to finish 8. in close Hold	1, 2, 1, 2

Repeat steps 1–8 if desired.

Note: On step 8 the man should lower his L heel into light contact with the floor.

LADY

Begin and end backing LOD.

	Count
1. Step on LF in place (Appel)	
2. Back RF, long step	1
3. Back LF (ball of foot) rising at end of step. Release hold with L hand and extend R arm forward	2
4. Close RF back to LF on balls of feet	1
5. Dance Basic Movement forward towards man, 6. small steps forward on LF, RF, LF, RF, 7. using pressure on the ball of each foot and gradually lowering to normal position, to finish in Close Hold 8.	2 1, 2, 1, 2

Repeat steps 1–8 if desired.

Note: On step 8 the lady should lower her R heel into light contact with the floor. On step 3 it is optional whether her L heel makes contact with or remains off the floor.

This fig. may be preceded by:

(1) The Sur Place.
(2) The Basic Movement Forward. } To face LOD

This fig. may be followed by:

(1) The Sur Place.
(2) The Separation repeated once.

Fallaway Ending to The Separation

MAN

Begin facing LOD and end facing diag. to centre.

		Count
1. Forward RF, OP		1
2. Forward LF, OP	⅛ turn R	2
3. Back and slightly to side RF in Fallaway		1
4. Back LF in Fallaway	⅛ turn R	2
5. Side RF		1
6. Close LF to RF		2
7. Side RF		1
8. Close LF to RF		2

LADY

Begin facing against LOD and end backing diag. to centre.

		Count
1. Forward LF, OP		1
2. Forward RF, OP	⅞ turn R	2
3. Back and slightly to side LF in Fallaway		1
4. Back RF in Fallaway	⅛ turn L	2
5. Side LF		1
6. Close RF to LF		2
7. Side LF		1
8. Close RF to LF		2

This fig. may be preceded by:

(1) The Separation.

This fig. may be followed by:

(1) The Sur Place.
(2) The Basic Movement.

Promenade Link

MAN

Begin facing LOD and end facing diag. to centre.

		Count
1. Appel on RF		1
2. Side LF in PP	¼	2
3. Forward and across RF in PP	turn L	1
4. Close LF to RF		2

Note: This figure may be commenced in other directions.

LADY

		Count
1. Appel on LF	⅛	1
2. Side RF in PP	turn R	2
3. Forward LF in PP	⅜	1
4. Close RF to LF	turn L	2

This fig. may be preceded by:

(1) The Sur Place.
(2) The Basic Movement.

This fig. may be followed by:

(1) The Sur Place.
(2) The Basic Movement.
(3) Chassés to the Right.

Note: Steps 3 and 4 may be used to complete figures which have ended in PP. In this case, alternative amounts of turn may be used.

22

Rock 'n' Roll

Rock 'n' Roll is a very interesting and fascinating dance, sometimes referred to as Single Beat Jive. It is a good idea for the beginner to learn Rock 'n' Roll before attempting the more difficult rhythm of Triple Beat Jive, which is fully explained in Chapter 23. Rock 'n' Roll music is easily recognizable with its accented off-beat, and it can be played in slow, medium or quick tempo. The ideal tempo for dancing is 40 to 46 bars per minute.

The *Hold* is similar to that for the Samba (see page 165) but is looser and more flexible, the arms being held a little lower. See description of the hold given for the Jive in Chapter 23 for further details of the 'Open Hold' which occurs in some of the following figures.

Basically the dance is very simple. The man begins all the figures with his left foot and the lady with her right.

The rhythm for all the basic figures is Slow, Slow, Quick, Quick (2 beats for each 'slow' step, and 1 beat for each 'quick' step).

All the steps are taken first on the ball of the foot, then on to the flat foot. When taking a 'slow' step sway the body very slightly towards the foot you are stepping with – e.g., side LF,

swaying body slightly to left.

With Rock 'n' Roll, the direction in which the dancer faces when he starts the dance does not matter as most of the figures are danced around the same spot. The dancer does not progress round the floor as with the other ballroom dances.

The usual abbreviations are used, and do not forget that s – a slow step – takes up 2 beats of the music and Q – a quick step – takes up 1 beat.

It will be helpful to the man if he remembers that the four foot movements of the Time Step (the first figure described) are repeated and danced in a similar manner in all the other figures. His steps may vary slightly but basically he dances the Time Step more or less continuously. It is the lady's steps which change and it is essential that the man should give a good strong lead with his right hand.

The Time Step

MAN

Begin with the hold described 'opened out' slightly, so that the lady's left hip is almost in contact with the man's right hip; the feet are 8–10 inches (20–25 cm) apart.

This floor-line effectively depicts a matador throwing his cape down in front of the bull.

1. Side LF almost in place — s
2. Side RF almost in place — s
3. Back with LF (across behind RF) — Q
4. Replace weight on to RF (small step) — Q

LADY

Begin as described in the man's step.

1. Side RF almost in place — s
2. Side LF almost in place — s
3. Back with RF (across behind LF) — Q
4. Replace weight on to LF (small step) — Q

The Time Step may be followed by the next figure described – the Breakaway. It may also be followed by the Arc.

The Breakaway (or Natural Break)

MAN

1. Side LF — s
2. Side RF, pushing your partner away from you with your R hand and then immediately releasing hold of her (with your R hand) — s
3. Back with LF (across behind RF) — Q
4. Replace the weight on to RF (small step) — Q
5. Forward LF (pulling lady towards you with L hand) — s
6. Side RF, regaining normal hold, turning approx. ¼ turn to R — s
7. Back with LF (across behind RF) — Q
8. Replace weight on to RF (small step) — Q

LADY

1. Side RF — s
2. Back LF, turning approx. ¼ turn to L to face partner (lady releasing hold with L hand) — s
3. Short step back with RF — Q
4. Replace weight on to LF (small step forward) — Q
5. Forward RF towards partner — s
6. Side LF, turning approx. ¼ turn to R and regaining normal hold — s
7. Back with RF across behind LF — Q
8. Replace weight on to LF (small step) — Q

The Arc

(Danced after a Time Step, or after the Breakaway)

MAN

1. Side LF, lifting L arm and leading partner to turn about ½ turn to R underneath your L arm — s
2. Replace weight on to RF (small step) — s
3. Back with LF (across behind RF) — Q
4. Replace weight on to RF (small step) — Q

LADY

1. Forward RF, turning to R for about ½ turn under partner's L arm — s
2. Back LF — s
3. Short step back RF — Q
4. Replace weight on to LF (small step forward) — Q

Follow this figure with the Loop (described below).

The Loop

(Danced after the Arc)

MAN

1. Side LF, lifting L arm and leading partner to turn about ¾ of a turn to L underneath your L arm — s
2. Replace weight on to RF (small step) — s
3. Back with LF (across behind RF) — Q
4. Replace weight on to RF (small step) — Q

LADY

1. Forward RF, turning to L for about ¾ of a turn under partner's L arm — s
2. Side LF, still turning slightly — s
3. Short step back RF — Q
4. Replace weight on to LF (small step forward) — Q

The Loop is followed by steps 5, 6, 7, 8 of the Breakaway.

With a little practice in joining the different figures together you will soon be able to improvise others and make a most enjoyable and exhilarating dance.

23

Jive (or American Swing)

The chapter on Rock 'n' Roll is a very good preparation for the beginner who wants to learn the Jive. The main difference between the two is that the Jive is danced in what is called *Triple Rhythm* as against the Single Rhythm of Rock 'n' Roll, that is, 'Q a Q' in place of the 'Slow' used in Rock 'n' Roll.

The Music is written in 4/4 time.

Two different rhythms form the basis of Jive:

(1) is based on one bar of music and has two steps timed QQ, followed by one Jive Chassé (in Triple Rhythm) timed Q a Q;

(2) is based on 1½ bars of music and has two steps timed QQ, followed by two Jive Chassés (in Triple Rhythm) timed Q a Q Q a Q.

The phonetic method of counting these rhythms is best interpreted by saying 'one, two' on the two single-beat steps, and on all Chassés 'three and four'. This is not, of course, musically correct, as if two Chassés take one bar of music, to say 'three a four, three a four' must obviously be wrong, as there is only one third and one fourth beat in any bar. Experience has proved, however, that this method of counting is excellent both for the pupil and for the teacher. This will be understood if you study the beat values and counts given below:

1-Bar Construction

	Step	Step	Jive Chassé
Count	1	2	3 a 4
OR	Q	Q	Q a Q
Beat Value:	1	1	¼ ¼ 1

1½-Bar Construction

	Step	Step	Jive Chassé	Jive Chassé
Count	1	2	3 a 4	3 a 4
OR	Q	Q	Q a Q	Q a Q
Beat Value:	1	1	¼ ¼ 1	¼ ¼ 1

There is also a *Double Rhythm* or *Two Beat Jive*, where the three steps used in the Triple Rhythm are replaced by a 'tap-step' movement counted 'QQ' or '3,4'. Part weight is placed on count 3, and full weight on count 4, completely omitting the change of weight on to the other foot on the 'a' count – see description of Jive Chassé. This Double Rhythm method is quite attractive, but should be used only occasionally as an interpretative variation of rhythm whilst dancing the normal Triple Rhythm Jive. In excess, the use of the Double Rhythm count gives an impression of laziness and lack of musical expression. All the following descriptions are therefore given in Triple Rhythm, which must be used for competitions and medal tests under the British Council of Ballroom Dancing rules, at a tempo of about 44 bars per minute. The music can, of course, be played much faster or much slower.

The Hold is similar to that for the Samba (see page 165) but is looser and more flexible, the arms being held a little lower. In the descriptions this is referred to as Normal Hold. Open Hold (used a great deal in Jive) is a position where the lady and man are apart, the man holding the lady's right hand in his left hand, with arms just above waist level and not quite straight at the elbow.

Leading. Many of the movements are led through a tension in the man's arms, to which the lady must respond by resisting with her arm-muscles ready to feel his lead. Unless the lady responds in this way, it is impossible for the man to lead such figures as the American Spin, therefore it is very important for the lady to remember never to have floppy arms when the man is leading her into any figure.

The Jive Chassé. A group of three steps, taken forward, back, sideways (to right or left), and turning (to right or left). A Chassé is counted 3 a 4, the moving foot being half closed towards the stationary foot on the second step. The feet are never closed on this 'a' count, and the actual movements of the feet should be kept very small.

Footwork. All steps are taken on the ball of the foot, with the heel just off (or lightly touching) the floor. The weight of the body should be kept rather forward and not be allowed to fall back into the heels, and the knees are flexed naturally. The hips should be kept free so that a very slight lateral lilt is felt as the weight is placed into the foot, particularly when a Jive Chassé is being danced sideways, as in Basic Movement. Heel leads on forward steps are not used, except very occasionally by the lady in advanced Jive 'styles'.

Alignment or Direction. The Jive does not progress around the ballroom (apart from the Walks), therefore the figures may begin facing in any direction.

As there are so many different kinds of music suitable for Jive, individual interpretations will vary from one dancer to another, and therefore the foot placings and amounts of turn given can only be considered approximate. The 'a' count is never accented by the Jive dancer as this gives a hurried and jerky expression to the Chassés, but any of the other beats may be stressed according to the music being played.

Jumps, kicks, flicks and skips . . . the Jive is an all-action dance.

Basic Movement

MAN

Begin with feet very slightly apart, weight on LF, in Normal Hold. End in Normal Hold.

	Count
1. Step on RF in place	1
2. Step on LF in place	2
3. Side RF	3
4. Move LF towards RF } Jive Chassé Sideways (to R)	'a'
5. Side RF (small step)	4

LADY

Begin with feet very slightly apart, weight on RF, in Normal Hold. End in Normal Hold.

	Count
1. Step on LF in place	1
2. Step on RF in place	2
3. Side LF	3
4. Move RF towards LF } Jive Chassé Sideways (to L)	'a'
5. Side LF (small step)	4

Note: Following the figure described above, and for the purpose of practising the rhythm, the Basic Movement can also be danced on man's LF and Lady's RF as follows:

MAN

	Count
1. Close LF almost up to RF	1
2. Step on RF in place	2
3. }	3
4. } Jive Chassé to L on LRL	'a'
5. }	4

LADY

	Count
1. Close RF almost up to LF	1
2. Step on LF in place	2
3. }	3
4. } Jive Chassé to R on RLR	'a'
5. }	4

The Basic Movement (commenced on man's RF) may be preceded by:

(1) The Basic Movement commenced with man's LF, as given in note.

(2) The Basic Movement in Fallaway.

(3) The Link.

(4) The Walk (on man's LRL turned to R to face lady).

(5) The Rock Basic (on man's LRL).

The Basic Movement (commenced on man's RF) may be followed by:

(1) The Basic Movement commenced with man's LF, as given in note.

(2) The Basic Movement in Fallaway.

(3) The Rock Basic (on man's LRL).

(4) The Change of Places R to L.

(5) The Change of Places R to L with Change of Hands.

Rock Basic

MAN

Begin and end in Normal Hold.

	Count
1. }	3
2. } Jive Chassé Sideways to Left (LRL)	'a'
3. }	4
4. }	3
5. } Jive Chassé Sideways to Right (RLR)	'a'
6. }	4

LADY

Begin and end in Normal Hold.

	Count
1. }	3
2. } Jive Chassé Sideways to Right (RLR)	'a'
3. }	4
4. }	3
5. } Jive Chassé Sideways to Left (LRL)	'a'
6. }	4

Note: The Rock Basic to R is often used by the man to commence the dance instead of using the Basic Movement, and steps 4–6 may also be danced following a Link, continuing with Basic Movement in Fallaway.

Basic Movement in Fallaway

MAN

Begin and end in Normal Hold.   Count

1. Cross LF loosely behind RF, turning slightly to L, leading lady to step back in Fallaway			1
2. Replace weight on RF, leading lady to commence her turn L			2
3. } Jive Chassé Sideways	}		3
4. } to Left (LRL),	} ⅛ turn R		'a'
5. } turning to face lady	}		4

LADY

Begin and end in Normal Hold.   Count

1. Cross RF loosely behind LF LF in Fallaway position, turning to R	⅛ to ¼ turn R	1
2. Replace weight on LF, commencing to turn L		2
3. } Jive Chassé Sideways	} completing	3
4. } to Right (RLR), continuing	} ⅛ turn to	'a'
5. } to turn L to face man	} ¼ turn L	4

Note: It is optional whether the heel lowers into light contact with (or remains just off) the floor on step 1.

This fig. may be preceded by:

(1) The Basic Movement.
(2) The Rock Basic (on man's RLR).
(3) The Whip.

This fig. may be followed by:

(1) The Basic Movement.
(2) The Rock Basic (on man's RLR).
(3) The Basic Throwaway.
(4) The Walks (on man's RLR if he omits turn R at end of Fallaway).
(5) The Change of Places R to L: man raises L arm on steps 3–5 of Fallaway, omits turn R, and continues with steps 6–8 of Change of Places R to L.
(6) The Change of Places R to L with Change of Hands: man omits turn to R on steps 3–5 of Fallaway and continues with steps 6–8 of Change of Hands.

Basic Throwaway

MAN

Begin in Normal Hold, end in Open Hold.   Count

1. } Dance two steps of Basic Movement, RL			1
2. }			2
3. Back and slightly to side RF leading lady away with R hand and then releasing hold	}	Jive Chassé Diag. Back, ⅛ turn R	3
4. Move LF back towards RF, extending L arm	}		'a'
5. Back and slightly to side RF (small step), retaining hold with L hand	}		4

LADY

Begin in Normal Hold, end in Open Hold.   Count

1. } Dance two steps of Basic Movement, LR			1
2. }			2
3. Back and slightly to side LF moving away from man	}	Jive Chassé Diag. Back, ⅛ turn L	3
4. Move RF back towards LF, extending R arm	}		'a'
5. Back and slightly to side LF (small step)	}		4

Note: At the end of this figure the lady and man should be approximately two feet (half a metre) apart, not quite facing each other, as they have opened out to a 'V-position' with a ¼ turn difference between them.

This fig. may be preceded by:

(1) The Basic Movement (beginning LF as man).
(2) The Basic Movement in Fallaway.
(3) The Link.
(4) The Walk (on man's LRL turned R to face lady).
(5) The Rock Basic (on man's LRL).

This fig. may be followed by:

(1) The Link (turning square to lady on steps 1–2).
(2) The Change of Places with Change of Hands (lady passing behind man).

The Walks

(In promenade)

MAN

Begin and end in Normal Hold. Dance steps 1–5 of Basic Movement in Fallaway (without turning to R on steps 3–5), and continue (in PP):

			Count
Right Foot Walk:			
6. Forward RF	⎱	leading lady with R	3
7. Move LF towards RF	⎬	hand to turn to her	'a'
8. Forward RF (small step)	⎰	R away from you	4
Left Foot Walk:			Count
9. Forward LF	⎱	leading lady with R	3
10. Move RF towards LF	⎬	hand to turn to her	'a'
11. Forward LF (small step)	⎰	L towards you	4

Repeat steps 6–11 *ad lib.*

Note: This figure moves gradually along the line of progression. The man's feet usually point slightly towards lady, causing his RF to be in a very slightly 'crossed' position on steps 6 to 8.

LADY

Begin and end in Normal Hold. Dance steps 1–5 of Basic Movement in Fallaway, turning to L on steps 3–5 to face man as usual, and continue (in PP):

				Count
6. Forward LF, turning away from man	¼ turn R		⎱	3
7. Move RF towards LF			⎬ Jive Chassé turning R	'a'
8. Forward LF (small step)			⎰	4
9. Forward and slightly to side RF turning towards man	⎱ ¼ turn L		⎱	3
10. Move LF towards RF			⎬ Jive Chassé turning L	'a'
11. Side RF (small step)			⎰	4

Repeat steps 6–11 *ad lib.*

Note: The feet and knees should be kept rather close to each other as the forward movements are danced (i.e. on steps 6 and 9).

This fig. may be preceded by:

(1) The Basic Movement.
(2) The Rock Basic (on man's RLR).
(3) The Whip.

This fig. may be followed by:

(1) The Basic Movement (man turns ⅛ R to face lady on steps 9–11 of Walks).
(2) The Whip, turning to face lady as in No. (1).
(3) Steps 6–8 of Change of Places R to L, taken after Left Foot Walk raising L arm.
(4) Steps 6–8 of Change of Places R to L with Change of Hands, taken after Left Foot Walk.
(5) The Rock Basic (on man's RLR), turning to face lady as in No. (1).

Change of Places Right to Left

MAN

Begin in Normal Hold, end in Open Hold.

			Count
1. Cross LF loosely behind RF turning slightly to L, leading lady to step back in Fallaway	⅛ turn L		1
2. Replace weight on RF, leading lady with R hand to commence her turn L			2
3. ⎫ Jive Chassé Forward (LRL) gradually			3
4. ⎬ raising L arm above head level, leading			'a'
5. ⎭ lady to continue her turn			4
6. ⎧ Lead lady to turn R under raised left arm, then release hold ⎫			3
7. ⎨ with R hand, dancing Jive Chassé Forward (RLR) turning ⎬ ⅛ turn L			'a'
8. ⎩ slightly L to face lady. Lower arm at end ⎭			4

Note: Steps 1–5 are the Basic Movement in Fallaway, but omitting the turn to R and raising L arm.

LADY

			Count
Begin in Normal Hold, end in Open Hold.			
1. Cross RF loosely behind LF in Fallaway position, turning to R	⅛ to ¼ turn R		1
2. Replace weight on LF, commencing to turn L			2
3. ⎫			3
4. ⎬ Jive Chassé Sideways (RLR) continuing to turn L, ⎫ completing ⅛ to ¼ turn L			'a'
5. ⎭ gradually raising R arm ⎭			4
6. ⎧ Turning R under raised arm, release hold with L hand, ⎫			3
7. ⎨ dancing Jive Chassé. Turning (LRL) moving away from ⎬ ¾ turn R			'a'
8. ⎩ man. End facing him and lower arm ⎭			4

Note: Steps 1–5 are the Basic Movement in Fallaway, but raising R arm. When the Change of Places R to L is danced naturally, the commencement of the turn to right will be felt at the end of step No. 5 on RF.

This fig. may be preceded by:

(1) The Basic Movement.
(2) The Rock Basic (on man's RLR).
(3) The Whip.
(4) The Walk on Left Foot (man raising L arm) into steps 6–8 of Change of Places R to L.

This fig. may be followed by:

(1) The Change of Places L to R.
(2) The American Spin (led with man's L hand).

Change of Places Left to Right

MAN

	Count
Begin and end in Open Hold.	
1. Back LF	1
2. Replace weight forward on RF, pulling lady gently towards you	2

		Count
3. Raising L arm above head level, lead lady	Approx. ¼	3
4. to turn L underneath arm, dancing Jive	turn R	'a'
5. Chassé in place (LRL) turning to		4
6. ⎫ Lowering L arm, allow lady to move		3
7. ⎬ away and dance a small Jive Chassé		'a'
8. ⎭ Diagonally Forward (RLR)		4

Note: On steps 6–8, although the man should 'follow' the lady in the same direction, he allows her to travel more so that they end about 2 feet (half a metre) apart.

LADY

Begin and end in Open Hold.

		Count
1. Back RF		1
2. Replace weight forward on LF, raising R arm		2
3. ⎫ Turning to L under raised right arm, dance		3
4. ⎬ Jive Chassé Turning (RLR). End almost	Just under ¾ turn L	'a'
5. ⎭ facing man		4
6. ⎫ Still turning slightly L, lower R arm		3
7. ⎬ dancing Jive Chassé Diagonally Back	completing the ¾ turn L	'a'
8. ⎭ (LRL) moving away from man		4

Note: If preceded by a figure where the lady has turned to the right (e.g. Change of Places Right to Left), the lady usually gets a continuance of turn to the R on step 1, and begins her turn to L on step 2.

This fig. may be preceded by:

(1) The Change of Places R to L.
(2) The American Spin, man then takes lady's R hand in his L hand on step 1 of Change of Places L to R.
(3) The Change of Hands, passing lady behind man's back.
(4) The Change of Places R to L with Change of Hands, then take lady's R hand in L as for No. (2).

This fig. may be followed by:

(1) The Link.
(2) The Change of Hands, passing lady behind man's back.
(3) The American Spin with man's L hand.
(4) The Change of Places L to R (normal) or releasing hold with L hand on step 2, regaining hold on step 6–8.

Change of Places Right to Left and Left to Right With Changes of Hands

MAN

The steps are the same as those given for Change of Places Right to Left and Left to Right, but the lead for the man is different and the arms are *not* raised above head level.

Right to Left: Steps 3–5:   lead with R hand as before but do not raise L arm

                Step 6:   lead lady to turn R then release hold with both hands

Left to Right: Step 1:   take lady's R hand in R hand (or 'shake hands hold'), at approximately waist level

                Step 2:   pull lady gently forward, leading her also to turn L, then release hold with R hand

                Steps 6–8:   take lady's R hand in L hand extending L arm forward to allow lady to move back

LADY

The steps are the same as those given for Change of Places Right to Left and Left to Right, but the lady does *not* raise her R arm. The lady must keep her R hand naturally forward in front of her after man has released hold with both hands. This enables him to catch her hand again easily to give her the lead for the following movement.

These figs. may be preceded by:

Right to Left Change of Hands:

(1) The Basic.
(2) The Rock Basic (man's RLR).
(3) The Whip.
(4) The Walk on man's LF into steps 6–8 of Change of Hands.

Left to Right Change of Hands:

(1) The American Spin.
(2) The Change of Places R to L with Change of Hands.

These figs. may be followed by:

Right to Left Change of Hands:

(1) The American Spin (led either with man's R or L hand).
(2) The Change of Places L to R with Change of Hands.
(3) The Change of Places L to R, man taking lady's R hand in L hand on step 1.

Left to Right Change of Hands:

(1) The Link.
(2) The Change of Hands passing lady behind man's back.
(3) The Change of Places L to R (normal) or releasing hold with L hand on step 2, regaining hold steps 6–8.

The Link

MAN

Begin in Open Hold, end in Normal Hold.

	Count
1. Back LF	1
2. Replace weight forward on RF	2
3. ⎫	3
4. ⎬ Jive Chassé Forward (LRL) towards lady	'a'
5. ⎭	4

LADY

Begin in Open Hold, end in Normal Hold.

	Count
1. Back RF	1
2. Replace weight forward on LF	2
3. ⎫	3
4. ⎬ Jive Chassé Forward (RLR) towards man	'a'
5. ⎭	4

Note: It is optional whether the heel lowers into light contact with (or remains just off) the floor on step 1.

This fig. may be preceded by:

(1) The Basic Throwaway (turning square to lady on Link).
(2) The Change of Places L to R.
(3) The Change of Places L to R with Change of Hands.

This fig. may be followed by:

(1) The Basic Movement.
(2) The Basic Throwaway.
(3) The Whip.
(4) The Rock Basic (steps 4–6).

The Whip

MAN

Begin and end in Normal Hold.

	Count
1. Cross RF loosely behind LF, turning to R and leading lady forward	1
2. Side LF (small step) still turning, lady outside on R side	2
3. } Jive Chassé Sideways (to R) on RLR,	3
4. } continuing to turn slightly, leading lady	'a'
5. } to end in Fallaway position	4

From ⅜ (minimum) up to ⅞ (maximum) turn R

LADY

Begin and end in Normal Hold.

	Count
1. Forward LF turning to R and preparing to step outside man on his R side	1
2. Forward RF, still turning, outside man on his R side	2
3. } Continuing to turn, dance a	3
4. } Jive Chassé Turning (to R) on LRL	'a'
5. } to end in Fallaway position	4

From ⅞ (minimum) up to 1⅛ (maximum) turn R

This fig. may be preceded by:

(1) The Link.
(2) The Walk (on man's LRL turned to face lady).
(3) The Basic Movement in Fallaway.

This fig. may be followed by:

(1) The Change of Places R to L.
(2) The Change of Places R to L with Change of Hands.
(3) The Basic Movement in Fallaway.
(4) The Walks.

Changes of Hands (Lady Passing Behind Man)

MAN

Begin and end in Open Hold. Man holds lady's R hand in his L hand.   Count

1. Back LF   1

2. Replace weight forward on RF   2

3. Forward LF commencing to turn L, changing lady's R hand to your R hand and leading
her to R side   3

4. Move RF towards LF continuing to turn   'a'

5. Forward LF (small step) still turning, moving R arm behind back (the man now has his back   ½ turn L
almost turned to lady)   4

6. Diagonally back RF still turning, changing lady's R hand into your L hand which is held
behind you   3

7. Move LF back towards RF still turning   'a'

8. Back RF still turning to end facing lady; L arm now held in front in normal position for
Open Hold   4

Note: When changing hands on step 3 the man should have the palm of his R hand facing downwards and place his hand over hers; on step 6 the man should have the palms of both hands uppermost behind his back and take his L hand under the lady's hand.

LADY

Begin and end in Open Hold.   Count

1. Back RF   1

2. Replace weight forward on LF   2

3.   3

4. Jive Chassé Forward (RLR) commencing to turn   'a'

5. R, to end almost facing man's back   ½ turn R   4

6. Jive Chassé turning (LRL) passing behind   3

7. man's back and moving slightly away to end   'a'

8. facing him   4

This fig. may be preceded by:

(1) The Change of Places L to R.

(2) The Basic Throwaway, man turning slightly L to face lady on steps 1–2 of Change of Hands.

(3) The Change of Places L to R with Change of Hands.

This fig. may be followed by:

(1) The Change of Places L to R.

(2) The Link.

American Spin

MAN

Begin and end in Open Hold position, not holding, but ready to take lady's R hand.

		Count
1.	Take lady's R hand into R hand and step back LF	1
2.	Replace weight forward on RF, gently pulling lady forward on to R arm	2
3.	Side LF (small step) and continue with rest of Jive	3
4.	Chassé on the spot (RL) bracing R arm against the	'a'
5.	forward pressure from the lady, releasing hold on step 5	4
6.		3
7.	Jive Chassé on the spot (RLR) whilst lady spins to the R	'a'
8.		4

Repeat *ad lib.*

Note: The action of pulling the lady forward on to the man's braced right arm and releasing the pressure and hold on step 5 should be sufficient to initiate the lady's spin to her right without any obvious 'pushing' action. The lady should then be able to maintain balance and dance on the spot for steps 5–8. This strong lead will make the left side of man's body move forward on steps 3 to 5, and the right side forward on steps 6 to 8.

LADY

Begin and end in Open Hold position, not holding, but ready to allow man to take R hand in his R hand.

	Count
1. Back RF	1
2. Replace weight forward on LF	2
3. Short step forward RF pushing forward with a braced R arm against man's arm	3
4. Replace weight back on to LF (arm still braced)	'a'
5. Replace weight forward on RF, arm still braced but immediately release hold with hand and turn strongly to R	Approx. ½ turn R — 4
6. Jive Chassé on the spot (LRL), continuing to turn R keeping knees close completing full turn	3 'a' 4

Repeat *ad lib.*

This *fig. may be preceded by:*

(1) The Change of Places R to L with Change of Hands.
(2) The Change of Places R to L, man leading first American Spin with his L hand.
(3) Another American Spin.

This *fig. may be followed by:*

(1) The Change of Places R to L with Change of Hands.
(2) The Change of Places L to R, taking lady's R hand in man's L on step 1.
(3) Another American Spin.

24

Disco Dancing

This type of dancing, which is an outcome of the Twist, has made the biggest impact on the public of any dance since the Charleston nearly seventy years ago. It has become immensely popular over the last few years and is danced by people of all ages in most ballrooms, dance halls and discotheques all over the world.

Disco Dancing differs from the other ballroom dances in many ways, perhaps the main distinction being that partners do not touch at all. It is very much a solo dance, danced on the spot with the partners facing each other.

In my opinion the dancing profession has been very lax in not laying down a few simple figures to act as a guide for those who wish to learn this form of rhythmic movement, which can be danced to 'Beat' music in 4/4 time – the type of music featured by most of the modern groups.

However, here is one simple figure which can be used as a basis for this type of dancing. The same foot movements can be used by both the man and the lady. Try the steps as follows:

1. Short step to side with RF   s
2. Close LF to RF keeping weight on RF   s
3. Short step to side with LF   s
4. Close RF to LF keeping weight on LF   s
Repeat *ad lib.*

When you have mastered these foot movements try making them more rhythmic by straightening and flexing the knee of the leg carrying the weight of the body on each step. When you can dance this continuously and rhythmically, try swinging the arms slightly from side to side on the counts of 1 and 3. To the right on 1, to the left on 3, and so on.

This figure can be adapted to form different patterns, forwards and backwards or turning slightly on each step.

When you have mastered this figure and can dance it well in an easy, relaxed manner, you should be quite capable of improvising and dancing other simple movements.

Reviser's Note: The British Council of Ballroom Dancing has published a superb and detailed technique for Disco/Freestyle Dancing. This was produced by a committee of leading experts; teachers of this style who were nominated by corporate members of the British Council of Ballroom Dancing. In some ways the technique and physiological detail is far ahead of that related to the other dance styles mentioned in this book.